UK Politics Today

(Third Edition)

Frank Cooney

Peter Fotheringham

Pulse Publications

CONTENTS

1	Elections	3
2	Voting Behaviour	14
3	Political Parties	31
4	Parliament	63
5	The Executive	83
6	Pressure Groups	99
7	Scottish Devolution & Electoral Systems	112
8	The Scottish Government	124
9	Local Government	141

ACKNOWLEDGEMENTS

The authors and publishers would like to thank the following for permission to reproduce copyright material:

The Press Association for photographs on pages 12, 16, 26, 36, 39, 42, 49, 53, 63, 66, 71, 74, 76, 78, 80, 82, 84, 85, 86, 90, 92, 93, 95, 99, 101, 104, 105, 108, 113, 115, 116, 128, 132, 133, 134, 138.

Paul Creaney for his contribution to chapters 8 and 9.

All rights reserved. No part of this publication may be reproduced, stored in a retrieval system, or transmitted in any form or by any means, electronic, mechanical, photocopying, recording or otherwise, without written permission from the publishers.

Published and typeset by
Pulse Publications
Braehead, Stewarton Road,
by Kilmaurs, Ayrshire KA3 2NH

Printed and bound by
Thomson Colour Printers

British Library Cataloguing-in-Publication Data
A Catalogue record for this book is available from the British Library

ISBN 978-1-905817-03-0
© Cooney & Fotheringham 2008

Chapter 1
Elections

What you will learn.
1. *The purpose of elections.*
2. *The different electoral systems used in the UK.*
3. *The effects of these systems on the distribution of power among the parties.*

ELECTIONS AND DEMOCRACY

Elections are central to democracy, linking citizens to the machinery of government. Elections permit the people collectively to decide who should govern them. British democracy is representative and indirect, meaning that the people do not rule or govern directly; rather the people are governed by the individuals they have elected to represent them in the legislature, the House of Commons. The leaders of the majority political party become members of the executive.

Democratisation, the process whereby countries become democratic, is characterised above all by two achievements—universal suffrage and free elections devoid of corruption. The process of democratisation in Britain took a long time. In the nineteenth century the right to vote was extended to most males. Women did not get the right to vote until the 1920s. Some people argue that contemporary Britain needs another round of democratisation, focusing particularly on reform of the electoral system which defines the electoral process and has a profound impact upon the composition of Parliament in general and government in particular.

Electoral systems have become controversial elements of contemporary British democracy for various reasons. Turnout has been declining in British general elections. The recent introduction of new and unfamiliar electoral systems was accompanied by a significant and largely unexpected increase in the number of spoilt ballot papers in the Scottish Parliament and Scottish local government elections of May 2007. Holding elections at weekends has been suggested as a means of encouraging and enabling more voters to go to the polls.

The electorate used to decide only who should represent them in the Commons and on local government councils, using only one electoral system—the first-past-the-post (FPTP), winner take all, system. Today's voters also take part in elections to the European Parliament and, if they live in Scotland, Wales or Northern Ireland, to the Scottish Parliament, the Welsh Assembly or the Northern Ireland Assembly (Stormont). Voters have had to get used to a variety of electoral systems, some of which incorporate the principle of proportional representation.

THE GENERAL ELECTION

The principal election in Britain is the general election which must be held at least once every five years. The Prime Minister may call a general election before the five-year period is up if that is likely to increase the government's chances of re-election. Formally the Prime Minister must ask the Monarch to dissolve Parliament before the election can be held. However, circumstances may leave him/her with little choice about the election date. Such was the case in May 1979 when James Callaghan went to the country after losing control of the House of Commons as a result of being defeated on a Motion of Confidence. The Prime Minister may also be forced to wait until almost the last possible moment of the five years allowed if opinion polls suggest that his or her party will not be re-elected (for instance, John Major in 1997). In 2001 Prime Minister Blair was forced to delay the date of the election by one month because of the foot and mouth crisis. The succession of Gordon Brown as Prime Minister in June 2007, without a general election

being required, led to speculation that he would call an election well in advance of the five years which would not be up until May 2010.

Constituencies

When a general election is held, all 646 Members of Parliament are elected. Every one of the 646 constituencies in Britain is represented by a single MP. Constituencies do not all have the same number of voters. Na H-Eileanan an Iar, formerly the Western Isles, has the smallest number (21,576 in 2005) while the Isle of Wight has the most voters (109,046 in 2005). In 2001 the average constituency had 69,892 voters in England, 66,170 in Northern Ireland 55,718 in Wales and 55,291 voters in Scotland. In 2005, after changes to take account of the significantly devolved government for Scotland, the average constituency had 69,873 voters in England, 65,276 in Scotland, 64,778 in Northern Ireland and 55,276 in Wales. The voters in each constituency choose one individual from a number of candidates for the job of MP in that constituency. Although voters are officially voting for an MP, they tend to think more about which party they support and who will form the government. The name of the party which the candidate represents is now noted beside his/her name on the ballot paper. In addition to selecting their own candidates, the major political parties effectively organise election campaigns.

Candidates & deposits

Under procedures established over many decades, candidates are required to submit their nomination papers, together with a deposit of £500, to the Returning Officer, who has responsibility for managing the smooth running of the election. The regulations require that any candidate who fails to gain at least 5% of the votes cast in the election will lose his or her deposit. This is a considerable sum of money for an individual to lose, although the amount has not been increased for many years. In 2005, a total of 3,555 candidates, 80% of them men, contested the election, of whom about 2,000 lost their deposits. In 1997 only one Labour candidate, three Conservatives and eleven Liberal Democrats lost their deposits, so the great majority of deposits lost were by the candidates of minor parties with no hope of winning seats.

Polling Stations

On general election day, polling stations up and down the country will be open from 7.00 a.m. until 10.00 p.m. Voting is fairly straightforward with the electors marking an 'X' beside the name of their preferred candidate. At the close of the polls the ballot boxes are carefully sealed and sent on to the numerous counting centres which have been set up. It is here that the votes are counted and the results announced. Any voting slips which are deemed to have been 'spoiled' are set aside and not counted. Results are announced from midnight onwards, with the outcome of the election usually being fairly clear by about 3.00 a.m.

THE PURPOSE OF ELECTIONS

What is it that voters hope to gain out of a general election?

? A change of Prime Minister and Cabinet?
? A change in the form of government?
? A new MP to represent their views at Westminster?
? Manifesto promises carried out?

The voting public will get some of these things. They certainly get a constituency MP who will represent them whether they voted for him/her or not. These constituency representatives select the government, and elections occasionally lead to a change in the party in power. That government will, during its lifetime, find time to carry out some of its manifesto promises. Since 1999 the election of the Scottish Parliament by the Additional Member System has given voters the chance to reject government based on one party only in favour of coalition government or even minority party government.

Selecting a government

Governments are chosen by the electoral process, even though in the British parliamentary system only members of the legislature (the MPs) are elected directly by the people. Which political party

Electoral Systems in Britain 2007

System	Election of:	Constituency Type: Single- or Multi-Member
First-Past-the-Post (FPTP)	House of Commons, Local Government Councils in England and Wales	Single
Additional Member System (AMS)	Scottish Parliament, Welsh Assembly	Single and Multi
Regional List	European Parliament (not N. Ireland)	Multi
Single Transferable Vote (STV)	Scottish Local Government Councils, N. Ireland Assembly, N. Ireland European Parliament	Multi

Table 1.1

makes up the government is effectively decided by the collective voice of individual voters who usually return to the Commons a majority party from whose ranks the Prime Minister, Cabinet and junior Ministers are drawn. The government receives legitimacy from its members being elected by the representatives of the people. The rule of law is much easier to achieve when those who make the law have been elected, even indirectly, by the people who must obey the law.

Power to the people?

The voice of the people is turned into political reality by the electoral system, i.e. by the rules governing general elections. The representation of parties in the legislature and the party composition of the government to emerge from the legislature after an election are influenced by:

- the way that a country is divided into constituencies,
- the number of representatives per constituency,
- the way votes are counted to decide who is elected.

Electoral systems are not neutral in their effects. Different rules lead to different results in terms of the number of parties with significant representation in the legislature and the number of parties represented in the government. Although the rules of an electoral system are important, changes in voting habits may lead to changes in election results without a change in the electoral system.

There may be conflict between two of the principal purposes of an election—representation of the people and the establishment of a government. How representative is the House of Commons and the government following a general election? What is the best type of government—one based on a single majority party or one based on a coalition of two or more parties none of which individually enjoys a majority in the legislature? We will see that the rules of an electoral system may profoundly influence the politics of a country like Scotland. The various electoral systems in use in Britain are summarised in Table 1.1.

THE HOUSE OF COMMONS ELECTORAL SYSTEM

Britain has had a long history of a strong two-party system providing single majority party government. Power has alternated between the two major parties at varying intervals. The rules of the electoral system contribute in no small measure to these central features of British politics. Reform of the electoral system itself has become a topical political issue in recent decades for a number of reasons.

- The apparent electoral invincibility of the Conservative Party from 1979 until 1992 led some to believe that the only way to overcome Conservative strength was to change the electoral system.
- The decisions to use different forms of proportional representation for elections to the European Parliament, Scottish Parliament and Welsh Assembly from 1999 onwards.
- The weakening of the Conservative and Labour vote which has meant that fewer people have actually supported the party forming the government. (See Table 1.3.)
- Calls for reform of the electoral system by the Liberal Democrats whose support has been increasing.
- An alarming fall in turnout in recent decades.

Plurality system

The electoral system used at British general elections depends on simple majorities rather than on proportion. It is popularly known as a first-past-the-post system (FPTP) or plurality system because the winning candidate is the one with the most votes in each single-member constituency. In other words the one winner in each constituency is the candidate with more votes than any other rival candidate. The winning number of votes need not be an absolute or overall majority. (See Table 1.2.)

	% Share of Vote	
	1992	1997
Liberal Democrats	**26.0**	17.5
Labour	25.1	**33.9**
Conservative	22.6	17.5
SNP	24.7	29.0

Table 1.2 *Figures in bold indicate the winning party*
Source: Times Guide to the House of Commons 1992 & 1997

Table 1.2 illustrates what can happen when four candidates are evenly matched. In 1992 Sir Russell Johnstone won the seat with only 26% of the votes cast. This highlights one of the criticisms of FPTP, namely that it creates a situation whereby many individual MPs and the victorious party overall, which goes on to form Her Majesty's Government, do not receive the support of a majority of the electorate. The people who vote for those parties which form the Opposition may still have their views represented by the opposition MPs. They will not, however, see these representatives in government. Since there are no prizes for coming second they get nothing in terms of power or influence. As we will see, those who get nothing make up a substantial proportion of the electorate.

Election results based on the first-past-the-post principle, such as those reported in Tables 1.2–1.4, give rise to claims that the electoral system used to elect members of the House of Commons is essentially unfair and that it leads to many individual votes being 'wasted'. The three most striking features of the general election results reported in Tables 1.2–1.4 are:

- Consistently clear discrepancies between the proportion of total votes gained by political parties and the proportion of seats they win in the House of Commons.
- The clear parliamentary majority achieved by one single party in thirteen of the seventeen elections since 1945. The exceptions are 1950, 1964, February 1974 and October 1974. (See column 9, Table 1.3.)
- The persistence of a two-party system at the parliamentary level in spite of the decline in the combined Conservative and Labour share of the popular vote from a high of 96.8% in 1951 to 67.6% in 2005. (Compare columns 3 and 6, Table 1.3.)

FEATURES OF FPTP

Table 1.3 illustrates trends in the percentage shares of votes and seats won by British political parties in general elections since 1945. The discrepancies between party shares of the popular vote and shares of seats in the legislature are used by many people to claim that the 'representative' character of British government is not as good as it could be or should be. There are three main conclusions to be drawn from Table 1.3.

All rewards to the victor

Firstly, the winning party always wins a bigger share of seats than of votes. In 2005, Labour won 35.2% of the popular vote and 54.9% of the seats in the House of Commons. The party coming second overall in the share of the popular vote usually benefits from the first-past-the-post system by winning proportionately more seats than votes though this has not been true of the Conservatives in Opposition since 1997. The impact of the electoral system is evident when the two-party or major-party share of the vote (i.e. the combined Conservative and Labour share) is compared with the major-party share of seats in the Commons. The decline in the popularity of the two major parties is shown in column 3. Conservative and Labour together won close to or more than 90% of the popular vote from 1945 until 1970. However, in the 1974 elections their share fell well below 80%. Their lowest share was recorded in 2005 when they won less than 70% of the popular vote. Column 6, which

THE BRITISH TWO-PARTY SYSTEM AND THE ELECTORAL SYSTEM: 1945–2005

	% Share of the Vote			% Share of Seats			Liberals		Overall
	Con. 1	Lab. 2	C+L 3	Con. 4	Lab. 5	C+L 6	%Votes 7	%Seats 8	Majority 9
1945	39.8	**47.8**	87.6	33.3	61.4	94.7	9.2	1.9	146
1950	43.5	**46.1**	89.6	47.7	50.4	98.1	9.1	1.4	5
1951	**48.0**	48.8	96.8	51.4	47.2	98.6	2.5	1.0	17
1955	**49.7**	46.4	96.1	54.7	43.9	98.6	2.7	1.0	58
1959	**49.4**	43.8	93.2	57.9	40.9	98.8	6.0	1.0	100
1964	43.4	**44.1**	87.5	48.1	50.3	98.4	11.2	1.4	4
1966	41.9	**47.9**	89.8	40.2	57.6	97.8	8.5	1.9	96
1970	**46.4**	43.0	89.4	52.4	45.6	98.0	7.5	1.0	30
1974	37.9	37.1	75.0	46.6	47.4	94.0	19.3	2.2	—
1974	35.8	**39.2**	75.0	43.5	50.2	93.7	18.3	2.0	3
1979	**43.9**	36.9	80.8	53.4	42.2	95.6	13.8	1.7	43
1983	**42.4**	27.6	70.0	61.0	32.2	93.2	25.4	3.6	144
1987	**43.4**	31.7	75.1	57.7	35.2	92.9	23.2	3.4	101
1992	**41.9**	34.4	76.3	51.6	41.6	93.2	17.9	3.1	21
1997	30.7	**43.2**	73.9	25.0	63.6	88.6	16.8	7.0	179
2001	31.7	**40.7**	72.4	25.1	62.6	87.7	18.8	7.9	167
2005	32.4	**35.2**	67.6	30.7	54.9	85.6	22.9	9.6	64

- The figures in bold denote the share of the vote of the party which won a majority of seats in the House of Commons. In 1974 (Feb.) no party won a parliamentary majority.
- Shares of votes and seats are based on results in the United Kingdom as a whole. Until 1970 Northern Ireland votes are included under the appropriate British parties. From 1974 this is not done because the Northern Ireland parties broke away from their British counterparts which did not, by and large, campaign in the province.

Table 1.3 Source: Butler and Butler *British Political Facts 1900–1994* and *Times Guide to the House of Commons 1997, 2001, 2005*

The Electoral System: A Scottish Dimension

	Percentage of votes				Percentage of seats				Number of seats			
	1992	1997	2001	2005	1992	1997	2001	2005	1992	1997	2001	2005
Labour	39.0	45.6	43.9	38.9	68.0	77.8	77.8	69.5	49	56	56	41
Conservatives	25.7	17.5	15.6	15.8	15.2	0	1.4	1.7	11	0	1	1
Liberal Democrats	13.1	13.0	16.4	22.6	12.5	13.9	13.9	18.6	9	10	10	11
SNP	21.5	22.1	20.0	17.7	4.2	8.3	6.9	10.2	3	6	5	6

Table 1.4

gives the major-party share of seats in the Commons, shows that, despite the decline in their share of the vote, the share of seats won by the two major parties has not declined to anything like the same extent.

Nevertheless, since 1974, the two major parties have been winning fewer seats than before. In 1997 the much stronger Liberal Democrat performance in winning forty six seats reduced the Conservative–Labour share of seats (88.6%) to less than 90% for the first time in the post-war era. That share was reduced further to 87.7% in 2001 and to 85.6% in 2005. Such trends suggest that the FPTP electoral system has protected the parliamentary representation of the two major parties from a long-term decline in their popular support.

The 'winning' party, i.e. the party with the most seats, nearly always wins more votes than any other party. However, in 1951 the Conservatives won more seats than Labour in spite of winning a slightly smaller share of the popular vote. This can happen because of single-member constituencies. A party winning some of its seats by large margins may win fewer seats but more votes than a party which wins its seats by narrower margins. In February 1974 these positions were reversed. The Conservatives, who had called the election after three years and eight months in office, won almost 230,000 more votes than Labour. This difference in number of votes represented less than 1% of the total vote in the United Kingdom. Nevertheless, the Conservatives won four seats fewer than Labour. In 2005 the Conservatives won 56,663 more votes than Labour in England—but ninety two fewer seats.

Third parties smothered

Secondly, the first-past-the-post system makes it difficult, though not impossible, for 'third' parties to gain significant representation in the House of Commons. In Table 1.3, columns 7 and 8 illustrate the mixed electoral fortunes of the most significant 'third force' in post-war British politics, the Liberals from 1945 to 1979, the Liberal/SDP Alliance in 1983 and 1987 and the Liberal Democrats since 1992. The liberal 'third force' has been winning a lot more votes than seats for many years. In 1951 the Liberals won six seats with 2.5% of the vote. In 1992 the Liberal Democrats won twenty three seats with 17.9% of the vote. In other words the third party vote share was seven times greater but its share of seats went up only four times. The 'third party' fared particularly badly in 1983 when it took the form of the Liberal/SDP Alliance (an alliance of the old Liberal Party and the newly formed Social Democratic Party which had broken away from Labour in 1981). The Alliance won 25.4% of the vote in Britain compared to Labour's 27.6%. Yet the Alliance won only twenty three seats (3.6%) compared to Labour's 209 (32.2%).

The Liberal Democrats' share of seats increased from 3.1% in 1992 to 9.6% in 2005. This increase reflects a change in Liberal Democrat strategy which involves 'targeting' seats with relatively small majorities. The Liberal Democrats were the main beneficiaries of the decline in the Labour vote in 2005; they gained several seats as younger voters, particularly students, moved away from Labour because of the Iraq War. (See Chapter 2 Voting Behaviour.)

The electoral system encourages long-term two-party domination at the parliamentary level, but a particular two-party system may not be indestructible. It took the Labour Party, established by the trade union movement in 1900, forty five years to win a general election. During that period Labour replaced the old Liberal Party as the second major party as it gained the support of an increasing proportion of the working class. To overcome the biases of the first-past-the-post electoral system, third parties have to attract support consistently from significant sections of the electorate such as a social class, or a nation or region, or supporters of a particular point of view. Labour accomplished this task very gradually during the first thirty years of the twentieth century. The Greens are seeking support from all sections of society on the basis of their stance on environmental issues.

The influence of third parties depends as much on the gap between the two major parties as on their own strength in the Commons. The narrower the margin between the major parties in the legislature and the smaller the winning party's overall majority, the greater is the influence of third parties represented in the Commons. The contemporary Conservative–Labour two-party system has tottered sometimes, particularly in the 1970s when on two occasions no party enjoyed a Commons majority. In the February 1974 election, no party won a parliamentary majority. Labour was able to form a government because the Liberals made it clear that they would not support the continuation of Edward Heath's Conservative government. In October 1974 Labour 'won' with a majority of only three. Labour lost its majority in by-elections and had to rely on a 'Lib-Lab Pact' to survive in Parliament until the summer of 1979.

Comfortable Government

Thirdly, the electoral system and the electorate usually combine to produce a government with a comfortable working overall majority in the House of Commons. (Column 9 in Table1.3.) A 'comfortable majority' is a variable which depends upon such factors as how the governing party fares in by-elections and whether a suitable opportunity arises for the government to call a general election which will increase its parliamentary majority. Labour's majority of five in 1950 was not sufficient to withstand a determined Conservative Opposition which forced all-night sittings and brought the government to its knees. The Labour government which won narrowly in 1964 after thirteen years of Conservative rule was able to call an election after eighteen months and win a large Commons majority. In contrast, the Labour government elected in October 1974 with an overall majority of three never identified a suitable opportunity to go to the country to strengthen its mandate.

The three Conservative victories in 1979, 1983 and 1987 were all 'comfortable'. The somewhat unexpected victory for the Conservatives under John Major in April 1992 provided a majority of twenty one which was whittled away by by-election defeats and the defection of three Conservative MPs until, at the beginning of 1997, the government lost its overall majority. However, Major's government survived some votes of confidence because the Ulster Unionists did not vote against it. A government without an overall majority can survive if some third party MPs vote for it or do not vote against it. Prime Minister Major was unable to call an election until the last possible moment in 1997 because the polls had suggested for several years that Labour would win.

Concentrated support

The plurality FPTP electoral system suits political parties with significant long-term support throughout British society (Labour and Conservative) or strong, if limited, regional support (the nationalist parties in parts of Scotland and Wales in 1974). Such support leads to particular parties coming first in certain types of constituency. For example, Labour dominates in the central cities such as Glasgow where all the seats have been won by Labour since 1987. It is not so favourable to parties whose vote is spread evenly but thinly throughout much of the country (the Liberal Democrats in England and the SNP since 1979 in British elections).

Table 1.4 illustrates further variations in the results possible in the first-past-the-post electoral system. Labour has been the dominant party in Scotland since 1959. Its dominance in terms of seats has grown in spite of the increase in support for the two smaller parties, the SNP and the Liberal Democrats, which now contest all Scottish constituencies. In 1966 Labour won almost 50% of the Scottish vote and forty six seats. In 1992 Labour won less than 40% of the vote but still won forty nine seats. Labour's social base has remained sufficiently loyal to ensure that Scotland contributes positively to Labour's overall strength in the Commons. The fall in seats won by Labour in 2005 was due mainly to the reduction in the number of Scottish MPs following devolution. In contrast, the Conservative Party, which won 50.1% of the Scottish vote in 1955, has experienced a massive loss of votes. This reduced its share of Commons seats to 15% (eleven out of seventy two) in 1992 and to no seats at all in 1997. The Conservatives won one seat in 2001 and 2005. The electoral system did not protect the Conservatives from the big loss of popular support. The long-term Conservative decline is due, in part, to the increase in support for the SNP and the Liberal Democrats whose strength has been most evident in the rural areas of Scotland outside the industrial and urbanised belt in central Scotland. The Conservatives have, since 1959, progressively lost out to Labour in urban and industrial Scotland.

All recent general elections, with the exception of 2005, highlight the fact that the Liberal Democrats won more seats than the SNP in spite of receiving a smaller share of the Scottish vote. In 2001 the SNP received 20% of the votes and the Liberal Democrats 16.4% yet in terms of seats the Liberal Democrats gained double the number of seats which the SNP received—ten to the SNP's five. Liberal Democrat voters tend to be concentrated in certain areas such as the Borders and the north of Scotland. The SNP tends to have more support than the Liberal Democrats in most parts of Scotland outside the seats loyal to the Liberal Democrats.

PROPORTIONAL REPRESENTATION (PR)

The Liberal Democrats and their predecessors have long been supporters of electoral reform, particularly proportional representation (PR). PR is based on the principle that every party winning an agreed minimum number of votes should be awarded a number of seats in the legislature. This number should be approximately proportional to the number of votes the party receives in the country as a whole. Some small parties, which gain very few votes, would not be awarded any seats at all, even under PR. In Scotland the FPTP electoral system used in British general elections works strongly in favour of Labour compared to what would happen under any type of proportional representation.

British general elections are still decided by first-past-the-post. However, the development of new institutions to be elected by British voters, the European and Scottish Parliaments in particular, opened the door to innovation in the design of electoral systems.

The Scottish Parliament has been elected by the Additional Member System since its inception in 1999 and Britain moved, also in 1999, to the National/Regional List system for elections to the European Parliament. Yet another electoral system, the Single Transferable Vote (STV), is used for the Northern Ireland Euro-constituency and, since 2007, in Scottish local government elections.

The Alternative Vote (AV)

The alternative vote is, in effect, only a modified form of the first-past-the-post system. It would not require any boundary changes and the constituencies would still return one MP. Where the alternative vote system would differ is that voters would have two votes instead of one. The voter would indicate his or her preference among the candidates. In this situation the winner would be that candidate who secured an absolute majority of the votes cast (more than 50%). Should this not happen after the first count, then the candidate with the fewest votes would be eliminated with his/her second preferences being distributed among the other candidates. If this did not produce a candidate with more than 50% of the votes, the procedure would be repeated until it did. The main criticism of the alternative vote system is that it fails to give a fairer share of the votes to the smaller political parties.

The Additional Member System (AMS)

The voter in the additional member system casts two votes. First the voter selects the candidate whom he/she wishes to represent him/her in the local constituency. The rationale here is to maintain a link between constituencies and their elected representatives. Therefore, seventy three Members of the Scottish Parliament (MSPs) are elected from seventy three single-member constituencies. These are the seventy two British parliamentary constituencies which were used in Scotland before 2005, with the Orkney and Shetland constituency having two seats allocated in the Scottish Parliament, one for each of the northern isles.

Under AMS the voter also has a second vote in a multi-member constituency, choosing between parties. Each has a regional list. These lists, which are not printed on the ballot paper, contain the names of candidates in order of preference as decided by the parties. This second ballot determines the overall composition of the legislature. Second ballot votes are counted in such a way as to ensure a high degree of proportionality in the overall allocation of seats to parties.

The most dramatic result of using the proportional AMS system rather than the FPTP system has been that no party has won a majority of Scottish Parliament seats. This lead to the emergence of a Labour and Liberal Democrat coalition government after the 1999 and 2003 elections, and of a minority SNP government after the 2007 election. The AMS system gives small parties a better chance of winning parliamentary representation. The Greens and the Scottish Socialist Party did particularly well in 2003 but fell back in 2007. The operation of the additional member electoral system in Scotland is explained in detail in Chapter 7.

National/Regional Party List

This form of PR has been used in many European countries and was employed for the first time in Great Britain (but not in Northern Ireland) in the 1999 elections to the European Parliament. Under this system, the electorate does not vote for individual party candidates but for party lists in multi-member constituencies. The candidates are selected and listed in order by the parties so it is known in advance which candidates will be elected depending on how successful each party has been. For elections to the European Parliament, Great Britain is divided into eleven multi-member constituencies. In 2004 nine English 'Euro' constituencies elected a total of sixty four MEPs. Scotland (seven MEPs) and Wales (four MEPs) each constitute one 'Euro' constituency.

As in the FPTP system individuals have only one vote. The counting system, which was used for the first time in Britain in 1999, is called the d'Hondt system. Seats are allocated among the parties in each 'Euro' constituency according to the following formula:

$$\frac{\text{Number of Votes}}{\text{Number of Seats Gained} + 1}$$

The operation of the regional list system is illustrated by working out the allocation of the seven Scottish MEPs in 2004. (See Table 1.5.) To allocate the first of

The Operation of the Party List Electoral System:
2004 European Parliament Elections in Scotland

	Votes	Share of Votes	Percentage of Seats	No. of Seats
Labour	310,865	26.4	28.6	2
SNP	231,505	19.7	28.6	2
Conservative	209,028	17.8	28.6	2
Liberal Democrat	154,178	13.1	14.3	1

Table 1.5

the seven Scottish 'Euro' seats in 2004 the number of votes gained by each party was divided by one. Labour was thus allocated the first seat because it had won the most votes in Scotland. In the second count Labour's total vote was divided by two according to the d'Hondt formula. This left the SNP with the largest number of votes, so it was allocated the second seat. Then the SNP total was divided by two, leaving the Conservatives as the strongest party in the third count. The three strongest parties had now had their vote totals halved. In the fourth count Labour's total divided by two still exceeded the Liberal Democrats' total, so Labour got the fourth seat. Labour's total vote was divided by three for the fifth count when the Liberal Democrats won the seat because their total vote now exceeded the reduced votes of the other parties. The Liberal Democrat vote was then divided by two, leaving the SNP with the highest total in the sixth count and the Conservatives with the highest total in the seventh and last count. Table 1.5 shows that the 2004 vote and related seat shares of Labour and the Liberal Democrats were strongly proportional whereas both the Conservatives and the SNP won the same number of 'Euro' seats as Labour with considerably fewer votes.

The impact of PR is evident if the 1994 and 2004 European results in Scotland are compared. In 1994 Labour won six of the then eight single-member 'Euro' constituencies and the SNP won two. In 2004 Labour, the Conservatives and the SNP each won two seats and the Liberal Democrats won one seat in the now seven-member Scottish 'Euro' constituency.

The degree of proportionality which may be achieved by the list system and the consequences for party representation are illustrated in Table 1.6 by comparing the results of the 1994, 1999 and 2004 European elections in Britain as a whole. In 1994 the first-past-the-post system based on the simple plurality rule in single-member constituencies was hugely favourable to Labour at a time when it led the Conservatives comfortably in the opinion polls. Labour won almost three-quarters of Britain's eighty seven Euro seats with only 44% of the popular vote. The Liberal Democrats suffered their usual fate: the plurality counting system did not turn their votes into seats. In Britain as a whole the 1999 and 2004 results were characterised by a much closer relationship between shares of votes and shares of seats. The new electoral system also helped the Greens and the UK Independence Party (opposed to membership of the European Union) to win seats which they were unlikely to do under first-past-the-post. The larger the number of seats per constituency the more proportional the results will be.

The Single Transferable Vote

This system is used in Northern Ireland for elections to both the European Parliament and the Northern Ireland Assembly. It was used in Scottish local government elections for the first time in May 2007. Using a quota system for counting votes and allocating seats in multi-member constituencies, STV usually introduces a high degree of proportionality into election results. Voters have a single vote but may express as many preferences as there are representatives to be elected from each constituency. In a five-member constituency voters rank their preferences among the total number of candidates standing using the figures 1–5. Often the number of candidates will be in double figures. Finding the winning candidates using STV is complicated. It is achieved by using a formula to calculate the minimum number of votes, known as the quota, required to win one of the several seats to be decided.

STV Formula

$$\text{Quota of Votes} = \frac{\text{Number of Votes Cast}}{\text{Number of Seats} + 1} + 1$$

In a five-member constituency where 180,000 votes were cast, a candidate would require 30,001 votes in order to be elected. (Work it out!) Candidates exceeding that total when votes are first counted are immediately declared elected. It is unlikely, though not impossible, that all five seats will be allocated in the first count. Certainly, no more than five candidates can win. If votes were evenly divided among six candidates with 30,000 each, none would be elected in the first count. In practice, votes are unevenly distributed with perhaps two or three candidates from the major parties securing immediate election. The second and subsequent preferences of voters are then taken into account to decide the allocation of the remaining seats. The 'surplus' votes of the first candidate or candidates elected are redistributed among the candidates not yet elected in proportion to the second preferences of all the voters who supported the

Euro Elections in Great Britain, 1994, 1999 & 2004

	% share of votes			% share of seats		
	1994	1999	2004	1994	1999	2004
Labour	44.2	28.0	22.6	73.8	34.5	25
Conservative	27.9	35.8	26.7	21.4	42.8	36
Liberal Democrats	16.7	12.7	14.9	2.4	11.9	16
UK Independence	0.8	7.0	16.2	0	3.6	16
Greens	3.2	6.3	6.2	0	2.4	2.7
Nationalists	4.3	4.6	2.4	2.4	4.7	4

Table 1.6

winning candidate. This process continues until the five seats are all filled.

STV in practice

The influence of STV on party representation in the legislature and the nature of executive government is illustrated in Table 1.7 by the results of the 2007 elections to the Northern Ireland Assembly. The Assembly has 108 seats elected in eighteen multi-member constituencies, with six representatives per constituency. The results indicate that the Democratic Unionist Party (DUP) and Sinn Fein are the strongest parties in contemporary Northern Ireland. The Ulster Unionists and the SDLP also attract considerable numbers of voters. The Alliance Party, which tries to bridge the religious divisions, won 5% of the vote. The choice of proportional representation in the form of STV was motivated by a desire to ensure 'fair' and significant representation for the many political forces in Ulster. It could be said that 'fairness' was achieved in the strong proportionality between the shares of votes and the shares of seats won by the parties. No party won a majority in the legislature and an Executive crossing party and religious lines was sworn in. Ian Paisley and Martin McGuiness took over as First Minister and Deputy First Minister respectively.

2007 Northern Ireland Assembly Election Results under STV

Party	Share of Votes (%)	Number of Seats	Share of Seats(%)
UUP	14.9	18	16.7
DUP	30.1	36	33.3
Alliance	5.2	7	6.5
SDLP	15.2	16	14.8
Sinn Fein	26.2	28	25.9
Others	8	3	2.8

Table 1.7

STV IN SCOTLAND 2007: "NO OVERALL CONTROL"

The STV system was introduced in Scotland in 2007 when local government councils were elected by this method. STV had an immediate and significant impact.

1. Councils will be ruled predominantly by coalitions at least until the next round of elections in 2011.
2. The tradition of Independents controlling councils in the rural areas was eroded.
3. The SNP became the largest party.

Scotland has thirty two local councils. In 2003 the traditional use of FPTP produced thirteen Labour-controlled councils, one Liberal Democrat council (Inverclyde), one SNP council (Angus), and six 'Independent'-controlled councils (a majority of councillors not claiming a party affiliation). On eleven councils there was 'no overall control'; in other words there was no majority for one party. Results in 2007, when STV was used at the local government level, were startlingly different. No fewer than twenty seven councils emerged with 'no overall control'. Only two councils, Glasgow and North Lanarkshire, were Labour-controlled after the 2007 elections. The three Island councils, Orkney, Shetland and the Western Isles, returned mainly Independents. Elsewhere Independent-controlled councils disappeared as political parties won seats. In 2003 Moray returned sixteen Independents and three SNP to a council of twenty six. In 2007 twelve Independents and nine SNP were elected.

The impact of STV is evident in the results recorded in Scotland's two largest cities. In Glasgow Labour won seventy one out of seventy eight council seats in 2003. Labour was reduced to forty five seats in 2007. SNP representation leapt from three to twenty two; the Greens entered the council for the first time winning five seats. Labour's majority on Glasgow City

Comparison of the Number of Councillors Elected in 2003 under FPTP and 2007 under STV by Party

Party	2003	2007	Difference
Labour	509	348	-161
SNP	176	363	+187
Liberal Democrat	174	166	-8
Conservative	122	143	+21
Green	0	8	+8
Others	241	194	-47
Total	1,222	1,222	0

Table 1.8 Source: Electoral Commission 2003; BBC 2007

Table 1.8 clearly highlights the dramatic impact of STV on the fortunes of the new largest parties, Labour and SNP. In 2003 Labour had more councillors than the combined number of SNP, Liberal Democrat, and Conservative councillors. However, in 2007 the SNP became the largest party. The Liberal Democrats failed to benefit from the new system in contrast with the Conservatives and the Greens.

Council fell from sixty four to eleven. In Edinburgh Labour lost its very narrow majority of two as voters divided evenly between the four main Scottish parties: Liberal Democrats (17), Labour (15), SNP (12) and Conservatives (11). Three Greens filled the remaining places.

The Great 2007 Scottish Elections 'Fiasco'

'Fiasco' was a commonly used media description of what happened in the elections of 3 May 2007 in Scotland. Four years earlier in 2003 Scottish voters entering the polling booth were handed three ballot papers: one to elect a constituency MSP from candidates in a single-member constituency; one to elect a regional list MSP from a list of parties in a multi-member constituency returning seven MSPs; and one to elect a local councillor. Citizens of the Glasgow area of Pollokshields thus voted in the Govan constituency in the first Scottish Parliament ballot; in the Glasgow region in the second Holyrood ballot; and in the Maxwell Park ward of Glasgow City Council. Every citizen had one vote and one separate ballot paper for each of the three decisions to be made.

In 2007 these exercises in democratic representation produced the alleged 'fiasco' of a large increase in spoilt ballot papers—voting slips deemed invalid and not to be counted. Democracy was widely believed to have been harmed by the clear confusion of many voters as to how to proceed in the privacy of the polling booth. The major change compared to 1999 and 2003 was that what had previously been two separate Scottish Parliament ballot papers were combined in one paper on which the voter had to record by the traditional 'X' in the two appropriate places his/her choice for constituency MSP and regional list MSP. Voters were also handed a separate ballot paper on which to record

A computer displays marks made on ballot papers around Edinburgh as counting staff count the votes in the local elections in Edinburgh on 4 May 2007.

their ranked preferences for local government councillors. The local government election employed the STV counting system in multi-member constituencies.

In Scotland as a whole there were 140,000 spoilt ballot papers in 2007 compared to 45,700 in 2003. No fewer than 7% of Scottish Parliament ballot papers were rejected. Blame was said to lie with the decision to place both elements of the AMS system on one ballot paper. The reason for so doing was to eliminate an alleged distinction between the two types of MSP elected, the constituency MSP linked to a particular locality and the list MSPs linked to a much larger region containing seven MSPs. It was claimed that list MSPs were accorded an inferior status in the public eye.

The Electoral Commission for Scotland set up an inquiry into why so many voters failed to cast valid votes.

ARGUMENTS FOR FIRST-PAST-THE-POST

1. Usually produces a strong government drawn from one party enjoying a majority in the House of Commons.
2. Single-party government allows the Prime Minister and Cabinet to pursue policies clearly stated in their manifesto without having to compromise with smaller parties in the coalitions associated with PR.
3. There is no tradition of coalition government in Britain. PR encourages coalitions or minority government which may allow minor parties to hold larger parties to ransom.
4. PR may lead to a coalition between a minor party or parties and the second largest party in Parliament. This leaves the largest section of public opinion unrepresented.
5. Coalitions encourage compromise so that fewer voters—mainly Conservative or Labour voters—get what they really want.
6. When an MP retires or dies a by-election is held to elect a new MP. This enables the public to show their disapproval of a government which has become unpopular. In February 2006 the Liberal Democrats won a 'safe' Labour seat in Dunfermline West. Labour's two by-election victories in July 2007 provided greater legitimacy for the government of Gordon Brown. (Tony Blair had been the Labour leader at the May 2005 election.)

ARGUMENTS AGAINST FIRST-PAST-THE-POST

1. It does not always produce decisive or fair results. In the February 1974 election the Conservatives gained more votes than Labour yet had fewer seats. (See Table 1.3.) In the 2005 election Labour formed a government with only 35.2% of the votes cast. *The Independent* newspaper described it as "the most unfair election result of all time" as this was the lowest ever winning party share of the vote.
2. Strong government does not always create good or fair government. The leader of the Ulster Unionists, when first-past-the-post was used in the elections in Northern Ireland, made the infamous statement; "a Protestant government for a Protestant people." This abuse of power denied Northern Irish Catholics their civil and political rights. Today in Northern Ireland, using a PR system (STV) has resulted in a power-sharing government between the Democratic Unionists and Sinn Fein. (See page 11.)
3. It can lead to a situation where the winning MP in a constituency can receive less than 30% of the vote. In 1992 the Liberal Democrat candidate in Inverness East, Nairn and Lochaber won with 26% of the vote. (See Table 1.2.)
4. It is argued that FPTP leads to voter apathy. All of Glasgow's constituencies are held by Labour and the Conservatives do very badly. Why should a Conservative voter bother to vote when his/her vote will be of no consequence?

ARGUMENTS FOR PROPORTIONAL REPRESENTATION

1. PR is 'fair' because it produces a close correlation between shares of votes and shares of seats and avoids such results as Labour winning 74% of European Parliament seats with 44% of the popular vote as happened in 1992.
2. PR gives minor parties more parliamentary representation and encourages voters to vote for them without feeling that their votes will be wasted. In the 2003 elections for the Scottish Parliament the AMS system enabled the Scottish Socialist Party, the Green Party, the Scottish Senior Citizens Unity Party and Independents to be represented.
3. Coalition government increases the percentage of the electorate supporting the government parties. The Liberal Democrats and Labour formed a coalition government in Scotland in the period 1999 – 2007 providing stable and effective government.
4. Coalition government gave Germany better government than Britain for many years.
5. Coalitions encourage consensus which is the result of compromise. In other words more voters get some of what they want and less of what they do not want.
6. It is argued that PR will reduce the number of 'wasted votes' and so encourage greater turnout.

ARGUMENTS AGAINST PROPORTIONAL REPRESENTATION

1. PR can create a government in which a minority party can implement its policies. The Liberal Democrats finished fourth in the 2003 Scottish election, yet formed a government with Labour—but they were not the voters' choice.
2. It can lead to unstable and weak government. It is not certain that the SNP minority administration elected in 2007 will get its policies implemented in the Scottish Parliament. The AMS is designed to ensure that no one party will have an overall majority in the Scottish Parliament. A party which had a 'landslide victory' in the first-past-the-post election of constituency MSPs would do very badly in the regional/list election of MSPs.
3. It does not always create a more representative Parliament. In the 2007 Scottish elections the number of MSPs outwith the four major parties decreased from seventeen to three.
4. It is argued that the AMS system creates conflict between the constituency MSP and the seven list MSPs. There is clear rivalry between the 'two classes' of MSPs
5. The regional list system makes parties more powerful than voters. Being placed first or second on your party's list will mean you have a very good chance of being elected to the Scottish Parliament (assuming you represent one of the major parties). Margo McDonald, a leading SNP figure, decided to stand as an Independent on the Lothian Regional list after she had been given a low place on her party's list.

Chapter 2
Voting Behaviour

What you will learn.
1. Voting patterns and explanation of voting behaviour.
2. The shaping of political attitudes through the media.

Voting behaviour—the ways in which individuals decide which political party to vote for—determines who governs us and, to a large extent, the policies they carry out in office. The study of voting behaviour raises complex issues. Which party an individual voter chooses is influenced by social and demographic factors, such as social class, age, sex, family background, neighbourhood, ethnic background, and region, and by the most powerful political issues of the day.

CONTINUITY AND CHANGE

British electoral patterns are characterised by a great deal of stability. The Conservative and Labour Parties have been the only two major parties in Britain for more than sixty years. The Conservatives won four elections in a row between 1979 and 1992, giving them control of British government for eighteen years. Labour won the next three general elections in 1997, 2001 and 2005. Labour has won a majority of Scottish seats at Westminster in all thirteen elections since 1959. Such continuities in election results are the product of a great deal of stability in individual voting behaviour over time. When a political party acquires major party status as Labour did in the first thirty years of the twentieth century, or loses an election in a landslide as the Conservatives did in 1997, it does not win or lose all its supporters overnight.

Many voters tend to acquire a loyalty to the party of their choice, a loyalty which is not easily or quickly overturned. Such loyalties explain why parties like the Liberals, and now the Liberal Democrats, find it difficult to achieve major party status. However, one of the interesting questions about voting behaviour as it changes from one generation to another is whether individual voters have become less loyal to parties than they used to be, and if this is the case, why.

In every general election result we see a mixture of continuity and change. The study of voting behaviour is concerned with identifying and explaining both the continuities and the changes which determine who wins elections and, ultimately, much of what political parties attempt to do in office when they win. The principal continuities and changes in the decisions of the British electorate in the seventeen elections since 1945 are illustrated on page 15.

Table 2.1 illustrates the theme of continuity and change by comparing the 1992 and 2005 British general election results in two areas—Scotland and the south-east of England (excluding Greater London). Continuity is represented by the fact that Labour was the strongest party in Scotland and the Conservatives were the strongest party in the south-east of England in both elections, although the winning party overall had changed from the Conservatives in 1992 to Labour in 2005. Clearly, in 2005, Scotland was a Labour stronghold and a Conservative political desert, while the South-east remained a Conservative stronghold even when Labour won comfortably elsewhere. Change is evident in 2005 in the Conservative decline in Scotland and in the limited Labour recovery and the moderate Liberal Democrat advance at the expense of the Conservatives in the south-east of England.

CONTINUITY & CHANGE

	1992		2005	
	% Votes	Seats	% Votes	Seats
Scotland				
Labour	40.0	49	39.5	*41
Conservative	26.0	11	15.8	1
SNP	22.0	3	17.7	6
Liberal Democrats	13.0	9	22.6	11
Total		72		59
South-east England				
Labour	21.0	3	25.5	27
Conservative	54.0	106	43.3	83
Liberal Democrats	23.0	0	25.5	7
Total		109		117

Table 2.1 *Includes the Speaker*

CONTINUITY and CHANGE IN BRITISH POLITICS

EVIDENCE OF A STABLE POLITICAL LANDSCAPE

(See Table 2.1 for more details of the 'continuities' listed below.)

1. The British electorate has consistently maintained a Conservative–Labour two-party system since 1945. Only these two parties have formed the British government during that period. Only once, in 1983, has a third party come within 5% of the vote of the weaker of the two major parties.

2. The Conservatives have twice won at least three elections in a row (in 1951, 1955 and 1959 and in 1979, 1983, 1987 and 1992), holding office for thirteen and eighteen years respectively. Labour has once won three consecutive elections: in 1997, 2001 and 2005.

3. The winning party has won more than 40% of the vote except in the two closely contested elections of 1974 and also in 2005.

4. The principal 'third party' challenge to Conservative and Labour domination of governmental office has consistently come from the Liberal and Liberal Democrat Parties. From 1945 until 1970 the Liberals only once, in 1966, won more than 10% of the popular vote. Since the February 1974 election the 'Liberal' challenge has averaged around 20% of the vote.

5. For most of the post-1945 period the degree of major party 'swing', i.e. the relative change in the Conservative and Labour shares of the popular vote, lay within a range of 1–4%, indicating that many individual voters remained loyal to one or other of the major parties for several elections. Britain possessed a stable electorate. Swing was much higher in American presidential elections.

EVIDENCE OF A CHANGING POLITICAL LANDSCAPE

1. Seven of the seventeen elections since 1945 have resulted in a change of government: 1945, 1951, 1964, 1970, 1974 February, 1979 and 1997.

2. The Conservative–Labour two-party system has been considerably weaker since 1974. Until 1970 the two major parties averaged 91.2% of the popular vote. Their combined share has averaged only 75.6% since the February 1974 election. This decline has been seen as evidence of 'partisan dealignment'. (See page 21.)

3. In 1997 the Liberal Democrats' share of seats more than doubled in spite of a slight fall in their popular vote share because they successfully 'targeted' seats they thought they had a realistic chance of winning. They were also helped by tactical voting on the part of Labour voters seeking to deny seats to the Conservatives.

4. The electorate has become more volatile since 1979 as more and more voters are changing the way they vote from election to election. Prior to Mrs Thatcher's first victory in 1979 the average gap between the votes of the two parties was a mere 3.4%. Since 1979 that gap has averaged 10.7%. The 1997 Labour landslide was based on a swing of 10%. Labour even won with swings of 15% a few seats which had been considered 'rock solid' Conservative seats.

5. Election 'turnout', the percentage of the registered electorate turning out to vote, has been falling. Prior to 1970, turnout did not fall below 75%. Since 1979 turnout has fallen below 75% in five elections. It reached a post-war low of 59.1% in 2001 when two voters in five did not go to the polls.

LABOUR'S THREE IN A ROW: 1997, 2001 and 2005

1997–A 'RECORD-BREAKING' ELECTION

Labour's 1997 landslide election victory was its first victory since October 1974. In several respects the results may be described as 'record-breaking'.

Labour: A Commons majority of 179 was Labour's biggest ever, as was the 13% margin by which it beat the Conservatives in the popular vote.

Conservatives: The Conservatives only received 30.7% of the popular vote, their lowest share since 1832. The 165 Conservative MPs returned was the smallest number since 1906. Seven Cabinet Ministers lost their seats. No Conservatives were returned from Scotland and Wales, leading to claims that these countries were 'Tory Free Zones'.

Liberal Democrats: The forty six Liberal Democrat MPs elected was the highest number since 1929.

The 1997 election also produced the highest 'swing' since 1945, 10% from Conservative to Labour.

2001–LANDSLIDE AND APATHY

The 2001 results look very similar to those of 1997. The shares of both votes and seats won by the two major parties hardly altered. The Conservatives enjoyed a net swing of 1.6% from Labour but could win only one more MP than in 1997. The small Conservative net gain of five seats from Labour was offset by a net loss of four seats to the Liberal Democrats. Only twenty one seats changed hands in Britain excluding Northern Ireland, the smallest number since 1910. Labour's Commons majority of 167 was only twelve down on its 1997 record majority.

The Liberal Democrats gained six seats overall, proportionately the biggest change in party fortunes. The 'third' party won almost three million votes fewer than its predecessor, the Liberal/SDP Alliance, had in 1983 but won more than twice as many seats, suggesting that the Liberal Democrats had learned to cope with the first-past-the-post electoral system by concentrating their campaign where they had a realistic chance of winning.

The electorate's verdict in 2001 repeated the Labour landslide of 1997, but British voting behaviour differed in one highly dramatic and significant way from preceding elections. This was in the unusually large drop in the numbers of voters making the effort to go to the polling station, giving rise to widespread concern about an apathetic electorate.

Turnout

Only 59.1% of the registered electorate voted on 7 June 2001, only 2% more than the record low turnout of 57% in 1918, a wartime election. Fewer than three out of every five voters made it to the polling booths. Only 25% of the registered electorate voted for the winning party. The drop of 12.2% relative to the 1997 figure, itself the lowest since 1945, was the largest recorded between two peacetime elections. Labour attracted 2.8 million fewer supporters than in 1997 and almost 800,000 fewer than when it lost in 1992. John Major's Conservative Party won almost 6 million more votes in 1992 than did William Hague's Party in 2001. Turnout failed to reach 50% in sixty eight constituencies. Low turnout was particularly marked among new and young voters. Only one-third of voters under 25 went to the polls but 70% of pensioners did so.

There are several theories to account for the long-term decline in turnout since the early 1970s and the dramatic falls in 1997 and 2001.

"The result was a foregone conclusion"

In 2001 the turnout of voters was the lowest since 1918.

Public opinion polls throughout the four years following New Labour's 1997 victory provided little or no hint of a Conservative revival in time for the next election. Polls taken close to the 2001 election gave Labour a very comfortable lead. Thus it is argued that many voters did not feel that they could make a difference or else felt that their particular votes were not needed by their preferred parties.

"The result is an instruction to do better"
The Prime Minister's own interpretation of voting behaviour in 2001 was based on an analysis of the low turnout which claimed that many voters had not been greatly impressed by the government's attempts to improve public services such as education, health and transport. Abstention was a way of warning the government that improvements were necessary before the next election if a third Labour victory was to be achieved.

"The end of ideology"
There have been several changes in the image of British politics as a contest between two class-based, ideologically divergent parties. Labour has more or less lost its socialist and trade union dominated image. The private finance initiative (PFI) to provide some public services is a far cry from the nationalised industries of the 1945–1979 era. Conservatives have accused Labour of 'stealing the Emperor's clothes'. The middle class has become the biggest class in our allegedly 'classless society'. In the post-industrial society the general public, who are the consumers of health, education and other services, are more concerned with the efficiency of these services than with the ideologies behind the policies of the various parties on these services. However, deciding how to vote by judging the relative efficiency of political parties in government is much more difficult than doing so out of an emotional commitment to a political ideology. Thus fewer observable policy differences between the parties and less ideological commitment on the part of voters combine to explain the long-term decline in turnout in general elections in many western capitalist democracies.

Turnout was higher where local or regional issues were stronger than national issues. Turnout was higher in Northern Ireland where the Good Friday Agreement divided both nationalists and loyalists. Turnout was 75% in Wyre Forest where an independent, Dr Richard Taylor, won a seemingly 'safe' Labour seat. Dr Taylor ran as a protest against developments in the NHS in his constituency.

Compulsory Voting?
The 2001 turnout immediately prompted calls for the introduction of compulsory voting by those who are worried that lower turnout cheapens or weakens British democracy.

THE 2005 GENERAL ELECTION

The electorate's verdict on 7 May 2005, which is summarised in Table 1.3, was not a repetition of Labour's landslide triumphs of 1997 and 2001. Labour did achieve an unprecedented third general election victory, albeit with its majority reduced to sixty four; and the Conservatives lost a third election in a row for the first time since 1910. Labour's 2005 vote, down by over a million on 2001, was not a ringing endorsement of the 'New' in New Labour or of 'Blairism'. Nevertheless, it was not a rejection of New Labour because the party emerged as the largest party in the country and in the House of Commons.

The main features of voting behaviour in 2005 were:

1. Labour's 35.2% share of the vote is the smallest share ever received by a party winning a Commons majority. Furthermore, its 21.6% of the registered electorate voting Labour is the smallest ever recorded by the party elected to govern. These low figures reflect declining turnout and increasing support for third and other political parties.

2. Labour's share of the vote fell by 5.5%. The main beneficiary was the Liberal Democrats whose vote share increased by 3.5%. The Tory vote share fell a long way short of the 40%+ which the party usually won before 1997. The thirty three seats gained by the Tories did not even bring them up to Labour's total of 209 in 1983, Labour's worst performance during its period in opposition from 1979. The Labour and Conservative vote combined, the major-party or two-party vote, fell below 70% for the first time in since 1945.

3. The sixty two Liberal Democrat seats constitute the third party's largest total since the Liberal Party won in 1923. The Liberal Democrats won over 20% of the vote for the first time since 1987.

4. The most dramatic and potentially far-reaching political change in 2005 occurred in Northern Ireland where the Democratic Unionist Party (DUP) replaced the Ulster Unionists as the dominant voice of Protestant opinion. (See page 18.)

5. In Scotland Labour lost seats mainly because of the reduction in the number of Scottish Westminster seats from seventy two to fifty nine to bring Scotland's post-devolution representation into line with England. Previously Scotland had had more seats than a strictly proportional allocation by population would have permitted. The Liberal Democrats gained and the SNP lost vote share compared to 2001. The Conservatives returned one MP to Westminster. (See Chapter 7.)

6. Turnout improved on 2001 but only slightly, moving up from 59% to 62%. It remained markedly lower than prior to 2001.

Hiccup or Transition ?

The issues raised by the electorate's collective verdict in 2005 were neatly summarised by Peter Riddell in *The Times Guide to the House of Commons 2005*: "The 2005 election looks a transitional contest: the end of Labour dominance, but only the start of a Conservative recovery, and a Liberal Democrat advance but not yet a breakthrough". The idea of a particular election as transitional implies that it was a stage in a change from one state of electoral politics, Labour domination, to a new and different state which might be a Conservative victory next time round or a 'hung Parliament' based on a Liberal Democrat breakthrough. Alternatively, the 2005 outcome could prove to be merely a temporary and limited 'hiccup' in Labour's domination of British politics and government which began in 1997. Historians will eventually explain the outcomes of future elections and evaluate the accuracy of Riddell's claims. The 2005 results should be explained before that happens using existing theories of voting behaviour.

NORTHERN IRELAND

The 2005 election produced its most dramatic political result in Northern Ireland where Protestant voters deserted the hitherto principal unionist party, the Ulster Unionists (UUP) led by David Trimble, in favour of the more hard-line Protestant party, the Democratic Unionists (DUP) led by Ian Paisley. Trimble subsequently resigned as the Ulster Unionist leader. There was also a further polarisation of the Ulster electorate along religious sectarian lines as the more moderate parties (the Ulster Unionists and the Social Democratic and Labour Party) lost votes to the more hard-line DUP and Sinn Fein (SF).

By far the most significant result was the emergence of the DUP for the first time as the province's strongest party in terms of both votes and seats. The DUP won half of Ulster's eighteen parliamentary seats as its vote rocketed from 22.5% to 33.7%, by far the largest rise for a significant party in any part of the United Kingdom. This was at the expense of the UUP who had played a leading part in the Peace Process and the reaching of the Good Friday Agreement. The DUP's electoral success reflected Protestant unease at the Peace Process and scepticism about the IRA's renouncing of violence as a means of achieving political ends. In 1997 the UUP won ten Ulster seats but has since lost out to the DUP as Ulster politics have polarised.

The Northern Ireland Vote: 2001 and 2005

Party	Votes (000s) 2001	Votes (000s) 2005	Votes (%) 2001	Votes (%) 2005	Seats 2001	Seats 2005
Ulster Unionist (UUP)	216,839	127,856	26.8	17.8	6	1
Democratic Unionist (DUP)	181,999	241,856	22.5	33.7	5	9
Social Democratic & Labour (SDLP)	169,865	125,626	21	17.5	3	3
Sinn Fein (SF)	175,933	174,530	21.7	24.3	4	5

Table 2.2

The election in 2005 saw the voters of Northern Ireland shift their support to more 'hard-line' parties. The DUP led by Ian Paisley (right), won the majority of loyalist support and Sinn Fein, led by Gerry Adams (left), won the majority of nationalist support.

Sinn Fein enjoyed a 2.6% increase in its share of the vote. Although Sinn Fein's vote total fell by 1,403 compared to 2001, this was due to the decline in the size of the Ulster electorate. Sinn Fein is now the second strongest party in terms of both votes and seats in Ulster.

Although the SDLP, the more moderate nationalist party, lost about 44,000 votes, it held on to three seats, losing one (Newry and Armagh) to Sinn Fein but gaining one (South Belfast) from the UUP. Before the election, pundits were predicting that the SDLP would lose three seats to Sinn Fein, but the SDLP resisted that challenge. The political polarisation of Ulster politics appears to be more marked on the Protestant side than on the nationalist side.

Turnout dropped dramatically in Northern Ireland from 68% in 2001 to 62.5% in 2005. In this respect, political behaviour across the Irish Sea was similar to the rest of the UK.

VOTING BEHAVIOUR

There are two very general types of explanation for individual voting behaviour and collective voting trends.

- The first emphasises long-term factors such as social class, occupation and religion.
- The second explanation focuses on the political context of particular elections such as the significant issues and personalities of the day which may influence individual voters. Issues tend to explain short-term changes such as Labour's defeat in 1979 which led to the Thatcherite era in British politics and the 'record' characteristics of the 1997 result. Issues may also be related to long-term continuity in so far as they provide a motive for individual allegiances to a party which are then sustained over a long period of time.

Class and Voting

Social class dominated explanations of voting behaviour until the 1970s and is still considered to be influential today. The dominance of social class among the various influences on the decisions of the British electorate was dramatically expressed in 1967 in a celebrated claim by the Oxford political scientist P J Pulzer:

> "Class is the basis of British party politics; all else is embellishment and detail."
> (PJ Pulzer *Political Representation and Elections in Britain* Allen & Unwin, 1967)

Pulzer's statement was widely accepted as an accurate description of the key characteristic of such elements of British party politics as voting behaviour, party membership and party policies. Studies of voting behaviour were discovering that many people voted for the same party throughout their lives and that choice of party was strongly linked to 'social class'. Given its central position in explanations of British political behaviour, it is essential to define 'social class'. (See above.)

Market Research Definition of Social Class

Class	Categories		Percentage in Category 1966	1992	2005
A	Higher Managerial	A+B	12	19	21
B	Lower Managerial				
C1	Skilled Supervisors		22	24	31
C2	Skilled Manual		37	27	22
D	Unskilled Manual/Manual	D+E	29	30	27
E	Residual/Unemployed/Poor				

Table 2.3 Categories A, B, and C1 constitute the non-manual 'middle class' categories, while C2, D and E make up the manual 'working class'.

WHAT IS SOCIAL CLASS?

A social class is generally taken to be a set of individuals who share certain social characteristics which collectively give them a similar attitude to life in general and to politics in particular. Individuals who are brought up in the same neighbourhood and who then live and work in similar conditions might be expected to develop similar views on politics (which party to support), sport (which team to support), religion (which church to attend), leisure activities (bingo or bridge) and so on. There are many social conditions which are included in lists of variables defining social classes: occupation, housing, education, income and wealth. Some individuals are born into poor families, others into wealthy families. The children of richer families tend to go to private, fee-paying schools and on to higher education; the children of less wealthy families are more likely to go to comprehensive schools and are less likely to go on to higher education.

Such a simple division of the population is not accurate enough for the purposes of political scientists. They have tended to make use of the social class categories employed by market research organisations in their efforts to find out why consumers buy certain products and not others. The market research definition of the British class structure uses six categories, namely A, B, C1, C2, D and E, which are based on a classification of occupations. These categories and their relative sizes are described in Table 2.3.

Table 2.3 illustrates a significant change in British social structure in the three decades between the late 1960s and the early 2000s. Britain is slowly becoming more middle class. The percentage of the workforce classified as middle class increased from 34% in 1966 to 43% in 1992 and to 52% in 2005. The two classes experiencing the most change have been the upper middle class (A+B) which has increased in size, and the skilled manual class which has reduced in size. Before the 1997 election this change in the relative sizes of the two principal social classes was considered to be a disadvantage for the Labour Party. This was partly responsible for Labour leaders after Michael Foot redesigning the policies, the image and the electoral strategies of the 'working-class party'.

The changing relationships between social class—as defined by the market research categories and illustrated in Table 2.3—and party support/voting behaviour are illustrated in Table 2.4 which covers four elections: 1992 (Conservative win with a small majority), 1997 and 2001 (Labour landslides) and 2005 (comfortable but not landslide Labour victory). The most basic evidence suggesting

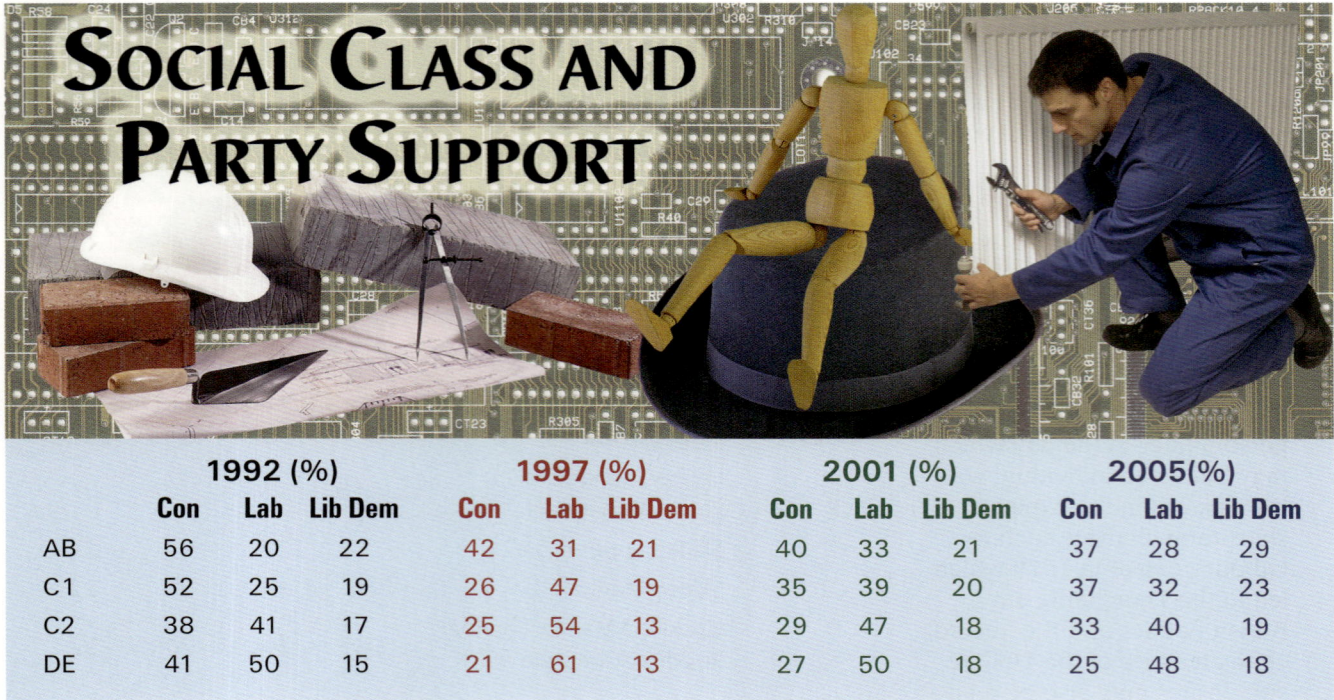

Social Class and Party Support

	1992 (%)			1997 (%)			2001 (%)			2005 (%)		
	Con	Lab	Lib Dem	Con	Lab	Lib Dem	Con	Lab	Lib Dem	Con	Lab	Lib Dem
AB	56	20	22	42	31	21	40	33	21	37	28	29
C1	52	25	19	26	47	19	35	39	20	37	32	23
C2	38	41	17	25	54	13	29	47	18	33	40	19
DE	41	50	15	21	61	13	27	50	18	25	48	18

Table 2.4 Source: Butler & Kavanagh *The British General Elections of 1992, 1997, 2001 and 2005*

that social class influences voting behaviour becomes visible when we look up and down the columns illustrating party support by class. Conservative support declines and Labour support increases each time as we move from AB through C1 and C2 to DE. However, the margins vary from year to year. The traditionally Labour skilled manual working class, C2, which had unusually been more Conservative than Labour in 1983 and 1987, became slightly more supportive of Labour in 1992 before moving decisively in Labour's favour again in 1997.

The 1997 election has been described above as a record-breaking election. The record-breaking theme may also be applied to the survey findings linking class to party support. For the first time ever the larger middle-class category, C1, gave more votes to Labour than to the Conservatives, and by a wide margin (21%). The highest social class, AB, remained faithful to the Conservatives, but for the first time fewer than 50% of ABs voted Conservative. There were now many more middle-class radicals (Labour voters in AB/C1) than working-class Conservatives (Conservative voters in C2/DE).

The 1997 links between class and party were substantially repeated in 2001 when Labour again trounced its main rivals. Labour's lead among lower middle class C1s was reduced but not overturned. The Conservatives recovered moderately and Labour lost ground slightly throughout the class structure except in the upper middle class AB where the Conservatives lost ground to both Labour and the Liberal Democrats.

In 2005 none of the classes gave more than 50% support to any of the parties. The unskilled working class, DE, was the most partisan, favouring Labour by a margin of 23%. The Conservative decline among ABs continued as the professional middle class opted in greater numbers for the Liberal Democrats. The Conservatives regained their position as the strongest party in the increasingly large C1 class.

The long-term links between social class and party support gave rise to the conventional wisdom that Labour was the 'natural party' of the working classes and the Conservatives the 'natural party' of the middle classes. These links were also expressed in the competing policies of the major parties. Labour adopted policies which could be said by and large to protect working-class interests while the Conservatives followed suit on behalf of the middle and upper classes. If voters are classed according to occupation, the proportion voting by class (percentage of working class voting Labour plus percentage of middle class voting Conservative) fell from over 60% in the 1960s to 41% in 2005. This weakening of class–party links, dramatised on occasion by the Conservatives leading Labour among C2s in 1983 and 1987 and Labour leading the Conservatives among C1s in 1997 and 2001, challenges the continuing relevance of the concept of 'natural class parties'. Falling turnout, a long-term decline in the combined Conservative–Labour or two-party vote, and more individuals crossing class lines when they vote have all contributed to a decline in class voting in Britain. This decline opens the way for other factors to exercise more influence on individual and collective voting behaviour.

RIVAL EXPLANATIONS OF SOCIAL CLASS AND VOTING TRENDS
Dealignment or Trendless Fluctuations?

British society and British voting patterns have changed since it was claimed in the 1960s that "class is the basis of British party politics". That claim has to be re-examined in the light of the changes in the links between social class and party support illustrated in Table 2.4.

Two rival explanations have been offered to explain the links between social class and party support illustrated in Table 2.4. One explanation is the dealignment thesis put forward by Professor Ivor Crewe and others. The second explanation put forward by Heath, Jowell and Curtice in How Britain Votes, published in 1985, focuses attention on problems inherent in efforts to define social class meaningfully.

Dealignment

Dealignment means a weakening relationship between social class and party support—a decline in the class basis of British politics. The evidence supporting the dealignment thesis may be seen in the fall in the proportion of the electorate voting for their natural class party from 64% in 1966 to 41% in 2005.

Crewe explained dealignment by distinguishing between an 'old' and a 'new' working class. Members of the 'old' working class still shared such definitive characteristics as

- an unskilled manual occupation in a traditional 'heavy' industry
- trade union membership
- living in council housing
- they were to be found in greater numbers in North Britain (north of England, Scotland and Wales) than in South Britain

Members of the 'new' working class were

- more likely to be skilled
- owner-occupiers
- working in newer 'high tech' industries
- located in the southern half of England

Two sets of evidence supported Crewe's division of the working class into two parts.

- Several social and political indicators suggested a growing 'North-South' divide.
- In the 1980s the skilled working class had moved from the Labour camp to the Conservative camp.

New definitions of Class

Heath et al challenged the dealignment thesis. First they focused attention on the widely accepted market research class categories in such a way as to strengthen the links between class and voting behaviour. Their new class categories are described below.

- *Salariat* (27%): managerial, supervisory and professional 'workers' with secure employment, relatively high income and some authority and autonomy.
- *Routine non-manual* (24%): clerks, salespersons and secretaries; subordinate position in the workplace but still 'white collar'.
- *Petty bourgeoisie* (8%): farmers, small proprietors and self-employed manual workers; essentially individuals who work for themselves and who are not subordinate within the workplace.
- *Foremen and technicians* (7%): 'blue-collar' elite, supervisory positions in the workplace.
- *Working class* (34%): rank-and-file skilled and semi-skilled manual occupations in industry and agriculture.

Heath et al argued that the voting behaviour of these redrawn class categories supported their view of social class in Britain. The most Conservative class between 1983 and 1992 was the 'petty bourgeoisie'. 'Foremen and technicians' were more evenly divided between the parties, moving from favouring the Conservatives in 1983 to favouring Labour in 1992. Both were more Conservative than the working class because their possession of some authority and independence allowed them to see themselves as closer to the 'salariat' in the workplace.

Heath et al concluded that there had not been a significant reduction in the links between social class and party support—that dealignment was not a satisfactory explanation. Rather the variations in the links between class and party support evident in voting behaviour since the 1970s, including 1997 when Labour took over from the Conservatives as the dominant party, suggest that the circumstances of each election might explain the result.

The Heath et al perspective on Class Voting in 2005

Social Class	Conservative	Labour	Liberal Democrat
Salariat	36	34	23
Routine non-manual	39	33	21
Self-employed	55	28	14
Foremen & technicians	29	39	24
Working class	21	51	20

Table 2.5

The Heath et al view of social class in Britain also demonstrates a relationship between class and party support in 2005. The strongest class–party links are found in the self-employed and working-class categories. Only these two classes are more than 50% in support of one party. The self-employed are strongly Conservative and the working class are strongly Labour. The two major parties are almost equally represented within the salariat which is the biggest category. Labour led the Conservatives among foremen (by 10%) and in the working class (by 30%). The Conservatives were 6% ahead of Labour in the routine non-manual group. Labour's large lead over the Conservatives among working-class voters overcame the Conservatives' much smaller advantage among the routine non-manual voters and the salariat. Liberal Democrat support does not have any class features except for the low support among the self-employed petty bourgeoisie.

Residence and Party Support 2005

	Lab	Con	Lib Dem
Homeowner	29	44	20
Mortgage Holder	36	31	25
Council Tenant	55	16	19
Private Renter	36	27	28

Table 2.7

The connection between political parties and type of housing is still clearly visible as illustrated in Table 2.7. In the 1997 Labour landslide homeowners had favoured Labour for the first time ever. In 2005 only homeowners whose mortgage was paid up favoured the Conservatives. The most partisan group were council tenants who were strong Labour supporters. Mortgage holders and private renters were more evenly divided between the parties. The Liberal Democrats fared best among private renters.

Ethnicity and Voting

About 5% of the British electorate is non-White. This group is composed of immigrants and the offspring of immigrants from Asia, Africa and the Caribbean. Table 2.6 clearly highlights the overwhelming allegiance to Labour of non-white ethnic voters in 1997, though a quarter of voters of Asian origin voted Conservative. The non-white vote in 2005 reaffirmed Labour's advantage with 56% opting for Labour and only 19% for the Conservatives who were 3% behind the Liberal Democrats.

Britain's participation in the Iraq War, which began in the spring of 2003, persuaded many Muslims who opposed the war to desert Labour in protest. Labour's vote dropped 5.5% overall in 2005; in constituencies where more than 10% of the voters were Muslim, Labour support fell by 10.6%. The Liberal Democrats were the main beneficiaries, their vote going up 8.8% in these constituencies. Bethnal Green and Bow, in Inner London, and Birmingham Sparkbrook have the largest Muslim electorates in Britain. George Galloway won the former and his Respect Party came second in the latter.

Asian & Black voting intentions 1997 (%)

	Asian	Black
Conservative	25	8
Labour	70	86
Liberal Democrat	4	4

Table 2.6 Source: based on Saggar (1997)

Age & Party Support

Age Group	Cons	Labour	Lib Dem
18–24	28	38	26
25–34	25	38	27
35–44	27	41	23
45–54	31	35	25
55–64	39	31	22
65+	41	35	18

Table 2.8 Source Butler & Kavanagh 2005

There are links between age and party support as shown in Table 2.8. The two older age groups favoured the Conservatives; the under-55s preferred Labour. A more spectacular link between age and political behaviour occurred in 2005. Turnout was much higher in the older age groups. OAPs (75%) were twice as likely to have voted as 18–24-year-olds (37%).

Student Activism

The voting behaviour of one social group stood out in 2005—that of college and university students who are defined narrowly by age but more broadly by lifestyle. The Liberal Democrats, whose vote rose 3.8% in Great Britain between 2001 and 2005, did particularly well in constituencies with the highest number of students. Their vote increased by an average of 8.6% in constituencies 15% of whose electorate were students. The Liberal Democrats recorded some spectacular and unexpected gains from Labour in Manchester Withington with a swing of 17.4% and Leeds NW, which has the highest number of students of any British constituency, with a 10% swing. The 'student factor' probably accounted for six Liberal Democrat gains from Labour in 2005. Students were galvanised into political action by issues such as the Iraq War and student fees. Only the Liberal Democrats of the three leading parties opposed the war.

Gender and Party Support 2005

	MORI 2005			British Election Study (BES)		
	Lab	Con	Lib Dem	Lab	Con	Lib Dem
Men	34	34	22	38	31	23
Women	38	32	23	37	34	21

Table 2.9

In 1992 the Conservatives were 9% ahead of Labour among women but only 4% ahead among men. In the 1997 and 2001 Labour landslides the gender gap had disappeared as men and women preferred Labour by similar margins. In 2005, as indicated in Table 2.9, different views of any gender gap were offered by different polling organisations. MORI, reported in Butler and Kavanagh, suggested a pro-Labour gender gap with women providing Labour's majority as men divided equally between the two major parties. The BES survey placed Labour ahead by 7% among men but by only 3% among women.

ISSUE VOTING

How can we explain the scale of the dramatic change in party electoral fortunes in 1997? Explanations based on socio-demographic factors—class, gender, age, residence etc.—remain relevant but do not tell the whole story. What influences could have been at work to produce the 1997 Labour landslide after eighteen years out of office?

Every election campaign has two principal points of reference for intending voters, some of whom are predisposed to support a particular party on class or other social grounds while others might be swayed by other political forces:

- **What** do the parties stand for on the pressing issues of the day?
- **Who** should form the government?

The 'what' may be defined in policy issue terms—what the parties say they stand for in their Manifestos in relation to policy areas such as health, education, law and order, the economy, foreign policy and so on. Voters may evaluate which policies are closest to their own views of what should be done before deciding how to vote. Many are influenced by impressions of how well each party has performed in office in the recent past. The 'who' includes the leading personalities in the election campaign, particularly images of rival party leaders such as the incumbent Prime Minister and the leader of the Opposition.

The 1992 and 1997 elections with their contrasting outcomes, offer an opportunity to examine the role of issues. Table 2.10 indicates that in 1992 the Conservatives were preferred on taxation, defence, law and order, the economy, and relations with Europe. Labour was preferred on education, the NHS and unemployment. The Conservatives' lead in 1992 on the issues on which they came out ahead as 'best able to handle a particular problem' was considerably greater than Labour's lead on its most favourable issues. Opinions had changed since 1987 but not sufficiently to get Labour elected.

In 1997 Labour overtook the Conservatives on both taxation and relations with Europe and increased its lead considerably on unemployment, the NHS and education. Labour's lead was greatest in relation to the NHS. The Conservatives were still ahead on defence and law and order but by greatly reduced margins. Labour was now regarded by many voters as the party they would prefer to carry out major government functions.

Why did public perceptions of how the rival parties would handle decisive issues change after 1992? After all, Labour had been ahead on issues before, though not nearly so decisively, and had lost the elections of 1987 and 1992.

According to John Curtice there was a drastic change in the public's perception of the strengths and weaknesses of the Conservative Party sometime following the 1992 election. (See Table 2.11.) The surveys were conducted in the spring and early summer of the years in question. In 1992, shortly after the closely contested general election, the Conservative image was much more positive than Labour's on party unity and on whether the parties were likely to offer strong and capable government. The parties were equally rated on 'moderation' which suggested that Labour had by then lost its radical left-wing image. By 1994 the Conservative image had been severely tarnished on both party unity and the ability to provide strong government. In contrast, Labour's image had improved so much that from 1994 onwards Labour was widely perceived as more moderate, more united and more likely to provide strong, capable government.

Curtice explains this dramatic switch in the public's perception of the attributes of the two major parties to 'Black Wednesday' in September 1992 when the Conservative government had to withdraw Britain from the European Exchange Rate Mechanism and accept devaluation of the pound. Conservative disunity on European issues was highlighted by Euro-sceptics rebelling in Parliament against the passage of the Maastricht Treaty and later on the issue of the single currency.

Issues and Preferred Party: 1992, 1997 and 2005

Issue	1992	1997	2005
NHS	Labour 17	Labour 49	Labour 14
Education	Labour 6	Labour 39	Labour 14
Law and Order	Conservative 22	Conservative 1	Conservative 12
Unemployment	Labour 19	Labour 38	Labour 15
Defence	Conservative 41	Conservative 8	Conservative 14
Taxation	Conservative 20	Labour 6	Conservative 6
Managing Economy	Conservative 29	Conservative 15	Labour 30
Relations with Europe	Conservative 34	Labour 6	Conservative 11
Asylum/Immigration			Conservative 41
Iraq			Liberal Democrat 20

The statistics indicate the percentage lead among voters of the named party over its nearest rival, usually Labour or Conservative.

Table 2.10 Source: 1992 and 1997, Dunleavy et al Developments in British Politics 5, page 50; 2005, Mori Polls

Although the Conservatives campaigned to 'Keep the Pound' at the election in 2001, the issue of Britain's place in Europe split the Party from the early 1990s. This disunity helped to create a lack of confidence among the voters about the Party's ability to govern.

The main issue in 1997 was the record of the Conservative Party in office rather than the positions of the parties on policy issues. The 1997 result has been interpreted as a negative judgement on the performance of the Conservative government elected in 1992. The result also supported a widespread view that governments lose elec-

IMAGES OF THE PARTIES, 1992–1996

Image		1992	1994	1995	1996
Moderation	Conservative	61	48	48	51
	Labour	61	72	76	74
Capable, strong government	Conservative	84	32	27	27
	Labour	35	60	67	62
Party unity	Conservative	67	10	8	9
	Labour	30	64	67	54

Table 2.11 Source: Based on data derived from John Curtice Anatomy of a Non-Landslide in The Politics Review *September 1997.*

tions rather than Oppositions winning them. However, Table 2.10 emphasises that by 1997 Labour had improved its standing on most issues of importance to voters.

Table 2.12 provides a view of how the electorate perceived the strengths and weaknesses of the parties in relation to the political issues which voters considered to be the most important to them in 2005. Labour was preferred on health care, education and unemployment whereas the Conservatives were preferred on law and order and defence. Labour's period in office has been seen by many as one of successful economic management leading to Labour being preferred on this issue in 2001 and 2005. The influx of immigrants from Africa, Asia and Eastern Europe has led to asylum and immigration becoming one of the most significant issues for many voters. In 2005, 37% of voters mentioned it as an issue likely to influence the way they voted. The Conservatives enjoyed a large lead, 41%, over Labour. Nevertheless, the immigration issue was less significant for many voters than health care, education and law and order.

The Iraq War and the environment were the only issues in 2005 on which voters preferred the Liberal Democrats, who opposed the war, to both major parties. The Liberal Democrats had a lead of 20% over the Conservatives and 29% over Labour on Iraq, which is consistent with the Liberal Democrat gains in the popular vote, and the capture of several parliamentary seats where the Iraq War issue influenced Muslim and student voters. (See pages 22–23.) However, the Iraq War came quite low down on the list of issues chosen by people as likely to influence their votes: only 18% said that it would influence the way they voted.

Although Labour clearly lost ground to the Conservatives in 2005 on most issues, it was still sufficiently ahead on several of the leading issues to be returned to power with a reduced majority in the Commons. Labour also stayed ahead of the Conservatives in terms of perceptions of the strengths and weaknesses of the rival candidates for the premiership, Blair and Howard. The 2005 campaign generated claims in the media and elsewhere that Tony Blair's image had slipped from being one of Labour's principal electoral assets in 1997 and 2001 to being more of a liability in 2005. Widespread public unease about the course the conflict in Iraq was taking was held to be responsible for the change in the Prime Minister's image. Support for this view of Blair may be found in a widely commented on feature of Labour's campaign, the much greater prominence given to the Chancellor, Gordon Brown. Blair and Brown were almost inseparable as Labour strategists decided that Brown had to be brought 'on board'. His 'reward' was that the Prime Minister acknowledged that he would not fight the next election as Labour leader, though he did not say at that point when he would stand down. Blair did say that the Chancellor was most likely to succeed him as Labour leader and Prime Minister.

The Conservatives, who remained firmly behind Labour in surveys of voting intention as the 2005 campaign unfolded, attempted to take advantage of Blair's weakening image. Their leader, Michael Howard, claimed that the Prime Minister could no longer be trusted because of misleading statements about

Preferred Party on Significant Issues, 2005
"Which party has the best policy on this issue?"

Issues Favourable to Labour			Issues Favourable to Conservatives		
Mentioned by		Labour Lead	Mentioned by		Conservative Lead
67%	Health care	14	56%	Law and Order	12
61%	Education	15	49%	Pensions	2
35%	Managing Economy	30	42%	Taxation	6
28%	Environment	6	37%	Asylum & Immigration	41
27%	Housing	20	19%	Europe	11
26%	Transport	21	19%	Defence	14
25%	Unemployment	31	18%	Iraq*	9

* The Liberal Democrats who opposed the war in Iraq, unlike the Conservatives, were preferred by 39% of the respondents compared to 19% preferring the Conservative stance and only 10% preferring the Labour government's policy.

Table 2.12 Source: Mori Polls

Public Images of Rival Leaders: Preferences as Prime Minister

Statement	All Voters	Men	Women
Blair has been a good PM overall	38	40	36
Blair has not been a good PM overall but still preferred to Howard	26	26	27
Blair not a good PM Howard is preferred	26	26	25

Table 2.13 Source: Populus Limited 2005, The Times 3 May 2005

weapons of mass destruction (WMD) in Iraq.

Table 2.13 illustrates the complexities of public perceptions of the two principal figures in the 2005 campaign. Blair was clearly preferred to Howard as the next Prime Minister even though a quarter of voters considered him not to have been a 'good PM overall'. Nearly two-thirds considered Blair either to have been 'a good PM' (38%) or at least preferred Blair to Howard (26%). During the campaign Blair's ratings improved more than Howard's which suggested that the negative tactic of attacking Blair's character did not work for the Conservatives.

GEOGRAPHICAL INFLUENCE

Regional and national variations in voting behaviour and election results have become a major focus of interest in recent years because of their political implications for the future of the United Kingdom. The Labour governments elected in 1950, 1964 and 1974 were dependent on winning a comfortable majority of Scottish and Welsh seats to overcome Conservative majorities in England. Nationalist electoral successes in Scotland and Wales in 1974 appeared to pose a potential threat to Labour's parliamentary standing and so prompted Labour's conversion to support for devolution. The establishment in 1999 of devolution for Scotland and Wales has not ended the debate about the future of the United Kingdom. The SNP's success in the 2007 Scottish Parliament elections raised questions about Scotland's constitutional status should SNP support increase further in future British and Scottish elections. What then have been the territorial dimensions within the British electorate in recent elections?

A North-South divide?

In the 1970s and 1980s British politics acquired increasingly territorial dimensions. The post-1979 combination of Labour dominance in Scotland and long-term Conservative government at Westminster raised the spectre of the 'Doomsday Scenario' whereby Scottish interests might be ignored by Conservatives in control of Westminster and Whitehall. Liberal Democrat seats were concentrated in Scotland from 1983 until their significant advance in England in 1997. Finally, there was increasing talk of a deepening North-South economic and political divide under Thatcherism. The Conservatives were much stronger electorally in the southern half of England, including the English

THE REFERENDUM DEBATE

Does the elected government have to accept the result of a referendum?

An interesting feature of the devolution saga is that a Labour government twice gave the device of the referendum a key role in the decision making process. (See Chapter 7.)

A referendum has two advantages:
● A referendum is democratic in that it gives 'the people' a direct role in the decision making process which adds legitimacy to the decision taken whether the answer is Yes or No. The Conservatives, who opposed devolution strenuously, quickly moved to accept the result of the devolution referendum in 1997.
● A referendum allows a government not to decide.

Basically, this means that difficult decisions may be put to the people and the government does not have to resign if the people reach a decision which the government does not really want. The British government resorted to referenda in 1975, 1979 and 1997 to decide on issues of constitutional reform.

On the other hand, the critics of referenda in a parliamentary system argue that a government which resorts to a referendum is renouncing its responsibility to legislate. There is a conflict over whether a government should carry out the decision reached by the people.

Midlands, than in northern Britain, including Scotland and Wales. The electoral division seemed to be accompanied by economic trends which saw lower unemployment and higher incomes in the South than in the North.

Studies of the territorial dimension in British elections generally refer to the four British nations and to nine standard English regions as shown in Figure 2.1. In 1987, the last Conservative landslide, the Conservatives were the dominant party in terms of votes and seats in the southern regions of England (South-east, South-west, East Anglia and Greater London) where Labour was desperately weak outside Inner London. The Conservatives almost monopolised constituencies in the South-east and the South-west of England, winning all but five out of 156 seats and over 50% of the popular vote. Rural East Anglia was just as strongly Conservative. Inner London, where Labour won twenty out of twenty nine seats, was an exception to Conservative dominance in the south of England. The Conservatives were the strongest party in Greater London and the Midlands where they won more than 40% of the vote and 60% of the seats.

Only in the northern regions of England did Labour win more seats than the Conservatives in 1987. However, Labour's margin of superiority, 94 seats out of 161 in the North-west (mainly Lancashire), Yorkshire and Humberside and The North (essentially the border region) was much smaller than the Conservative margin in its southern stronghold. Scotland and Wales were even less sympathetic to the Tories than the north of England.

The 1997, 2001 and 2005 elections produced comparable territorial patterns even though the overall fortunes of the parties had changed radically. A North-South divide was still visible, although by 1997 Labour was the dominant electoral force in Britain as a whole. This 'divide' is illustrated by the 2005 election results in Table 2.14. The much weaker Conservative performance was relatively in line with, but a pale reflection of, the regional patterns of support evident in 1987. The percentage of votes gained by

Territorial Variations in British Voting Behaviour 2005
A North to South Perspective

Nation/Region	No. of Seats	Labour No.	Labour %	Conservative No.	Conservative %	Lib. Dem. No.	Lib. Dem. %
Scotland	59	41	69	1	1	11	19
Wales	40	29	73	3	7	4	10
North of England	36	32	89	2	5	2	6
N W England	70	57	81	8	11	5	7
Yorkshire and Humberside	56	44	79	9	16	3	5
Midlands	103	64	62	34	33	4	4
Greater London	74	44	59	21	28	8	11
South-east and East Anglia	139	32	23	98	70	9	6
South-west	51	13	25	22	43	16	31
Total	628	356	57	198	31	62	10

* The nationalist parties won six seats in Scotland and three in Wales. Three Independents were elected, one each in Inner London, Wales and the West Midlands.

Table 2.14

NUMBER OF SEATS IN ENGLISH REGIONS

		1987	2005
South of England	South-east (excluding Greater London)	108	117
	Greater London (Outer & Inner London)	84	74
	South-west	48	51
English Midlands	West Midlands	58	59
	East Midlands	42	44
	East Anglia	20	22
North of England	Yorkshire and Humberside	54	56
	North-west	73	70
	Northern England	34	36
	(England)	(521)	(529)

Table 2.15

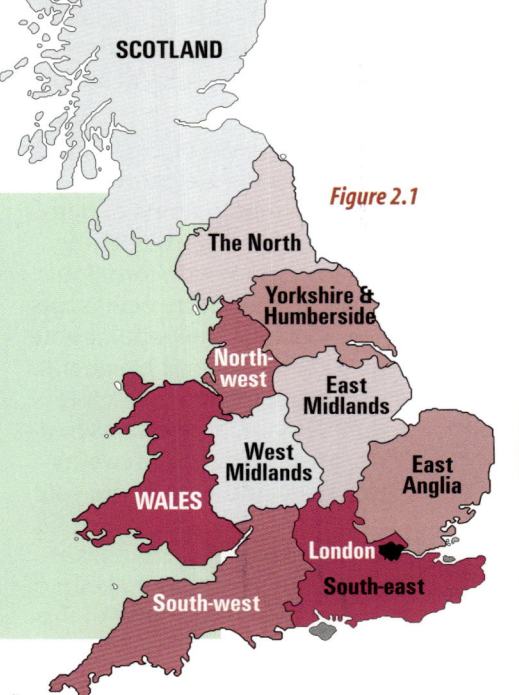

Figure 2.1

27 UK Politics Today

the Conservatives and their share of seats falls and Labour's share rises as we move northwards. Indeed, the electoral divide between North and South shifted because Greater London and the English Midlands became solid Labour territory in 1997. The Conservatives lost three-quarters of their seats in the suburban constituencies of Outer London. They lost half their seats in the English Midlands. Labour's electoral superiority in the northern regions of England in the lean election years of the 1980s and early 1990s was dramatically extended in 1997 and now exceeds the Labour lead in Scotland and Wales where Labour's parliamentary strength has been whittled away by SNP, Plaid Cmyru and Liberal Democrat gains.

Table 2.14 suggests that a simple North-South divide does not adequately summarise the territorial divisions in British general elections. Rather, there are variations within both North and South leading to a four-way division:

1. The Labour heartland lies in Scotland, Wales and the northern regions of England.
2. Labour's next source of strength lies in the English Midlands and Greater London, although a Conservative landslide could eliminate Labour's parliamentary majority in these regions.
3. The Conservatives dominate in the South-east of England and East Anglia where they capture most rural and suburban seats.
4. The South-west of England now supports a clear three-party system in terms of both votes and seats. In 1987 the Conservatives won forty four of the region's forty eight seats and 50.6% of the popular vote. In 2005 the Liberal Democrats won sixteen seats, two more than Labour, as the Conservatives were reduced to twenty two seats and 43% of the vote.

There has also been a significant change in the territorial makeup of the Liberal Democrat Party in the House of Commons. In 1987 more than half of the twenty two seats won by the Liberal Democrats were Scottish (ten) and Welsh (two). In 2005 they won forty seven of their sixty two seats in England. Although they won seats in all English regions their strength was concentrated in 'southern' Britain. (See Table 2.14.) The Liberal Democrats have not made any significant advances in Scotland since 1983. (See Table 7.1.) Nevertheless, the last two Liberal Democrat leaders were Scots—Charles Kennedy and Menzies Campbell.

The geographical divisions in British voting may be explained in part by the class factor. The clue here is the presence of the Labour stronghold of Inner London at the height of Conservative electoral dominance in the 1980s. Inner London remained true to Labour because there were enough working-class voters in its inner city constituencies. Similarly Scotland, Wales and the north of England have more working-class constituencies than their southern counterparts.

However, the territorial divisions are not simply a mirror image of social divisions because the differences are greater than social factors alone would lead us to expect. Even here the explanation relies on class. It was established in the 1960s that the minority class in constituencies which were strongly working class or middle class crossed the party line to a greater extent than in constituencies where the classes were more evenly matched.

Economic trends were also significant. The 'South' generally experienced less unemployment and attracted a higher proportion of the supervisory and skilled jobs in new industries based on technology. The 'North', where unemployment rates were higher, had more than its share of unskilled jobs in heavy industries which were dying out.

Another clue lies in Crewe's 'old'–'new' working class distinction.

Members of the 'new' working class, who were more inclined to vote Conservative than their 'old' working-class brethren, were more likely to be found in the 'South' than in the 'North'.

Scottish and Welsh support for Labour and hostility to the Conservatives is also explained by political issues such as devolution. Conservative intransigence on this issue in the face of support for devolution from the other parties added to the forces turning voters away from the Tories.

THE MEDIA AND ELECTIONS

The British press is politically much more partisan than television because of the strict rules governing television and radio. The BBC's public status requires it to be non-partisan and this requirement is extended to the other television channels. There is no equivalent of the BBC in the newspaper world which is permitted to be partisan.

Historically the British press has been predominantly Conservative in political orientation. In 1945 the circulation of pro-Conservative newspapers reached 6.7 million compared to 4.4 million for pro-Labour papers. In 1992 the Conservative advantage in press support reached its climax. There were 8.7 million readers of newspapers favouring the Conservatives compared to 3.3 million readers of pro-Labour papers. Partisanship on the part of the press was seen at its most dramatic in the *Sun's* 1992 election day headline:

> "If Kinnock wins today will the last person to leave Britain please put out the lights".

Some former Conservative supporters did not share the *Sun's* viewpoint. *The Independent* refused to endorse any party. *The Financial Times* was not in favour of a Conservative victory but did not feel able to recommend voters to elect a Labour government.

There were several reasons for the strong Conservative allegiance of

Ownership and Political Allegiance of Major British Newspapers

Newspaper	Owners	Circulation (August 2007)	Party Preferences and/or Endorsements			
			1992	1997	2001	2005
Daily Mail	Daily Mail & General Trust Group	2,339,278	Con	Con	Con	Con + anti Labour tactical voting
Express	Northern & Shell	827,491	Con	Con	Lab	Con
Mirror	Trinity Mirror	1,582,290	Lab	Lab	Lab	Lab
Sun	News International	3,158,045	Con	Lab	Lab	Lab
Independent		239,834	None	Lab	Lab	Lab + more LD MPs
Times	News International	638,820	Con	Eurosceptic	Lab	Lab
Financial Times	Pearson	426,830	None	Lab	Lab	Lab
Telegraph	Telegraph Group/ Barclay Brothers	887,664	Con	Con	Con	Con
Guardian	Guardian Group	355,750	Lab	Lab	Lab	Lab + more LD MPs

Table 2.16 Source: MediaGuardian.co.uk

the British press for almost fifty years following World War II. Newspaper owners are in business to make money and have accordingly supported the party most favourable to a free market capitalist system. That party was the Conservative Party for most newspaper owners. They also wanted to oppose the regulatory image of 'Old' Labour before it jettisoned much of that image along with Clause IV. Certainly at election time most of the press called on its readers to vote Conservative. Often Labour support was confined to the *Mirror* and *The Guardian*.

The 1997 election marked a significant turnaround in the party preferences of Britain's newspapers. For most of the Thatcher years Labour support was confined to *The Guardian* and the *Mirror*. In 1997 no fewer than eleven of nineteen major daily and Sunday newspapers preferred Blair and New Labour to Major and the warring Conservatives. The *Sun*, so hostile to Labour in 1992, now recommended its 3 million plus readers to vote Labour. The *Independent* felt able to endorse Labour as did The Financial Times. The *Daily Mail*, the *Daily Express* and *The Telegraph* remained loyal to the Conservatives. *The Times*, by now tending to favour Blair and New Labour but opposed to their stance on European issues, took the independent line of recommending its readers to vote for 'Eurosceptic' candidates irrespective of their party affiliation.

By 2001 only *The Telegraph* and the *Mail* supported the Conservatives. This turnaround was due to several factors.

- The Conservative government's internal conflicts over European issues after the 1992 election and Labour's 1997 landslide contributed to a decline of the Conservatives' image as the natural party of government.

- Labour leaders, including Blair and Brown, undertook a clear campaign to convert media barons to the view that 'New Labour', having dropped Clause IV and its longstanding socialist image, was now the natural party of government.
- Labour maintained a comfortable lead over the Conservatives in public opinion polls between the 1997 and 2001 elections so that a Labour victory in 2001 was widely regarded as a foregone conclusion. In such circumstances clinging to a Conservative partisan preference when the party was in the doldrums no longer made sense to some newspaper owners and editors.

The changes in Labour's internal politics symbolised by the popular usage of the term 'New Labour' and evident in constitutional changes (removal of Clause IV and decline in trade union influence) persuaded many people, newspaper owners as well as voters, that Labour could be trusted to govern effectively. Labour leaders like Blair and Brown contributed to the view that the press did indeed influence the formation of political opinion by undertaking a clear campaign to persuade 'media moguls' and others in the newspaper fraternity that New Labour is located ideologically in the centre ground of British politics, no longer on the socialist left. What mattered now, Labour leaders argued, was not ideological space between the parties, because there was none, but the ability of the parties to govern Britain effectively. That campaign was successful. Shortly after the 1997 election the allegiance of the previously Conservative *Daily Express* changed to Labour because the Labour peer, Lord Hollick, took control of the paper. Hollick sold the *Express* in 2001 after the election, and the paper switched back to supporting the Conservatives in 2005.

The 2005 election brought some change in the partisan preferences of newspapers. The *Daily Express* returned to the Conservative camp while *The Independent* urged the election of more Liberal Democrats. *The Guardian* opted for a return of a Labour Government along with more Liberal Democrat MPs. The *Daily Mail* remained true to the Conservatives but allowed tactical support at constituency level for Liberal Democrat candidates if that was likely to defeat Labour. The Labour supporting press, including the 'Sundays', had 16 million readers compared to 10 million reading the Conservative press.

Most studies of the political influence of the press during election campaigns have found that the Conservatives benefited to some extent from the media bias in their favour. However, that benefit was limited and did not prevent Labour winning elections in 1945, 1950, 1964, 1966 and 1974. The main question was whether the press made the difference when Labour or the Conservatives won narrowly. Was Labour's majority reduced to uncomfortable proportions in 1950, 1964 and 1974 by press comment? Did the press ensure Conservative victories in 1951 and 1970?

Whether the changes in the partisan allegiance of sections of the press will be permanent remains to be seen. A feature of British party politics in recent decades has been an intensification of internal disputes over policy issues. This has opened the way for newspapers to be generally supportive of a political party but opposed to some of its policies. If a referendum is held on whether Britain should join the European common currency it is likely that some newspapers will oppose joining while maintaining their general support for Labour. Others may revert back to a previous Conservative allegiance.

The influence of newspapers on voting behaviour and on election results is difficult to evaluate. There are distinct correlations between the partisan stances of particular papers and the partisan preferences of their readers. In 1997, 72% of readers of the traditionally pro-Labour *Mirror* voted Labour and 57% of the strongly Conservative *Telegraph* voted Conservative. Only readers of the *Daily Mail*, the *Daily Express*, *The Telegraph* and *The Times* preferred the Conservatives.

Do these readers vote for their preferred party because they are influenced by the paper's clear political stance or do they buy the paper because they already support its preferred political party? Not all readers are aware of the partisan preference of the papers they read. In 1979, 68% of *Sun* readers did not know its partisan stance, so it is not clear if the press changes the way that individuals vote. It has been argued that the main political impact of the press is on committed voters. In other words, reading a paper which reflects the individual's own political views reinforces those views. In 2005 only *The Times* and *The Financial Times* were out of step with their readers as to party preference. Both papers called for a Labour victory whereas their readers preferred the Conservatives to Labour, although narrowly among FT readers. The 'split personality' stance of *The Guardian* and *The Independent* in 2005, return a Labour Government *and* more Liberal Democrats, may have influenced some of their readers to vote for the Liberal Democrats.

Newspapers act like pressure groups from time to time. In 2007 *The Times* publicised the plight of Iraqis who were acting as interpreters to British armed forces in Basra. These individuals were becoming targets for armed groups opposed to the 'occupation' of Iraq and it was feared that many interpreters would be sought out and killed after the British left Iraq. *The Times* called for interpreters who wished to settle in Britain to be allowed to do so. After a few weeks the government agreed.

Further discussion of the role of the media is found in Chapter 6.

Chapter 3
Political Parties

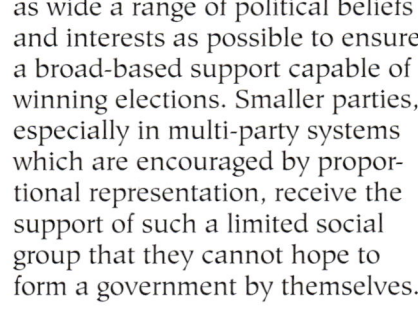

What you will learn.
1. The functions of political parties in a democracy.
2. The changing ideological beliefs of the major parties.
3. How the major parties are organised.

The electoral system, described in Chapter 1, ensures that Britain enjoys 'representative democracy'. The voters, whose behaviour was analysed in Chapter 2, have to be organised. The political institutions which have developed throughout the world in order to organise elections and voters are called political parties.

THE BRITISH PARTY SYSTEM

Political parties contest elections, organise voters by giving them meaningful choices, represent them in the legislature, and organise the business of government once the electorate has had its say. The members and supporters of a political party share distinctive ideas and philosophies. It is this which provides the bond that in turn allows for the pursuit of agreed policies and objectives. This is not to say that political differences will not emerge within a party. Intraparty differences—conflicts over policy positions within individual parties—are often as significant as interparty differences between rival parties. It could be argued that internal Conservative Party differences over the EU and a single European currency were the crucial factors in the heavy Conservative defeats in 1997 and 2001.

Political parties represent the views of their members and supporters in Parliament. Parties compete in elections in the hope that they will be able to form the government in order to implement agreed policies. In performing the functions of 'electioneering' and representation, political parties effectively organise the democratic process.

The range of parties in any country reflects its social composition, taking in class, religious, national and regional, linguistic, ideological and other divisions. Countries with several major social divisions tend to generate several significant or major political parties. Countries with a limited number of social divisions generate fewer major parties. Parties may be broadly or narrowly based. Comprehensive or 'catch all' parties, common to two-party systems, try to cover as wide a range of political beliefs and interests as possible to ensure a broad-based support capable of winning elections. Smaller parties, especially in multi-party systems which are encouraged by proportional representation, receive the support of such a limited social group that they cannot hope to form a government by themselves.

There are many commentators who argue that the political parties have become much too influential—particularly in the way in which the majority party dominates Parliamentary procedures and Parliamentary business. Nevertheless, although parties have become much more centralised and disciplined, they still offer many ordinary people the opportunity to become involved in the political process.

Parties have remained the principal organisers of the political process in Britain, even on the few occasions when referenda have been used as the mechanism for achieving some popular control over major decisions. The decision to hold referenda in 1975, 1979 and 1997 led to parties temporarily abandoning strict party discipline as cross-party alliances emerged to campaign for or against the questions being put to the electorate.

The Herald Election 2005
EXPLAINED: SCOTLAND'S VOTE FOR WESTMINSTER

2005 General Election in Scotland

	Share of Votes (%)	Number of seats
Labour	38.9	40
SNP	17.7	6
Conservative	15.8	1
Liberal Democrat	22.6	11

Table 3.1

GENERAL ELECTION RESULTS 1974–2005

Election Results		Con.	Labour	Lib.[2]	Others
February 1974	Votes (millions)	11.9	11.7	6.1	1.7
	Seats	296	*301*	14	24
	% Vote	38.0	37.0	19.0	6.0
October 1974	Votes (millions)	10.4	11.5	5.3	1.9
	Seats	276	*319*	13	27
	% Vote	36.0	39.0	18.0	7.0
1979	Votes (millions)	13.7	11.5	4.3	1.7
	Seats	*339*	268	11	17
	% Vote	43.9	36.9	13.8	4.0
1983[1]	Votes (millions)	13.0	8.4	7.8	1.0
	Seats	*397*	209	23	21
	% Vote	42.0	27.6	25.4	3.0
1987	Votes (millions)	13.7	10.0	7.3	1.4
	Seats	*375*	229	22	23
	% vote	42.3	30.8	22.6	4.4
1992[1]	Votes (millions)	14	11.5	5.99	2.1
	Seats	*336*	271	20	24
	% Vote	41.9	34.4	17.8	5.9
1997[1]	Votes (millions)	9.6	13.5	5.2	
	Seats	165	*419*	46	29
	% Vote	30.7	43.2	16.8	5.8
2001	Votes (millions)	8.35	10.74	4.82	
	Seats	166	*413*	52	29
	% Vote	31.7	40.7	18.7	6.5
2005[1]	Votes (millions)	8.77	9.54	5.98	–
	Seats	198	*355*	62	31
	% Vote	32.3	35.2	22.1	10.4

000 Denotes government
1 Number of seats increased to 650 in 1983, 651 in 1992, 659 in 1997 and fell to 641 in 2005
2 Liberal/SDP Alliance in 1983 and 1987; Liberal Democrats from 1992

Table 3.2

A TWO-PARTY SYSTEM?

The number of parties in any country with a parliamentary system has significant implications for the nature of government and also for the range of opinions represented in both the government and the legislature. It should be noted that

- the fewer the number of major parties, the less likely it is that a country will have a coalition or minority government;
- the greater the number of parties winning parliamentary seats, the stronger is the ability of every party to represent faithfully the views of its supporters in the electorate.

Historically, the British electorate has preferred a two-party system. The Labour and Conservative Parties have dominated political life since the 1930s. The last Liberal to hold Prime Ministerial office was David Lloyd George, who was Prime Minister from 1916–1922. Governmental office has been confined to Conservative and Labour since 1945. In only one of the seventeen general elections since 1945 has one of the two major parties failed to win a parliamentary majority, although the governing party has lost its majority on occasion in between general elections. Nevertheless, many other parties do exist, some of which win seats at general elections. The situation whereby a third party determines which major party should hold office after a general election has arisen only once in fifty years. In February 1974, a minority Labour government was formed after the Liberals decided to support Labour in the Commons rather than the Conservative administration led by Edward Heath.

The 1997, 2001 and 2005 election results provide contradictory evidence in relation to the issue of whether Britain still has a two-party system. In 2005 the Labour and Conservative Parties, the two 'major parties', won their lowest combined share of parliamentary seats in the post-war period—85.6%—and their lowest percentage of votes—67.5%. The Liberal Democrats won the largest number of seats, sixty two, to go to a third party since 1945. Nevertheless, Labour won the election with a comfortable working majority in the Commons.

Divergence in Scotland and Wales

There are national and regional variations in the strength of 'two-partyism'. Indeed, one could argue that the 'British' two-party system is an English phenomenon only. It cannot be applied at all to Northern Ireland which has its own party system. In Scotland the Conservatives, a major British party, did not win any seats in 1997 and only one in 2001 and 2005, coming fourth in the popular vote in 2005. In Wales they have not won any seats since 1992.

Scotland and Wales no longer support a Labour–Conservative two-party system. Instead, Scotland and Wales may be said to have one-party dominant, four-party systems under the first-past-the-post electoral system still used in British parliamentary elections.

IDEOLOGY AND POLICY

Ideological and policy differences between British political parties have long been expressed in terms of a spectrum running from left to right. Thirty years ago Labour was thought of as left of centre, the Conservatives as right of centre and the Liberals as the centre party. For most of the fifty-year period following the Second World War these ideological party images were defined in relation to economic issues and the role of the state in society.

Ideologically Labour was a socialist party. It stood for a redistribution of wealth in society in order to reduce major differences between the rich and the poor. Labour believed that the state should provide health and welfare for its citizens and should control the economy to achieve its aims. Labour promised radical reforms of both society and the economy.

The Conservative Party was opposed to socialism. It believed in leaving most economic decision making in the hands of the market economy while accepting the welfare state, the NHS and certain aspects of a mixed economy. Ideologically the Conservatives preferred gradual evolutionary change to radical reform.

Consensus

In spite of ideological differences and intense electoral competition from 1945 until the late 1970s, British politics were characterised as 'consensus politics'. There was a broad range of agreement over a number of key economic and social policies such as a mixed economy, the welfare state and the nationalisation of some, if not all, public utilities.

The 1970s proved to be a decisive turning point in British politics. After the long period of Conservative government from 1951 to 1964, the electorate rejected Labour in 1970, the Conservatives in 1974 and Labour again in 1979. British governments during that period experienced major economic problems. They were confronted by rising rates of inflation and found themselves having to choose between low inflation and low unemployment instead of being able to achieve both simultaneously. The humiliation of electoral defeat stimulated both parties to develop new policies in opposition. The 'post-war consensus' came to an end. It gave way to ideological polarisation, a divergence rather than a convergence in the ideological beliefs of the major parties.

Polarisation

Conservative defeat in the two 1974 elections was followed by the right-wing Margaret Thatcher replacing the moderate Edward Heath as leader in 1975 and by a radical policy rethink. Mrs Thatcher's name and her policies gave rise to the theme which was to dominate British politics for more than a decade after the Conservatives regained power in 1979. Her policy programme was summed up as 'Thatcherism'; her supporters were the 'Thatcherites'. 'Thatcherism' was considered to be radical and neo-liberal rather than conservative and evolutionary. It echoed Ronald Reagan's famous dictum that "Government is the problem, not the solution".

Electoral defeat in 1979 led to the Labour Party moving to the left because of discontent with the record of the Wilson and Callaghan governments. The left wing demanded, and temporarily achieved, a more socialist programme including a unilateralist defence policy and a commitment to withdraw from the EEC. However, successive electoral defeats in 1983, 1987 and 1992 forced Labour leaders Neil Kinnock, John Smith and Tony Blair to bring Labour policies into the ideological centre ground. By 1997 the change was so dramatic and the left so marginalised that Labour was commonly referred to as 'New Labour'.

THE CONSERVATIVE PARTY

Thatcherism: Ending the consensus

From May 1979 until May 1997 British politics and government were dominated by the Conservative Party which won four elections in a row (1979, 1983, 1987 and 1992). For much of that period, until she was forced out of office in November 1990, the dominant figure was Britain's first female Prime Minister. 'Thatcherism', the decisive radical policies associated with Mrs Thatcher and her supporters on the 'dry' wing of the Conservative Party, constituted a policy agenda which ended the 'post-war consensus' and changed the face of British politics. If 'conservatism' is associated primarily with preserving the status quo, then Mrs Thatcher was clearly less 'conservative' than her predecessors Harold Macmillan and Edward Heath were.

(continued on page 36)

THE POLITICAL SPECTRUM

Left

- Public ownership of large industries, especially utilities like water and gas.
- Big government—providing for needs of all in community through free health care, free education and social security.
- Workers' rights are defended.
- Community needs are given priority over individual needs.
- Promotion of greater equality by means of a redistribution of resources from the wealthy to the poorer sections of society.

Centre

- A mixed economy with public and private ownership.
- Toleration of opposing viewpoints with each individual guaranteed freedom to live as he or she wishes.
- Acceptance of the marketplace as a means of organising the economy but belief that the government has a duty to intervene to ensure that individuals are not exploited.
- Support given to the existence of a Bill of Rights.

Right

- All industries should be run by private companies without government interference. The marketplace is supreme in making economic decisions.
- The individual should be able to decide how to live his/her life free from government restrictions.
- Small government—each person is responsible for her/his own life and the government should not be involved in providing services.
- Government should only support the destitute.
- Government role should be limited to defence, providing a strong money supply, controlling relations with other nations.
- Patriotism and authority are stresse with strong support given to social discipline and law and order.

Post-war consensus based on the Welfare State

Left	Centre	Right	Left	Centre	Right
	LABOUR			CONSERVATIVE	
		LIBERAL			

Polarisation in the 1980s

Left	Centre	Right	Left	Centre	Right
LABOUR					CONSERVATIVE
		LIBERAL/SDP			

The early 1990s—return to a new consensus based on the market

Left	Centre	Right	Left	Centre	Right
	LABOUR			CONSERVATIVE	
	LIBERAL DEMOCRATS				

Late 1990s onwards— New Labour, New Consensus

Left	Centre	Right	Left	Centre	Right
	LABOUR			CONSERVATIVE	
	LIBERAL DEMOCRATS				

Both major parties are themselves made up of competing groups or factions which disagree about policy and ideology. In spite of often bitter internal conflicts over policy, British MPs rarely change their party allegiance. When any do so this is an indication of ideological conflict within the party. In June 2007 the Conservative MP, Quentin Davies, defected to the Labour Party. He accused David Cameron of being "superficial, unreliable and lacking conviction".

Why do we need POLITICAL PARTIES?

Political parties fulfil a great many functions which can be summarised as follows.

Candidate Selection

Political parties select election candidates. Candidates at an election need the back-up of a political party if they are to have any chance of being elected to Parliament. Voters tend to vote for a particular party rather than for a particular candidate. Only one Independent was elected in 1997, the first since 1950. Martin Bell, who was a widely recognised BBC reporter, was elected as an anti-sleaze candidate in Tatton. This unusual Independent success was made possible by the tacit support of the Labour and Liberal Democrat Parties. Their candidates stood down in what had been considered to be a safe Conservative seat in order to secure the defeat of Neil Hamilton who had been accused of committing 'sleaze'. In 2001 the voters of Wyre Forest elected an Independent MP, Richard Taylor, who stood on a local health issue—'Save Kidderminster Hospital'.

Electioneering

Parties provide the money required for an election campaign. They publicise their policies and their candidates nationally and also locally where their members and supporters may canvass, deliver leaflets and so on.

Policy Making

Parties make elections meaningful by publicising their rival positions on the most important issues of the day. Most voters have a rough idea of what the different parties intend to do if elected. The parties encourage this awareness by publishing Election Manifestos which state their policy programmes. This allows voters to choose a party whose policies are closest to their own point of view. American parties pay much less attention to policy making than to electioneering, whereas British parties focus strongly on the policy making function.

Governing

Government is organised by the winning party whose most senior MPs take control of government Departments. This is why British government is frequently described as 'party government'.

Organising the Parliamentary Process

With the aid of the Whip System (see page 77) parties organise the business of the House of Commons. This allows both government and opposition to be effective. As we shall see in Chapters 4 and 5, the British Constitution, in the shape of the conventions of ministerial responsibility to Parliament, encourages centralised and disciplined parliamentary parties.

The party functions listed so far describe what political parties do on their own behalf. Parties, however, also perform functions for the benefit of the political system and of society as a whole.

Representation

Parties represent the views and expectations of those who participate in politics. Through elections, parties ensure that Britain maintains a representative form of indirect democracy, although it should be noted that parties in office have been tempted occasionally in recent decades to resort to the more direct form of democracy provided by referenda. The people have been asked to state their collective view on issues such as membership of the European Community and devolution for Scotland and Wales. By the procedures of elections and referenda, parties help to ensure that government is legitimate because through these methods it receives the consent of the people who are being governed.

Underlying the policies outlined opposite, which were implemented in stages as the 1980s unfolded, was a basic determination to reduce the role of government and to replace much of the public sector of the mixed economy, for example utilities and railways, with a privatisation programme.

Efforts to capture the essence of Thatcherism have used terms such as 'individualism' and 'laissez-faire'. Mrs Thatcher demanded that individuals be allowed to make their own choices whenever possible. Conservative educational reforms such as allowing schools to opt out of local authority control in favour of grant maintained status applied the principle of individual choice to education. The preference for market decision making over the bureaucratic alternative was behind the attempt to create a market within the NHS known as an 'internal market'. GPs became 'fundholders' who could 'shop around' for the best hospital treatment for their patients. Catering and cleaning services were put out to tender. Hospitals could become Hospital Trusts, independent of regional hospital boards. Thatcher's ideological belief in the primacy of the market was clearly evident in the 'privatisation' of publicly owned utilities such as communications, electricity and water.

Tory 'wets', who lost influence progressively as the Thatcherite agenda unfolded, called for a return to 'One Nation Conservatism'. The Conservative Party had long claimed that it represented the interests of the whole nation, hence 'one nation', while accusing Labour of representing narrow class interests, basically trade union interests. A frequent criticism of Thatcherism was that its free market and 'anti-state' principles were enlarging the gap between rich and poor and so were contributing to 'two nations'.

Thatcherism frequently combined ideological and political objectives. Council house sales were justified ideologically by references to the desirability of a property owning democracy. However, they also reduced the role of local government, which was often Labour-controlled in urban areas, and they increased the number of owner-occupiers who were more likely than council house tenants to vote Conservative. Industrial relations reform could be justified for its own sake, but it could also be seen as weakening the powers of unions and their leaders who were strong supporters of the Labour Party. Legislation was introduced to force the unions towards greater internal democracy and to require ballots of union members before a strike could be called.

The main elements in the Thatcherite agenda included:
o Monetarism
o Trade union reform
o Community Charge (Poll Tax)
o Control of inflation
o Reducing income tax
o Sale of council houses
o Consumer choice
o Privatisation
o Greater reliance on the market
o Internal markets applied to education and the NHS

FROM MAJOR TO CAMERON

In 1990 Mrs Thatcher was replaced by John Major and although he won the 1992 election, it was clear that the Conservatives were a party in decline. John Major failed to control different factions of the party especially over Europe. (See page 84.) The party's image was further weakened by a number of allegations of 'sleaze' involving Conservative MPs. The Conservatives lost the 1997 election by a massive margin. John Major resigned as Conservative Party leader to be succeeded by the youthful William Hague (36), who proclaimed himself a Thatcherite and defeated the moderate Ken Clarke in the third ballot.

William Hague 1997 – 2001

Hague reorganised the party through his 'Fresh Future' proposals. His reforms were based on the principles of democratisation. Every party member now had the opportunity "to be involved in the decision making process of the party." (See page 38.) This enabled Scottish and Welsh party members to participate in the election of a new leader in 2001.

Hague set out to unite his party and to make it more attractive to the electorate. A problem for the Conservatives was that New Labour was implementing many of the Conservatives' policies—privatisation, low income tax etc. This made it difficult for Hague to put 'clear blue water' between the Conservatives and New Labour.

Hague tried to reduce party divisions over Europe by stating that the Conservatives would not join the single European currency for at least ten years. The return to Parliament in 1999 of Michael Portillo, a genuine leadership rival to Hague, further weakened Hague's authority. The 2001 election was another disaster for the Conservatives who made a net gain of only one seat. Hague resigned as party leader and, using the new rules, Iain Duncan Smith became the new leader defeating the moderate Ken Clarke.

UK Politics Today

The new system had elected a leader who was not the favoured choice of Conservative MPs. (Clarke had topped the poll among MPs.) Party members had also ignored the fact that Clarke was more appealing to voters than Duncan Smith.

Smith and Howard

Iain Duncan Smith appointed an overwhelmingly right-wing and Eurosceptic Shadow Cabinet. This was no surprise because as a committed Eurosceptic Duncan Smith was a constant thorn in the side of John Major's 1992 – 1997 government, doing his best to disrupt Major's pro-Europe policies. Duncan Smith was regarded as an ineffective leader and in October 2003 he lost the support of his fellow MPs and resigned as party leader.

The Conservatives turned to Michael Howard who had held high office in both the Thatcher and Major governments. In November 2003 he was elected unopposed as party leader. Howard brought stability and unity to a party exhausted after thirteen years of turmoil following the overthrow of Margaret Thatcher and eager to unite and rally around a strong leader. The Conservatives lost the 2005 election and Howard announced he would stand down "sooner rather than later" as he would be "too old" to lead the party into the next general election. He described the 2005 election as "the beginning of a recovery" with the Conservatives gaining thirty three seats. Despite announcing his future resignation, Howard reshuffled his Shadow Cabinet appointing David Cameron as Shadow Education Minister. This appointment cleared the way for David Cameron to run for the Conservative Party leadership. However, Howard failed to reform the party leadership election process. (He wished to reduce the influence of party activists and strengthen the role of MPs.) In December 2006 David Cameron was elected as the Conservative Party leader.

Built to Last

The 2006 'Built to Last' document included eight statements of Conservative values.

1. We will put economic stability and fiscal responsibility first. They must come before tax cuts. Over time we will share the proceeds of growth between public services and lower taxes.
2. There is such a thing as society; it's not just the same as the state. The right test for our policies is that they help the most disadvantaged in society, not the rich.
3. The quality of life matters, as well as the quantity of money. We will enhance our environment … We will support the choices that women make about their work and home lives.
4. Public services for everyone must be guaranteed by the state, not necessarily run by the state. We will improve the NHS and schools for everyone, not help a few to opt out.
5. It is our moral duty to make poverty history.
6. Security and freedom must go hand in hand.
7. We understand the limitations of government, but are not limited in our aspirations for government. We believe in the role of government as a force for good … It should support families and marriage.
8. We believe that government should be closer to the people, not further away. We want to see more local democracy instead of more centralisation.

Adapted from *Politics Review* September 2006

People Power is at our core—David Cameron

The changes I am leading in the Conservative Party today have two vital characteristics: modernity and long-term thinking.

Modernity matters because if we allow ourselves to be marooned on the wrong side of social and cultural change, the result is simply irrelevance and opposition. For too long, Tony Blair and New Labour laid claim to the future while the Conservative Party seemed stuck in the past. Today the position is reversed as we lead the political agenda into new areas such as the environment and wellbeing.

I am determined to ensure that the modern Conservative Party arrives at the next election with a serious long-term plan for government. Our policy development process is neither a shallow aping of New Labour nor an abandonment of Conservative beliefs. Instead it is driven by a distinctive aim: to bring benefits of Conservative values to all of the people all of the time, not just some of the people some of the time.

So we will apply our traditional Conservative belief in sound money to the benefit of all, by putting economic stability before short-term tax cuts. We will replace Labour's mismanagement of the health service with an approach rooted in Conservatism: trusting people and decentralising power.

Similarly, at a time of declining social mobility and chronic educational underperformance, we will best achieve our vision of opportunity for all by applying traditional Conservative belief in high standards and firm discipline throughout the state education system, rather than going back to the 11-plus and some mythical policy of "grammar school in every town." The debate can be tough but I'm determined to see the Conservative Party get to the right place on these issues. We must ensure that Conservative values and beliefs benefit all, not just some of the people.

Adapted from *The Observer*, June 2007

Reform of the CONSERVATIVE PARTY

STRUCTURE	MEMBERSHIP	POLICY	ORGANISATION IN PARLIAMENT	LEADERSHIP ELECTION
OLD — There were separate party structures for MPs, Central Office and the National Union (the party's volunteers). The main central body of the party was the National Union of Conservative and Unionist Associations.	Members belonged to a Constituency Party only. There were no national figures for membership. It is estimated that total membership had fallen from over a million in 1979 to under 400,000 by 1997.	This was decided by the Cabinet or Shadow Cabinet and the Conservative Party leader. No other body had the power to make policy.	Conservative MPs met as the 1922 Committee and discipline was enforced by the Party Whips. Disunity in Parliament under John Major made it difficult for the Whips to impose their authority. Withdrawal of the Whip was not used and, consequently, dissent and improper conduct by a minority of Conservative MPs went officially unpunished.	Only MPs voted for the Party leader.
NEW — There is now a unified party structure under a single governing body entitled The Board of Management. This body is responsible for all matters relating to party organisation and management, with direct powers over Central Office. It has the power to: • refuse membership to anyone; • replace constituency officers; • disband local associations. It also oversees campaigning and organises the Party Conference. It is chaired by the Party Chairperson who is appointed by the leader.	Such was the disarray of the party that in 1997 there were no precise figures for membership. A national membership database has been set up. This is intended to aid recruitment and identify areas and local parties which are failing to enlist young members.	Two new bodies—The National Conservative Convention and The Conservative Political Forum—were set up. Both allow members to influence policy, but they remain advisory. Hague attempted to make the party more democratic by the use of direct ballots of party members on specific policy issues. Since 1997 there have been four ballots and in every case party members have overwhelmingly endorsed the proposals of their leader.	An Ethics Committee can impose penalties for misconduct, including expulsion from the party. Tighter discipline has been imposed on MPs. Peter Temple Morris, a pro-European Conservative MP, publicly disagreed with Hague's declaration that Britain would remain outside a single European currency for the lifetime of two Parliaments. The Party Whip was withdrawn from him in 1997 and in 1998 he 'crossed the floor' and joined Labour.	A new two-stage process to elect the Conservative leader was introduced: Stage 1 involves only Conservative MPs; Stage 2 involves grass roots members of the Party. (See Figure 3.2.)

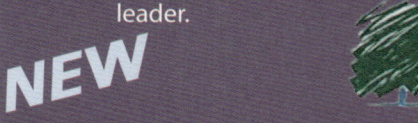

Perceptions of the Conservative Party October 2005

With which party do you associate the following statements?

	With the Conservatives	With Labour
It appeals to one section of society rather than society as a whole	48%	20%
It seems old-fashioned and stuck in the past	44%	10%
It is extreme	40%	17%

Table 3.3 Source: YouGov 2005

Compassionate Conservatism

While both Duncan Smith and Howard spoke of "compassionate Conservatism", this was not reflected in the 2001 and 2005 Conservative Election Manifestos which reflected traditional rightwing issues such as tax cuts, immigration and Europe. Cameron claimed he was returning to "the one-nation Conservatism" associated with the nineteenth century Conservative Prime Minister Disraeli and with the twentieth century leader Harold McMillan. Cameron called for a "more together society" and indicated the importance of public services in tackling poverty.

David Cameron made no secret of his belief that he was the new 'Tony Blair' of British politics—a youthful leader, not associated with the years in the electoral wilderness and party infighting and determined to broaden his party's appeal beyond its traditional support. Like Blair in the past, Cameron engaged in challenging traditional party values and set out to move the party into the middle ground of British politics. The YouGov 2005 opinion poll provided bleak reading for the Conservatives. (See Table 3.3.)

The party document *Built to Last*, published in August 2006, reflected 'compassionate' or 'modern' Conservatism. (See page 37.) Cameron claimed to be a "Liberal Conservative" and "not a deeply ideological person." Many of the policies that featured in the 2005 Manifesto were dropped. The Party abandoned its traditional support for the creation of grammar schools (to the fury of some Tories.) Furthermore, it pledged to maintain the NHS (a patient passport under which the individual cost of a private operation would be shared equally between the state and the private patient was discarded). Cameron also focused on issues not normally associated with Conservatism such as 'work-life balance', 'social justice', 'environment', and 'alternative family structures.'

Traditionalists within the Party were uneasy with these radical changes. The row over grammar schools in the summer of 2007 highlighted the end of the 'honeymoon period' for David Cameron. The resignation of Tony Blair, who was replaced by Gordon Brown in June 2007, created further unease. The July 2007 opinion polls displayed a surge for Labour (39%), giving them a four point lead over the Tories at 35%. While Cameron was hoping that under Mr Brown Labour would lurch, to the left, Brown was hoping that Mr Cameron's Conservatives would collapse under the weight of their internal disunity.

The Daily Telegraph's letters page reflects grass-root sTory opinion much of which was critical of Cameron. He was accused of being "all spin and no substance". One disgruntled letter stated, "I have always voted for the Conservative Party but after Cameron's speech there is no longer the option to do so. The choice is now between New Labour and newer Labour." Lord Tebbit, former Conservative Party chair stated that "the Party is aping Blair at precisely the moment when Blair is discredited."

David Cameron made no secret of his belief that he was the new 'Tony Blair' of British politics.

The Conservatives' poor results in the two July 2007 by-elections intensified the pressure on David Cameron. *The Observer* newspaper's comment article had as its headline "Could Cameron turn out to be the Tories' Kinnock?" and it continued, "Worse still for the Tory leader, Conservative MPs are echoing Labour's attack that he's just a superficial opportunist."

The Conservatives had expected Labour to win comfortably in Tony Blair's old seat in County Durham, but they had not expected to come third. In the Labour seat of Ealing Southhall, David Cameron had high hopes of winning Labour voters back to the Conservatives. He had visited the constituency five times and the Conservative candidate Tony Lit, an Asian businessman, had been chosen by the leadership and was even described on the ballot as representing "David Cameron's Conservatives." Labour's majority in Ealing Southall was reduced from 11,440 to 5,070. However, it was the Liberal Democrat candidate who benefited, coming second with the Conservatives trailing behind in third place.

Cameron's Shadow Cabinet reshuffle was also criticised, especially removing David Willetts as his spokesperson on schools after the right-wing backlash over grammar schools. The Prime Minister, Gordon Brown, is reported to have said: "It is not leadership to try to have a Clause Four moment and then sack the man who tried to draft it for you." To add to his worries further, opinion polls confirmed the 'Brown Bounce' and gave Labour 41% to the Conservatives' 35%. Satisfaction with Brown as leader was up sixteen points to 36%, while Cameron fell from 35% to 31%.

THE LABOUR PARTY: FROM 'OLD' TO 'NEW'

The period from 1979–1983 witnessed a disastrous split within the Labour Party between the left wing who wished more radical policies and the moderates on the right who wished, for example, to retain Britain's nuclear deterrent and to remain within the European Community. The low point was the desertion of leading right-wingers such as Roy Jenkins and Shirley Williams who formed a new party called the Social Democrats. In 1983 the ineffectual Michael Foot was replaced by Neil Kinnock who set out to make Labour once again electable. A further general election defeat in 1987 led to the defeat of the 'left' at the 1987 Labour Party Conference. Tony Benn's challenge to Kinnock's leadership was easily beaten and the policy review which followed abandoned the extreme left-wing policies which were not favoured by the electorate. The 1992 general election displayed the progress Labour had made towards becoming electable. John Major's Conservative majority had been reduced to twenty two.

From Smith to Blair

Kinnock resigned as leader after the 1992 election and a Scot, John Smith, a centre right candidate, became the new leader. John Smith was determined to continue Kinnock's policy of modernisation and the 1993 Conference reduced the influence of the trade unions, introducing One Member One Vote in the election of party leader and in the selection of parliamentary candidates.

Tragically, in 1994 John Smith died. In the ensuing leadership election the centre right of the party, now popularly known as 'New Labour', won handsomely in the person of Tony Blair who defeated Margaret Beckett and John Prescott, winning over 50% of the vote in all three parts of the electoral college. John Prescott won the contest for deputy leader, defeating Margaret Beckett. Although Prescott represented 'Old' Labour through his working-class and trade union background, he was by no means on the party's hard left.

Rewriting Clause IV

Tony Blair set about implementing further reforms to ensure that Labour's past failures and image would not lead to a fifth Conservative victory. Blair was determined to change Labour's policy image. His principal achievement was the removal of the famous, or notorious, Clause IV from the Labour Party Constitution.

Clause IV symbolised a commitment to socialism, to public ownership and to an interventionist state. It was an article of faith for the majority of Labour Party members for most of the twentieth cen-

---

Conservative Social Justice Review *Breakthrough Britain* **July 2007**

The policy group commissioned by Cameron and chaired by former Tory leader Iain Duncan Smith unveiled nearly 200 recommendations for tackling social breakdown. This report will form the basis of policy making for the next Conservative general election manifesto.

The Key Proposals
- Setting up a transferable tax allowance, making it easier for one parent to stay at home to look after children or elderly parents and boosting incomes by £20 per week.
- Enabling parents to 'frontload' child benefit with up to £2,800 per year up to the age of 3, less when the child is older.
- Expecting single parents to work sixteen hours a week when their youngest child reaches 5 and thirty hours a week when their youngest child reaches 11.
- Raising the tax on alcohol to tackle binge drinking.
- Cannabis to be a class B drug again.
- Raising the gambling age limit to 18.
- Failing state schools to be taken over by parents and charities with pupils in disadvantaged schools getting £500 for extra tuition—academic, musical or sporting.
- Making volunteering part of the school curriculum and rewarding youngsters who undertake community work with tickets for pop concerts.

"To secure for the workers by hand or by brain the full fruits of their industry and the most equitable distribution thereof that may be possible upon the basis of the common ownership of the means of production, distribution and exchange, and the best obtainable system of popular administration and control of each industry or service".
The Constitution of the Labour Party Clause IV (4)

Labour 1988

The Labour Party is a democratic socialist party. It believes that by the strength of our common endeavour we achieve more than we achieve alone, so as to create for each of us the means to realise our true potential and for all of us a community in which power, wealth and opportunity are in the hands of the many not the few, where the rights we enjoy reflect the duties we owe, and where we live together, freely, in a spirit of solidarity, tolerance and respect.

Labour
www.labour.org.uk

Labour Party membership cards. The card above contains the original Clause IV. Today the card has an extract from the reformed Clause IV.

Clause IV revised
The new Clause IV is much longer than its predecessor. Its main points are summarised below.

1. Labour is proclaimed to be a "democratic socialist party". This is an intriguing claim because in the early eighties, leaders of the Labour Right defected to form the 'Social Democratic Party'. This term 'softens' the socialist commitment without jettisoning it altogether. It emphasises the democratic component which might have been obscured by charges of trade union dominance.

2. It also reflects the political philosophy associated with Blair— 'communitarianism'. In addition to calling for "power, wealth and opportunity" to be "in the hands of the many not the few", the new Clause IV also emphasises the "duties we owe" to the whole community. This community emphasis contrasts sharply with the individualism associated with Thatcherism.

3. Whereas the old Clause IV stressed "common ownership" and "popular administration and control of each industry or service", the new version refers to "a thriving private sector and high quality public services" and, unlike the old version, to "the enterprise of the market" and to the "rigour of competition".

4. Core values compatible with 'socialism' are retained: a "just society", an "open democracy", a "healthy environment".

5. The trade union link is not rejected. Labour is pledged to "work with trade unions and other affiliated organisations".

tury and it was printed on every individual party membership card.

In April 1995 a special Party Conference voted by a two to one majority to replace totally Clause IV with a new statement of Labour's core values. Constituency Associations were particularly favourable suggesting that the left-wing activists who had been dominant there in the early 1980s had given way to enthusiastic supporters of the new leader. The unions, whose political ideology had been clear in the original Clause IV, supported the change by 55% to 45%.

The Labour Party of 1980 was hardly recognisable in the party which won the 1997 election so decisively. Indeed, the cartoonists' depiction of 'Tony' as 'Tory' Blair was merely a humorous way of stating a widespread belief that Labour had moved significantly to the right. Blair himself denied the cartoonists' view, preferring to emphasise that New Labour was attempting to establish a "Third Way" between the socialism of Old Labour and the selfish individualism of Thatcherism. Many Labour supporters still believe in core values which they claim to be compatible with 'socialism' such as equality of opportunity, and a more even distribution of wealth.

'The control freaks'

A major criticism of Blair's leadership and New Labour was its dictatorial behaviour in trying to control both the views of party members and the selection of Labour candidates to serve the public.

In 1998 Blair interfered in Welsh politics to ensure that his favoured candidate, Alun Michael, became the Welsh Labour Party leader. His leadership was unpopular and in 2000 he was replaced by the Welsh people's real choice, Rhodri Morgan.

Blair ensured that Ken Livingstone, a left-wing Labour MP, would not be Labour's candidate for the May 2000 London Mayor elections. Liv-

Dennis Canavan challenged and defeated the Labour Party after spending his political life fighting for the party. The voters put the individual before the party.

The Scottish experience

The sleaze in local government affairs in Scotland, involving Labour councillors especially in the West of Scotland, was used to justify vigorous selection procedures for the selection of Labour candidates for the new Scottish Parliament. However, the party members in charge of selection procedures used their powers to exclude several MPs and leading activists who displayed a left-wing (and independent) record. Dennis Canavan, the popular MP for Falkirk West, was rejected as being "unsuitable". This infuriated Canavan and the electorate of Falkirk West. After much soul-searching, Canavan stood as an Independent in the Scottish Parliament elections and won the largest majority of any candidate.

ingstone stood as an Independent and defeated the Labour candidate, Frank Dobson, to become Mayor of London.

BLAIR ERA 1997–2007

On the morning after his historic 1997 victory Blair stated: "We campaigned as New Labour and we shall govern as New Labour." Two further election victories were to follow, making him the most

THE BLAIR YEARS: 1997 - 2007

"What he (Blair) has done is force the Conservatives onto New Labour's ground. Blair's generation of Labour politicians felt compelled to accept the Thatcherite settlement on the economy. He, in turn, forced the Tories to accept a new, more social democratic consensus that government has a responsibility to invest in public services and deliver social justice."
The Observer, May 2007

"Just after the 1997 election an old colleague of mine said: come on Tony, now we've won again can't we drop all this New Labour and do what we believe in? I said: 'It's worse than you think. I really do believe in it.' "
Tony Blair at the Labour Party Conference, September 2001

1997
May 2 — After 18 years in the political wilderness, Labour achieves a landslide victory with a majority of 179 seats
May 6 — Gordon Brown, Chancellor of the Exchequer, gives the Bank of England the freedom to set interest rates independently of the government

1998
July — Parliament passes the *Crime and Disorder Act* to curb anti-social behaviour through the introduction of ASBOs in England and Wales

1999
May — Opening of the Welsh Assembly
July — Opening of the Scottish Parliament

2001
January — Peter Mandelson resigns from the Cabinet for a second time, following his involvement in a passport application for an Indian businessman
May — Labour wins a second election victory with a slightly reduced majority of 167

2002
February — British forces help to end the civil war in Sierra Leone
September — The first city academy, funded partly by private investors, opens in Kent. Blair publishes the government dossier alleged to contain evidence of Iraqi weapons of mass destruction

2003
February — Over a million people demonstrate in London against the invasion of Iraq
March — Parliament votes by 412 to 149 for military action in Iraq. Robin Cook, opposed to the war, gives his resignation speech in the House of Commons

2004
December — David Blunkett resigns as Home Secretary after he is linked to a visa application for the nanny of his ex-lover

2005
May — Tony Blair wins historic third general election with a significantly reduced majority of 66, and the lowest ever percentage of the vote for a winning British party
July — Suicide bombers attack the London transport system, leaving 52 people dead
November — The government suffers its first Commons defeat when MPs reject proposals for terror suspects to be held for up to 90 days without charge

2006
January — Prime Minister suffers another Commons defeat over proposed religious hate laws
March — Scotland Yard announces that it is launching an investigation into the 'cash for honours' allegations
September — Blair gives his final conference speech as party leader. He praises Brown but does not endorse him as a successor

2007
May — Blair announces that he will resign as Prime Minister on 27 June 2007
24 June — Gordon Brown becomes the new leader of the Labour Party
27 June — Gordon Brown becomes Prime Minister

UK Politics Today

THE MAIN POINTS OF NEW LABOUR'S THIRD WAY

- Acceptance that the market economy has a crucial role in creating individual and collective wealth.
- Rejection of the traditional left-wing view that only the public sector can provide public services. In the health service for example, the private sector can work with the NHS to improve health provision.
- Emphasis on community and moral responsibility rather than selfish individualism.
- A continual belief in social inclusion through "a hand up not a hand out." Individuals have an obligation to use welfare provision as an opportunity to improve their life chances. Provision of an enabling state rather than a nanny state.
- Pursuit of consensus and progress rather than ideological conflict.

2007 LABOUR PARTY DEPUTY LEADERSHIP ELECTION

While Gordon Brown was appointed leader of the Labour Party without having to go through a leadership contest (he was the only candidate), the appointment of deputy leader was an exciting and close contest with six candidates taking part.

The elections took place using the Alternative Vote System in an electoral college, with a third of the votes allocated to MPs and MEPs, a third to individual members of the Labour Party and a third to trade union members. The system used is complicated and time consuming. The last place candidate is eliminated in a series of rounds and their second preference is reallocated until one candidate gets more than 50% of the vote.

In the first round, Harriet Harman was the first choice among Labour Party members but only the fifth choice of union members. Alan Johnson was the first choice overall in the second to fourth rounds but failed to reach the 50% required. In the final ballot (see below) Harriet Harman achieved 50.4% to Alan Johnson's 49.6% and so became deputy leader. Harman's victory was achieved by her greater popularity among individual party members as Alan Johnson had the greatest support from MPs and affiliated organisations. In 1998 Ms Harman was sacked from Mr Blair's first Cabinet after public disputes with her Minister, Frank Field.

Round 5

Candidate	Members of Affiliated Organisations	Individual Members	MPs/MEPs	Total
Harman	16.18%	18.83%	15.42%	50.43%
Johnson	17.15%	14.50%	17.91%	49.56%

Table 3.4

successful Labour leader ever. The changes to the Labour Party, begun by Neil Kinnock and John Smith, and consolidated by Tony Blair, had transformed a divided and unelectable party into the natural party of government—the third way had become the only way!

The Third Way

Supporters of New Labour would argue that much of the Third Way approach promotes, according to Peter Mandelson, "a moral outlook that Keir Hardie and Clement Atlee would have shared." (See The Third Way, above.) Public spending on education and in health for example, have been considerably increased. Welfare reforms such as the New Deal have retained a safety net for the unemployed, while encouraging the individual to take up employment. The Minimum Wage which was opposed by the Conservatives and by big business reflects New Labour's social democracy agenda. However, critics argue that reforms such as the introduction of university tuition fees and the involvement of the private sector in the delivery of public services have been stolen from the Conservative Party. The electoral dominance of Labour enabled Blair to ignore criticism from the left wing of the party over such policies as the Public-Private Partnership agreements, the reintroduction of the internal market in the NHS and, above all, his decision to involve British troops in Iraq. In 2003, for instance, 139 Labour MPs defied the Whip and rebelled over Iraq.

By the 2005 election the war had damaged Blair and he needed the credibility of Brown whose trust ratings were now far superior to those of the Prime Minister. The police investigation into the accusation that Labour sold peerages in exchange for donations to the party further diminished Blair's credibility. He became the first Prime Minister to be interviewed— twice—in a criminal investigation. (See page 55.)

Blair's announcement that he would stand down before the next election encouraged greater opposition within the Labour Party. His reduced majority in 2005 provided greater opportunities for Parliament to challenge his policies and in November 2005 Tony Blair received his first ever defeat in the Commons on the government's proposals to allow the detention of suspected terrorists for ninety days. In January 2006 the Prime Minister suffered another Commons defeat on proposed religious hate laws.

Blair's relationship with his Chancellor, Gordon Brown, was a stormy one. Brown's view was that he, not Blair, should have been the leader of the Labour Party in 1994 after the death of John Smith. Blair conceded vast powers to Brown to try to appease the other man's frustrated ambition to lead the party and the country. Nevertheless, Blair and Brown were the rock on which New Labour was built and despite their differences the rock stood firm. Brown's control of the Treasury and the budgets for other departments gave him tremendous power in domestic affairs.

Blair's relationship with the Labour Party was a complex one. Many within the party did not like or trust him. His appointment of John Prescott, who represented the centre left tradition of the party, as deputy leader was mere window dressing. His greatest achievement was to lead a centre left party in directions it often did not wish to follow. (At present, David Cameron is trying to move a centre right party to the middle ground.) Under Blair, Labour went from being a party that had been four time losers into one that was three time winners. What more can a party ask of its leader?

GORDON BROWN: CONTINUITY AND CHANGE

The Conservatives' hopes that Gordon Brown would move Labour to the left, enabling David Cameron to win back former Conservative voters, has not materialised. In July 2007 Gordon Brown informed Labour's National Policy Forum that there would be no u-turn from Blairism. He stated: "We will and must be modern, not backwards-looking; appeal to the mainstream, not the fringe; listen to the British people, not speaking just to ourselves." He made no apology for attempting to form a government of all the talents (he had offered the post of Northern Ireland Secretary to the former Liberal Democrat leader, Paddy Ashdown, who had declined). At the Policy Forum meeting he went further and appealed to moderate Conservatives, who may be having doubts about the effectiveness of Cameron's attempts to transform 'the nasty party', to join Labour.

Brown appointed a strong and experienced Cabinet with David Milliband, 41, as Foreign Secretary and Jacqui Smith, 44, one of the original 'Blair babes' as Home Secretary. The terrorist attacks of June 2007 and Brown's announcement of constitutional reform and "a change to the face of British politics" enabled him to display a firm and forward-looking government. Labour held on to its two seats in the July 2007 by-elections and more importantly the Conservatives failed to make any breakthrough with the Liberal Democrats taking second place in both by-elections leaving the Conservatives a disappointing third.

THE LIBERAL DEMOCRATS: REFORMING THE CENTRE

The Liberal Party, the forerunner of today's Liberal Democrats, was classified as a 'minor' political party from the 1920s. It last won a parliamentary majority in 1906, last won more seats than Labour in 1923 and its vote was reduced to less than 3% in the 1950s. The Liberals won only a handful of seats, usually less than ten, from 1945 until the 1970s when they enjoyed a 'revival' which suggested that the two-party system was weakening. However, the Liberals were the perennial 'victims' of the electoral system as their share of seats failed to match their share of votes. The party was electorally strongest in or near the 'Celtic fringes'. Its leadership has come from Scotland (Jo Grimond, David Steel, Charles Kennedy and Menzies Campbell) and south-west England (Jeremy Thorpe and Paddy Ashdown).

What does it mean to be a Liberal?

"Three simple words—freedom, justice and honesty—sum up what the Liberal Democrats stand for.
FREEDOM – because everybody should have the opportunities they need to make the most of their lives.
JUSTICE – because freedom depends on fairness.
HONESTY – because where fairness has a cost, like investing in schools, hospitals and pensions, we explain how it will be paid for.
Liberal Democrats believe that the role of democratic government is to protect and strengthen liberty, to redress the balance between the powerful and the weak, between rich and poor and between immediate gains and long-term environmental costs. We believe in a society in which every citizen shares rights and responsibilities."

(Adapted from Liberal Democrat election literature)

The Liberals were perceived as the party of the centre—not socialist but not conservative either. The close election of February 1974 demonstrated that the Liberals were closer in spirit to Labour than to the Conservatives. The Liberals indicated that they would rather support a Labour government than the continuation of Heath's Conservative administration when neither of the two major parties won an overall majority in the Commons. When the Labour government lost its overall majority in the Commons in 1976, it survived with the support of the Liberals who participated in an informal 'Lib-Lab Pact' which gave the party some influence but no positions in the government. The Conservative victory in 1979 ended the period of Liberal influence.

In 1988 the Liberal Party merged with the Social Democratic Party—a right-wing breakaway from the Labour Party. The respective parties had formed an electoral alliance to fight the 1983 and 1987 general elections but had failed to 'break the mould' of British politics. Paddy Ashdown became the leader in July 1988, replacing David Steel.

Radical Liberals

The Liberal Democrats, like Labour, had to adjust to Conservative electoral success. With Labour moving into the centre ground under Smith and Blair, the Liberal Democrats sought ways of redefining their old 'radical' image. Their chosen strategy was to stand aside from Labour's "we shall not raise income tax" platform. Instead, the Liberal Democrats took the bold step of promising to raise income tax by a penny in the pound in order to increase spending on education. The Liberal Democrats also retained their radical stance on constitutional issues, joining with Labour in the Scottish Constitutional Convention in support of devolution.

In 1997 the Liberal Democrats benefited from a concentration of effort and resources in seats they had a realistic chance of winning. They enjoyed their most successful election of the post-1945 era, winning forty six seats—more than double their 1992 total—in spite of not raising their share of the popular vote. This was the most successful third party performance since 1929. Ironically, the size of Labour's majority meant that the new government would be unlikely to have any need of Liberal Democrat support in order to survive in office.

The Liberal Democrat gains were almost all from the Conservatives. Their objective, which was established by the 1997 result, was to continue the process of replacing the Conservatives as the second major party. This objective was achieved in Scotland in 1997 at the parliamentary level.

The relationship which Paddy Ashdown's and the Liberal Democrats had with the Labour Party was based on constructive opposition. After Labour's victory in the 1997 general election a 'Joint Cabinet Committee' (JCC), which included senior Labour and Liberal Democrat politicians, was created to discuss the implementation of the two parties' shared commitment for constitutional change. Blair appointed the Liberal Democrat peer Roy Jenkins to conduct a review of the case for electoral reform. However, Blair ignored the Jenkins Commission's recommendation that a system of proportional representation should replace first-past-the-post for general elections. Nevertheless, the Liberal Democrats could take comfort from the introduction of PR systems for the Scottish and Welsh Parliaments and for elections to the European Parliament. In 1999 the Liberal Democrats, under the leadership of Jim Wallace, formed a coalition government with Labour in the new Scottish Parliament.

Charles Kennedy

Paddy Ashdown resigned in 1999 and Charles Kennedy defeated Simon Hughes to become the new leader in August of that year. Kennedy's 'laid back' style was criticised by some but clearly not by the voters as the party won sixty two seats in the 2005 election, its greatest number of seats since the 1920s. However, many within the party were unhappy with its move to the right in an attempt to win over dissatisfied Conservative voters. The Liberal Democrats only won three seats from the Conservatives, and so critics claimed that this strategy had failed. Under the party's rules a leader must stand for re-election within a year of the general election. Kennedy, aware of the growing discontent within the party, moved quickly to organise a leadership election and he was re-elected unopposed as party leader. This was to be a short-lived triumph as he was forced to resign in January 2006 (See election of Menzies Campbell.)

Menzies Campbell

Charles Kennedy was 39 when he became leader in 1999; in contrast Menzies Campbell was 64

MAKING LIBERAL DEMOCRAT POLICY

The Federal Conference

The supreme policy making body is the Federal Conference. Representatives from every local party are elected to attend the Federal Conference where policy decisions are made on national and 'English' issues. The English Party delegates its policy making powers to the Federal Conference. The Conference can make decisions about foreign affairs and English domestic issues such as transport and education but the Scottish Conference deals with Scottish domestic issues.

The Federal Committees

(The Executive, Policy and Conference Committees) Membership comes from members of the Parliamentary Party, the three 'state Parties' and councillors. At least a third of each committee must be women.

The Election of Sir Menzies Campbell

In January 2006, the Liberal Democrats were engaged in a battle for the leadership and future direction of their party. Yet, in May 2005, they had achieved the highest number of third party MPs since the 1920s. Charles Kennedy was popular with both voters and party members. However, his forced admission of alcoholism led to his senior MPs demanding that he resign.

Four candidates entered the leadership contest. However, Mark Oaten, Home Affairs spokesperson, quickly withdrew from the race after revelations of a sexual scandal appeared in the *News of the World*. This left three candidates: Sir Menzies Campbell, deputy party leader and Foreign Affairs spokesperson; Chris Huhne, Treasury spokesperson, with a keen interest in environmental issues; and Simon Hughes, Legal Affairs spokesperson and Liberal Democrat President, who represented the left wing of the party. He had unsuccessfully stood against Charles Kennedy in 1999.

It was clear that the Party wanted a 'safe pair of hands' and Campbell was elected with 58% of the votes. With 52,036 party members participating, the Liberal Democrats hailed the election as "a triumph for party democracy".

Liberal Democrat Leadership Contest 2006

First round
Menzies Campbell	23,264
Chris Huhne	16,691
Simon Hughes	12,081

Simon Hughes was eliminated and his second preference votes were redistributed.

Second Round
Menzies Campbell	29,697
Chris Huhne	21,628

The leader is elected by every paid-up member of the party on a one member, one vote basis, using the Single Transferable Vote system.

Powers of the Party Leader
While the Federal Conference must give formal approval, the party leader has a great deal of influence over the formulation of policy. Most major party proposals stem from the Federal Policy Committee which is dominated by the party leadership. The policy committee and the party leadership are responsible for drawing up the party's election manifesto.

---

when he became leader in March 2006. Campbell was regarded as a 'safe pair of hands' and the Liberal Democrats received a boost when in February 2006 they won the Dunfermline by-election which had been regarded as a safe Labour seat. (Campbell was acting leader at the time.) Sir Menzies Campbell had been consistent in his hostility towards the UK's involvement in Iraq.

Sir Menzies Campbell regarded himself as a moderate social liberal standing between the more right-wing policies of Charles Kennedy and the more left-wing policies of Simon Hughes. The key issue which faces Liberal Democrat leaders is where to position the party. The internal division is not detrimental as party policies (see pages 55–61) tend to reflect both wings of the party. Campbell was aware that David Cameron was moving the Conservatives more to the centre. The two by-elections of July 2007 in Sedgefield and Ealing Southall were regarded as a key test for Menzies Campbell's leadership—a poor showing would have intensified the pressure for him to stand down. To the delight of Campbell and his party, the Liberal Democrats came second in both constituencies. The Conservatives, not the Liberal Democrats, had been squeezed out.

In October 2007 Menzies Campbell resigned as party leader. Media-inspired concern about his age and poor poll ratings for the party had undermined his leadership. Gordon Brown's decision not to call a general election in 2007 'persuaded' Campbell that it was time to step down.

Two candidates emerged to compete for the vacant leadership—Chris Huhne and Nick Clegg. Their backgrounds were almost identical. They both went to the same public school and university, both were Euro MPs and both were part of the new 2005 Liberal Democrats parliamentary intake. Chris Huhne, 53, stood against Menzies Campbell in the 2006 leadership contest. Nick Clegg at 40 was by far the younger candidate and this was the only difference between them. Both opposed Trident and Identity Cards. In December 2007 Nick Clegg (see photograph opposite) became the new leader of the Liberal Democrats.

THE ORGANISATION OF POLITICAL PARTIES

The study of party organisation focuses attention on where power lies within a political party. Who controls the major parties? This is a vital question because whoever controls the majority party also controls the government.

There are several levels of party organisation common to most major parties. Logically, one starts with individual, dues-paying, card-carrying members. Individual members belong to and participate in the activities of local organisations which are formed around the basic electoral unit in Britain, the parliamentary constituency. In the case of the Labour Party one has to add 'affiliated organisations' to the membership list. These include trade unions, socialist societies, fabian societies and young socialists.

Individual members, constituency associations and affiliated organisations constitute the grass roots of the party, sometimes known as the 'party in the country'. The main function of party members is to select the parliamentary candidate who will become the local MP if the party wins the constituency in the general election.

One might expect that the mass membership would be in charge of what a democratic political party does in terms of policy making and governing the country. However, that expectation ignores the need for 'organisation', both at the grass roots and in Parliament. In common with other large groups, political parties must be extremely well organised in order to be efficient. This is essential for any group whose members are drawn from all parts of Britain and is especially important for political parties whose members may disagree with each other over important political points. The need to be organised in the interests of efficiency extends to the party's successful parliamentary candidates. Thus the parliamentary parties are organised into leaders (the Cabinet and the Shadow Cabinet) and backbench supporters. Conservative backbench MPs belong to the 1922 Committee; Labour MPs are members of the Parliamentary Labour Party (PLP).

THE STRUCTURE AND ORGANISATION OF THE LABOUR PARTY

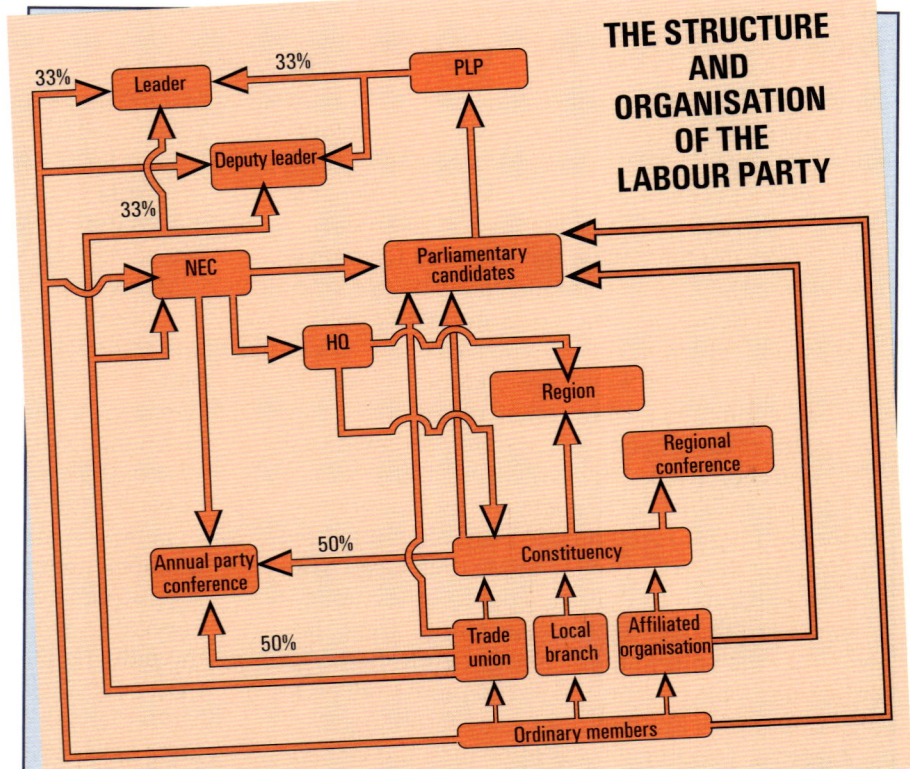

Figure 3.1

LABOUR'S POLICY FORUM SYSTEM

The national policy forum (NPF) consists of 175 members from across the party and meets three times a year. The Joint Policy Commission (JPC) is chaired by the party leader and includes Ministers, MPs, MEPs and national party officials. The NPF and JPC appoint specialist policy commissions to develop policies. This system operates a two-year policy cycle.

Year One

1. The NPF and JPC appoint specialist policy commissions which send policy proposals to constituency parties (CLPs) and affiliated bodies (ABs).
2. CLPs and ABs set up policy forums to discuss policy proposals and report back to the policy commissions.
3. The NPF and JPC examine the views of CLPs and ABs and prepare summaries for consideration by Party Conference.

Year Two

1. The NPF and JPC produce a second summary of forum reports based on conference debates.
2. The revised summary is sent to CLPs and ABs for comments.
3. The NPF and JPC produce final policy proposals which are presented to and endorsed by the Conference.

Constituency Organisation

What are the links between grassroots organisations in the country and the parties in Parliament? At this point it is worth emphasising that the Conservative Party was established about seventy years before the Labour Party. The rea-

PARTNERSHIP IN POWER

Blair used the euphoria of the May 1997 victory to push through a series of party reforms called 'Partnership in Power' (PIP). At the October 1997 Conference, PIP set up new machinery for agreeing party policy which strengthened the leadership's position. Under the old system the National Executive Committee (NEC) had formal responsibility for policy making between Conferences and party policy was determined largely by votes cast at Conference. Partnership in Power has created new bodies to work within a two-year 'rolling programme'. After two years of discussion, policies are presented to the NEC and then passed on to the Conference for a final decision. Officials highlight the fact that previously local parties would have been offered a three-minute slot at Conference to argue their case. Now they are able to feed their viewpoints to the policy commission throughout the year. Critics argue, however, that the policy reports are written from the government's point of view and spend more time praising current policies than discussing future ones.

Margaret McDonagh was appointed the General Secretary of the Labour Party in October 1998 representing the change in style between Old and New Labour. All previous Labour General Secretaries had been men, usually from a trade union background. McDonagh, a Labour Party organiser since the early 1980s, had campaigned for Blair in his quest for the Labour leadership in 1994 and in the successful bid to rewrite Clause IV in 1994–95. She claims that PIP makes the party more democratic: "We have a party whose members, from bottom to top, are involved in its decisions".

However, many party activists disagree with this statement. Left-wing MPs such as Dianne Abbott claimed the forums (see box on page 47) are a "smoke screen for autocratic decision making." They argue that top-up fees, foundation hospitals and support for the Iraq war were imposed after no discussion within the forum system.

Labour's annual Conference has been reduced to a rubber-stamp status, mostly ratifying forum proposals prepared by party officials committed to New Labour. Even Conference-backed motions such as the reduction in the use of the private finance initiative (2002) and the renationalisation of railways (2004) have had little impact and were ignored. In 2000 Gordon Brown stated: "the policy of this government is not to be decided by a few composite motions: we have a responsibility to the people and not just the party."

---

sons behind the origins of each party were completely different and their contemporary organisation reflects these differences in origin.

The Conservative Party proper, consisting of Conservative MPs only, can trace its origins back to the 1830s. Conservative MPs were organised within the House of Commons before the great nineteenth century reforms of the electoral system and the consequent extension of the franchise made it essential that parliamentary candidates be supported by party organisations in the country. Constituency parties were necessary to encourage a party's supporters within the increasing number of voters to come out on polling day. Conservative Party Associations were created to serve the Parliamentary Party.

The Conservative Central Office was established as long ago as 1871 to give some degree of coherence to Conservative electoral efforts across the country. Because

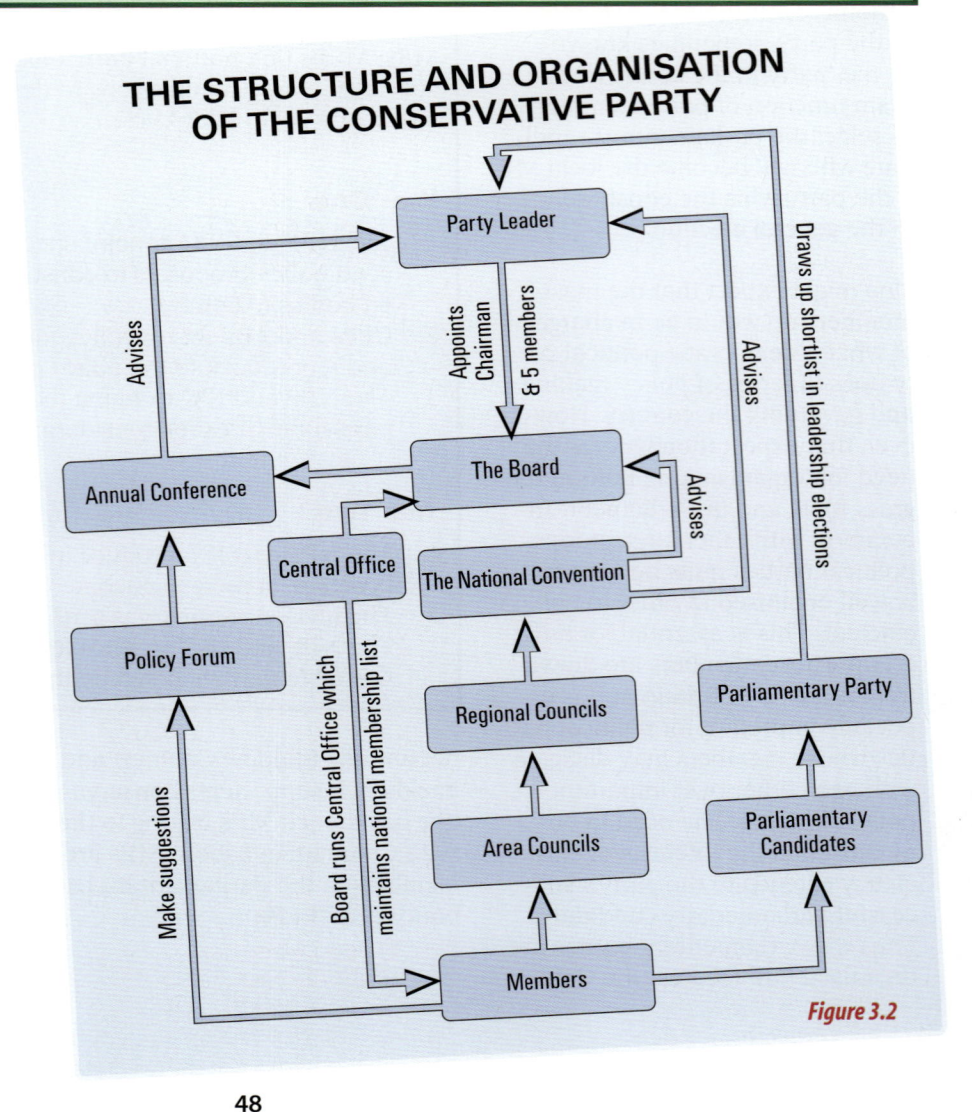

THE STRUCTURE AND ORGANISATION OF THE CONSERVATIVE PARTY

Figure 3.2

Delegates to the Labour Party Conference represent the constituency parties, the trade unions and various socialist societies. It is an opportunity for the leadership to communicate with the public as there is extensive television coverage of the debates.

the Constituency Associations and the Central Office were established to serve the Parliamentary Party before the onset of fully-fledged democracy, they have remained, for the most part, subservient to the Parliamentary Party. The reforms introduced by William Hague have made the party structure more democratic. (See Figure 3.2 and page 38.)

In common with the reforms introduced to Labour, this system has a network of policy forums and the mechanism of all-party referendums on policy issues. However, the forum system ensured a much more right-wing 2001 Conservative Manifesto which "respected party democracy but retarded party recovery."

Michael Howard's accession to the leadership of the Conservative Party owed nothing to party democracy as he was the only candidate. Howard diminished the role of party forums and he stated that only he and his most senior colleagues would draw up policies for the 2005 general election. (There was no party referendum for the 2005 Manifesto in contrast to 2001 when a referendum was held. Michael Howard proposed a change to the method of electing the leader of the Party but this was rejected by the Party. (See Howard's reform proposals.)

The Labour Party was established in 1900 as the Labour Representation Committee as a result of a Trades Union Council resolution in 1899. In other words, it was organised by political forces outside Parliament. The objective was to ensure that the labour movement and the working class were represented in Parliament. At this time more and more working-class men were becoming eligible to vote. However, the two major parties, the Conservatives and the Liberals, were middle-class parties. Labour Party membership could be acquired through individuals joining the party directly or through membership of an affiliated trade union. These historical events explain why important Labour Party decisions are taken by MPs, Constituency Labour Parties (CLPs), and trade unions and also why Labour has a more complex and decentralised organisational structure than the Conservative Party.

The conventional wisdom has been that the Conservative Party is more centralised and easier to control than the Labour Party. Such a claim might have been true of the Conservative Party under Margaret Thatcher and the Labour Party under Michael Foot, yet few would claim that it accurately portrayed the Conservative Party under John Major or the Labour Party under Tony Blair.

Both major parties have a number of organisations and procedures which give the grass roots some say in decision making but allow the leaders to control the party as a whole most of the time. MPs are the most obvious links between the parties in the country and their party in Parliament. MPs tend to be loyal to the parliamentary leadership, partly because loyalty may lead to promotion and partly because disloyalty would weaken the party in the fight for political supremacy.

Party Conference

The next link is the national party conference which is common to all parties, major and minor. The

UK Politics Today

> ### THE OCTOBER 2005 CONSERVATIVE PARTY CONFERENCE
> The traditional view of the Conservative Conference as being of no political importance and simply an orchestrated performance of devotion to the party leader clearly did not apply to this Conference. With Howard standing down, it provided an opportunity for the candidates for party leader to demonstrate their credentials. Each candidate was allocated fifteen minutes to outline his vision for the party. The contest was a disaster for the clear favourite, David Davis, and a triumph for the young outsider, David Cameron. Davis's presentation lacked sparkle and reassurance. In contrast, Cameron won over the delegates in a speech low on substance but high on charm and charisma.
>
> The conference had a direct impact on the outcome of the leadership election—it created an unstoppable Cameron bandwagon and a fatally wounded Davis. In December 2005 Cameron became the new leader. (See page 51.)
>
> Howard did Cameron a favour. If he had simply resigned in May 2005 instead of staying on to attempt to change the election rules, then the election would have been held before the Tory Conference and David Davis would have won the leadership election!

major parties hold annual party conferences in the early autumn. These act both as rallies of the faithful and as decision making bodies. The Conservative Conference, which is heavily stage-managed, is usually devoted to demonstrating support for the leader and for the policies decided by the Cabinet or Shadow Cabinet.

Until recently, the Labour Party Conference was much less subject to control by the leadership. The Labour Party Constitution states that Party policies making up the Labour Programme should be approved by the Conference, subject to receiving two-thirds support. The election manifesto, which consists of policies from the programme, has to be agreed between the parliamentary leadership and the National Executive Committee of the party. The Labour leadership submits its policy programme to the Conference and both CLPs and affiliated organisations may submit resolutions which may or may not agree with the leadership's point of view. Voting on resolutions is carried out by delegates from both CLPs and affiliated organisations such as trade unions who cast a number of votes determined by the size of their respective memberships. This means that the trade unions dominate voting as there are many more Labour members through trade union membership than through individual members joining the party directly.

Labour retains a federal organisation in that despite the introduction of 'one member, one vote', various posts are decided by an electoral college of trade unions, constituency associations, MPs, and others. The federal organisation limits the power of Labour leaders compared to their Conservative counterparts. Once elected, the Conservative leader in Opposition has a free hand in relation to choosing the Shadow Cabinet and deciding party policy. The Labour Shadow Cabinet is selected by a vote of the Parliamentary Labour Party (PLP). Labour Prime Ministers are not subject to such limitations, since they select their own Cabinet colleagues. However, the organisational and policy reforms accomplished by Labour leaders since the mid-1980s strongly suggest that in the long run the parliamentary party prevails over the party in the country and the affiliated organisations.

SELECTING THE PARTY LEADERS

Both of the major parties have reformed the leadership selection process in recent times, Labour in 1981 and the Conservatives in 2001. Both parties allow for challenges to be made to the incumbent leader. Leadership elections provide an indication of the degree of ideological or policy conflict within the major parties.

The Labour Party

The Labour leader used to be elected by the PLP with only a simple absolute majority being required for victory. Michael Foot was the last Labour leader to be chosen only by MPs. He defeated Denis Healey in November 1980 which has been compared with the 1997 Tory leadership contest. Foot, a left-winger, defeated Healey who was regarded as the representative of the centre-right leadership which had failed by losing the 1979 general election.

The Labour leader and deputy leader are now chosen by an electoral college representing three elements of the party inside and without Parliament—Labour MPs, the membership organised in Constituency Parties (CLPs), and members of trade unions affiliated to the Party. This reform was carried out in 1981 when the left wing of the party, which was in favour of extra-parliamentary controls over the leadership in the House of Commons, was dominant. The CLPs and the unions, the party without Parliament, were each given a 'constituency' within a tripartite electoral college. MPs and the CLPs were each given 30% and the unions received 40% of the votes in the college. In 1992 the three electoral college constituencies were made equal. It was also decided at that time to make the leadership election process more democratic by requiring both CLPs and trade unions to consult with their individual memberships in accordance with the principle of 'one member, one vote' (OMOV). The operation of the electoral college may be explained by examining the result of the 1994 contest which established Tony Blair as the leader.

Within the constituency section, every CLP has one vote which is assigned to the leadership candidate who wins the ballot of individual members. Within the trade union section, every affiliated union is assigned a share of the overall trade union vote (one-third of the total electoral college) based on the size of its membership. Every affiliated union holds a postal ballot of its members and its electoral college votes are divided between the candidates according to their share of the postal ballot. Tony Blair won a majority in each section of the Party. John Prescott was the runner-up. His strongest support came from the trade union membership which reflected his own working-class and trade union background.

The Conservative Party

The Conservative leadership election process has been much more competitive and controversial than Labour's in recent decades. The Conservative leader has been elected only since 1965 when Edward Heath succeeded Sir Alec Douglas Home who stood down following Labour's victory in the 1964 general election. Until then the Conservative leader was said to 'evolve' from a consultation process held within the Party. However, the absence of a clear-cut electoral procedure led to difficulties in 1957 and 1963 when the Conservative leader resigned while holding the office of Prime Minister. In controversial circumstances on both occasions, the leadership issue was settled when the Queen appointed the new Prime Minister. It was argued that the Conservative Party was unnecessarily involving the Monarch in the political process which was held to be contrary to constitutional principles.

The Conservatives adopted a complicated election procedure confined to MPs. In order to ensure that the elected leader would enjoy strong support after the election, a sizable majority was required to win on the first ballot—an absolute majority plus 15% more of the vote than the runner-up. This majority was accomplished only once in the five contests using this system between 1965 and 2001. This was in 1989 when Mrs Thatcher was opposed by a virtual unknown in what amounted to a protest against her leadership style. In 1990 Mrs Thatcher was forced out of office after failing by only a single vote to attract the 15% margin over Michael Heseltine. In the second ballot new candidates were allowed to enter the contest. At this stage an overall majority was required for victory. A third ballot may have been held if necessary. This third ballot was confined to the leading three candidates in the second ballot. At this stage preferential voting was used if there were more than two candidates.

The Conservative leadership election procedures

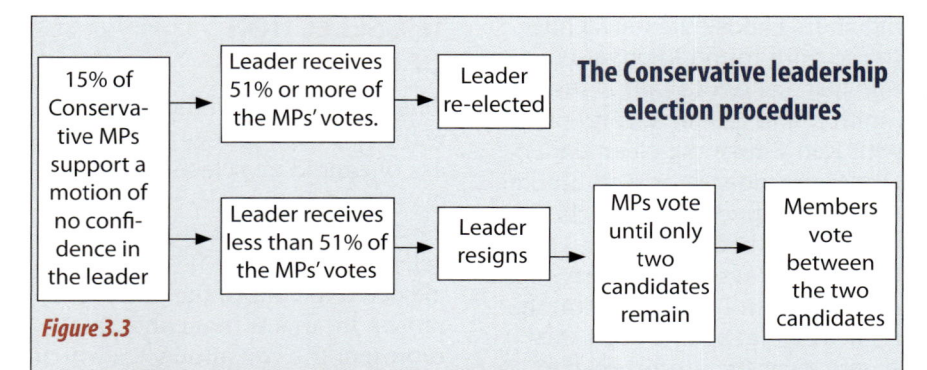

Figure 3.3

THE ELECTION OF DAVID CAMERON

Four candidates participated in the first stage: David Cameron, Ken Clarke, David Davis and Liam Fox. The favourite at this stage, David Davis, came top in the first ballot in October 2005. Kenneth Clarke, having come last, was eliminated. In the second ballot David Cameron won with a clear margin and it became a straight contest between David Cameron and David Davis. Under the rules for electing Conservative Party leaders, MPs decide which two candidates go forward to the second phase, whereby the 270,000 party members choose the new leader.

A six week campaign followed with David Cameron impressing the Tory faithful. The results of the ballot in December 2005 gave an impressive victory to Cameron. He received 134,446 votes to Davis's 64,398 votes.

First Round Voting
David Davis   62
David Cameron   56
Liam Fox   42
Kenneth Clarke   38

Second Round Voting
David Cameron   90
David Davis   57
Liam Fox   51

Final Stage
David Cameron   134,446 (68%)
David Davis   64,398 (32%)
Turnout   198,844 (78%)

Margaret Thatcher challenged and defeated Edward Heath in 1975. Thatcher herself was opposed by Sir Antony Meyer in 1989 and then forced out of office in 1990 as a result of the challenge from Michael Heseltine, although the winner was John Major who entered the contest after Mrs Thatcher's withdrawal. John Major resigned immediately after the 1997 election defeat to be succeeded, after three ballots, by William Hague.

The election of Iain Duncan Smith

Iain Duncan Smith was the first Conservative leader to be elected under the new system. (See Figure 3.3.) MPs decide which two candidates go forward to the second stage whereby the 270,000 party members choose the new leader. In the third round Michael Portillo just lost out to Iain Duncan Smith (54 to 53) for second place with Ken Clarke the clear leader. Under the old system Ken Clarke, a 'Conservative heavy-weight', would have become leader. Under the new system the party faithful chose Iain Duncan Smith, the right-wing, inexperienced Eurosceptic over the pro-European Ken Clarke by 155,933 to 100,864. John Major, who had endorsed Ken Clarke, accused Iain Duncan Smith of having done "immense damage" to his government by voting against his European policies.

Howard's Reform Proposals

Howard proposed to change the rules for the election of party leader which, if agreed to, would be used to choose his successor.

Reasons for change
- The system in use enabled a leader to be chosen who was not the first choice of MPs.
- The system was costly and time-consuming.
- The system created leaders liked by party members but not by the general public. The core support of the Conservatives tended to be more extreme than the party's MPs.

Instead of the 'first ballot' taking place among MPs, as was put in place by the 1998 reform, Howard proposed that it would take place among members of the Conservative National Convention (the 633 constituency chairs and the 244 national regional officers). The two most popular candidates would go forward to the second ballot and Conservative MPs would elect the leader. The proposal failed to achieve the two-thirds majority required in the Constitutional College and so the 1998 system was retained.

THE SELECTION OF CANDIDATES

One of the potential battlegrounds within political parties is the process of candidate selection. Whoever controls the selection of candidates, and the process of reselection of sitting MPs, could be expected to control the party. The reason for this is that candidates represent the constituencies which elect them and democratic theory assumes that there should be an element of local control over who should be selected to represent both party and constituency.

There are elements of local and central control in the candidate selection procedures of the two major British parties. The Conservatives maintain a list of candidates approved by a committee under the control of the party leader. Would-be candidates are subjected to interview before they can get onto the approved list. They are then eligible to be selected by a constituency party. A shortlist of candidates is drawn up by the committee before the full membership of a local Conservative Constituency Association meets to listen to these candidates, one of whom will be selected by a vote of the individual party members present.

Labour Party organisation at the constituency level is more complex than Conservative organisation. A CLP (Constituency Labour Party) may include a number of branches based on local government wards and some affiliated organisations such as trade unions. Both the branches and the affiliated organisations may propose individuals as candidates. Labour Party headquarters in London maintains lists of candidates who may be approached by CLPs. A shortlist is determined by the CLP's executive committee and the candidate is then chosen by a vote of the individual members of the constituency party.

Both of the major parties have experienced internal conflicts over candidate selection, especially at the stage of the reselection of sitting MPs. If an MP's general ideological position or his/her position on a particularly divisive policy issue is at odds with the majority of members in the constituency party then the MP may be in trouble. In the early 1980s when Labour introduced the mandatory reselection of sitting members it was feared that this would lead to the deselection of right-wing and centrist MPs out of step with left-wing majorities among the party activists who would turn up and vote at CLP meetings. In the event, although there have been a number of deselections, these fears were unrealised. Labour acted to deselect left-wing Militant candidates who caused problems during the 'modernisation' of the party under John Smith and Tony Blair.

SCOTTISH NATIONAL PARTY

The Scottish National Party (SNP) elected Alex Salmond as its leader in 2004. The leader is elected on a one member one vote basis so all members (around 12,000) participate in the leadership election. Salmond won convincingly, with Nicola Sturgeon as his deputy, leaving the party in the strange position of having a leader whose parliamentary seat was in Westminster not in Edinburgh. In the 2007 Scottish Parliament election Salmond won the Gordon constituency and with his party having the largest number of MSPs, he became First Minister. (See chapter 8.) Salmond had resigned as party leader in 2000 and had been replaced by John Swinney who stood down in 2004.

The SNP is a centre left political party which campaigns for Scottish independence. It is the largest party in the Scottish Parliament having forty seven seats. The SNP's income mostly comes from membership fees and fund-raising activities, although in the early 2000s it received funding from prominent Scottish businessmen such as Tom Farmer.

Party Organisation

Local branches are drawn together to form parliamentary constituency associations. Branches are responsible for selecting local candidates, and branches and constituency associations send representatives to the National Council and the Annual National Conference. The National Council is the governing body of the SNP which meets at least twice a year. The annual National Conference is responsible for making policy and electing the party's office bearers. The National Executive Committee is the senior body of the party, and is elected at the National Conference.

Party Unity and Division

Party members are united in their desire to make Scotland independent. However, they differ on how this should be achieved. Alex Salmond himself was expelled from the party in 1982 for being "too left wing." (He was readmitted in 1983). Salmond has been criticised for being authoritarian and for stifling party democracy by critics such as Margo MacDonald (now an Independent MSP). The creation of the Scottish Parliament and the (narrow) SNP victory in 2007 supports those within the party who favour a gradualist step-by-step approach to independence gained through greater degrees of devolution. In contrast the fundamentalist wing of the party wishes to have a more forceful emphasis on Scottish independence and fears that the devolved Parliament may distract both party members and the public from the goal of independence.

Scottish Parliament Results 2007

Party	Const	Regn	+/-	Total
SNP	21	26	+20	47
Labour	37	9	-4	46
Conservative	4	13	-1	17
Liberal Democrats	11	5	-1	16
Others	0	3	-14	3

Table 3.5

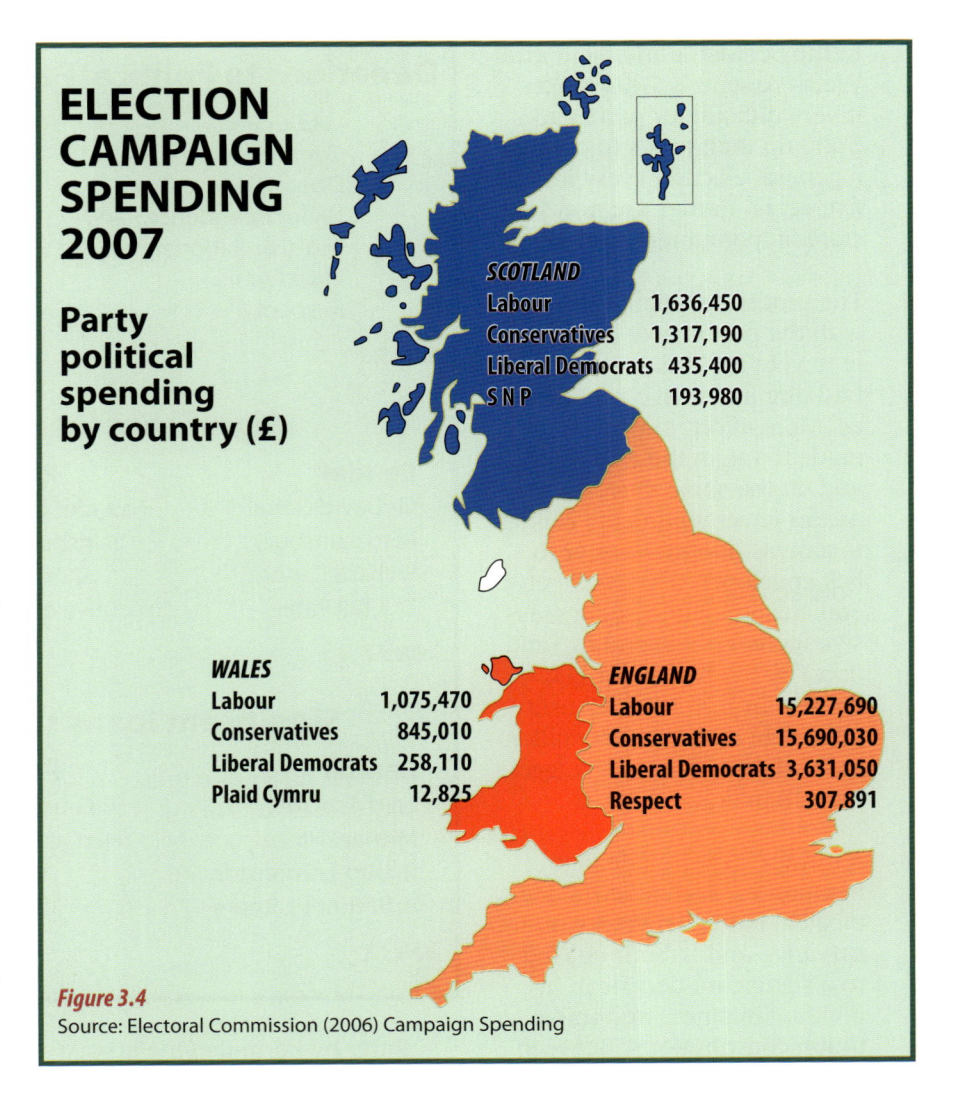

ELECTION CAMPAIGN SPENDING 2007

Party political spending by country (£)

SCOTLAND
- Labour: 1,636,450
- Conservatives: 1,317,190
- Liberal Democrats: 435,400
- SNP: 193,980

WALES
- Labour: 1,075,470
- Conservatives: 845,010
- Liberal Democrats: 258,110
- Plaid Cymru: 12,825

ENGLAND
- Labour: 15,227,690
- Conservatives: 15,690,030
- Liberal Democrats: 3,631,050
- Respect: 307,891

Figure 3.4
Source: Electoral Commission (2006) Campaign Spending

PARTY FINANCE & FUNDING

Political parties need large amounts of income to finance the party's organisation and to cover their election campaigns. (See Figure 3.4.) Until recently both major parties relied heavily on one particular source of finance: Labour received most of its money from the trade unions while the Conservatives relied upon 'big business'. It is clear that there is a crisis in party funding with a growing public perception that parties can be bought and that sleaze is a major issue. The arrest of Lord Levy, Blair's chief fundraiser, in 2006 reinforced this perception of sleaze.

Why are party finances in such a mess?

1. Parties are fighting more elections than ever. In addition to local government, Westminster and European elections, they now have to contest elections

Bernie Ecclestone, who controls F1 Motor Racing, donated £1million to the Labour Party before the 1997 election. Suspicions were voiced about the reasons for the donation and whether this gave him influence over government decisions regarding tobacco sponsorship.

to the Scottish Parliament and Welsh Assembly. This makes it very difficult for parties to build up their funds to contest a general election every four or five years. Parties are now in a state of 'permanent campaign'.

2. The process of dealignment, with the public now less likely to vote for 'their party' has had dire financial consequences. More effort now has to be made to target the electorate and, at the same time, there are far fewer volunteers willing to canvas door-to-door or to lick envelopes. The 2005 general election witnessed a massive increase in spending (and debt) by the two major UK parties. In July 2006, Conservative debt stood at £15 million and Labour's debt at a staggering £28 million.

3. A further impact of dealignment and a decline in the ideological battle between Conservative and Labour has led to a significant decline in individual business and trade union contributions. Between 1997 and 2006 membership of the Labour Party fell by 50%, with the Conservatives suffering a similar fate. By 2006 Labour raised only 8% of its income from membership subscriptions, the Conservatives 10% and the Liberal Democrats 30%. Trade union membership has fallen from 13 million in 1979 to 9 million today, thus reducing this important source of income to Labour. The Conservatives have also witnessed a significant reduction in income from company donations which represented 60% of Conservative Party income in 1981, but which is estimated to represent just 30% today.

4. The *Political Parties Elections and Referendums Act 2000*. The cash for questions scandal among Conservative MPs in the mid-1990s and the £1million donation to the Labour Party by Formula One boss, Bernie Ecclestone, in 1997 led to restrictions in party funding. Under the 2000 Act parties have to publish the names of those donating over £5,000. A new scandal broke out in 2006 concerning loans to the Labour Party. (See page 53.) This 'cash for peerages' scandal will further discourage wealthy individuals from sponsoring political parties.

Donations to Political Parties (January – June 2005)

Labour Party	£13,916,237
Conservative Party	£14,242,376
Liberal Democrats	£5,377,969
UK Independence Party	£574,956
Scottish National Party	£159,585
Plaid Cymru	£44,290
Respect	£35,458

Table 3.6

Significant loans to Labour 2005

Lender	Position	Amount
Sir David Garrard	Founder of Minerva Property	£2.3 million
Lord Sainsbury	Sainsbury's Supermarket	£2 million
Richard Caring	Clothing magnate	£2 million
Dr Chai Patel	Executive of Priory Health Group	£1.5 million

Table 3.7

Significant loans to Conservatives 2005

Lender	Position	Amount
Lord Ashcroft	Former Party Chair	£3.5 million
Michael Hinze	Hedge Fund consultant	£2.5 million
Robert Edmonston	Car dealer	£2 million
Arbuthnot Latham	City banker	£2 million

Table 3.8

The Phillips Report

In March 2006 the Prime Minister set up a Review of the Funding of Political Parties, chaired by Sir Hayden Phillips. The Prime Minister hoped to limit the damage created by the 'cash for peerages' crisis. The remit of the review was:

1. To examine the case for state funding of political parties, including whether it should be increased in return for a cap on the size of donations.

2. To consider how party funding could be more transparent.

In March 2007, the Phillips Report made its recommendations

- Donations to parties should be limited to £50,000 from any one source. During the 2005 general election the two main parties spent about £90 million as against £65 million for the 2001 election. The parties had ignored the controls on general election campaign expenditure introduced in 2001.

- Legislation must be introduced to ensure that political parties abide by the agreed limits. The role and powers of the Electoral Commission as a regulator must be strengthened.

- Expenditure on general election campaigns has progressively grown and should now be reduced in line with a new spending control regime to be agreed between the parties. Each should cut its spending by £20 million over the life of a full parliament.

- Political parties should receive greater financial support from the public purse. This should be measured by their performance at the ballot box. Eligible parties should receive 50p each year for every vote cast for them in the most recent general election, and 25p for every vote cast for them in the most recent elections for the devolved administrations in Scotland and Wales and for the European Parliament. Additionally, a matched funding scheme should be introduced to encourage the parties to recruit paying supporters. Eligible parties would be invited to establish a registered internet subscriber scheme, through which any voter could subscribe a minimum of £5 to support the party. Each subscription would be matched with £5 of public funding.

- Eligibility for public funding to political parties would be based on their ability to command enough support to win two seats at Westminster, Edinburgh, Cardiff or the European Parliament. Those parties not eligible for public funding would not be subject to the limits on donations.

- The estimated annual cost would be £23.4 million.

- The three largest parties should meet to reach consensus on the above recommendations.

CASH FOR HONOURS SCANDALS 2006–2007

It is ironic that Labour came to power in 1997 with the promise to "clean up" British politics and to restore the public's faith in politicians. In 2006–2007, the party was engulfed in a claim that honours were being given in return for party donations. In March 2006 the Prime Minister admitted that he had not informed the House of Lords' Appointment Commission that the Labour Party had received £14 million in loans before the general election. The police became involved and two associates of Tony Blair, Des Smith and Lord Levy, were arrested and questioned. The Prime Minister and other leading party members were interviewed by the police but no one was charged.

The public were not impressed and a YouGov poll of voter opinion made depressing reading for Labour. (See below.) The government reacted by setting up a review of the funding of political parties chaired by Sir Hayden Phillips and by stating that all loans had to be declared in party accounts. In July 2007 it was announced that Lord Levy, Ruth Turner and Christopher Evans would not face criminal charges after the Crown Prosecution Service ruled that there was not enough evidence.

1. **Do you suspect that Labour raised money by offering 'cash for peerages'?**
   Yes: 65%   No: 9%   Don't know: 25%

2. **Has the Blair government reformed party funding so as to end sleaze?**
   Yes: 6%   No: 78%   Don't know: 16%

3. **Do you think it is wrong that those who give loans to parties should not have to declare them?**
   Yes: 87%   No: 3%   Don't know: 10%

Source: YouGov. July 2006

"The status quo is not acceptable. The public wants reform. The system needs reform. The parties know that reform is necessary. Our parliamentary democracy cannot operate effectively without strong and healthy political parties. Limiting donations to, and spending by, political parties will help restore public confidence in our party system. Further public funding of parties is the cost we have to pay to secure a healthier politics."

(Sir Hayden Phillips)

THE POLICIES OF THE MAIN POLITICAL PARTIES

The creation of devolved bodies in Scotland and Wales now ensures that a significant number of the policies of the main UK parties apply only to England. Policy areas such as Education and Health and some Law and Order issues are now the responsibility of the Scottish Parliament and Welsh Assembly. Pages 61–62 highlight the policies of the main political parties in the 2005 general election and the 2007 Scottish Parliament election in the selected areas of education, law and order, taxation and Europe.

EDUCATION

Labour

In 1997 Tony Blair famously announced that his priority would be "Education, Education, Education". His ten-year focus on education led to a significant increase in spending across all of the United Kingdom. In England and Wales government spending per pupil doubled from £2,500 in 1997 to over £5,000 in 2007.

However, Blair's enthusiasm for reforming state schools was not always popular among his own backbenchers. In policy terms his education reforms were an evolution and rebranding of the existing Tory agenda with a generous injection of cash. The city academies which were supposed to transform inner city education were based on the city technology colleges first introduced under Margaret Thatcher. The 2007 Labour Manifesto promised to increase the number of academies to 200 by 2010 in places where state schools are failing in the inner cities. Each city academy is centrally funded and is run by a business sponsor who has to put up £2 million. To his critics within the Labour Party, Blair highlighted that parents were queuing up to get their children into them and that schools which have become city academies have seen an improvement four times the national average in their GCSE results.

The foundation schools proposed by Labour are similar to the Conservatives' grant maintained schools. A simple vote by a state school governing body would enable schools to escape the control of local authorities and to become independent schools that do not charge fees. Foundation schools would have control over budgets, assets, recruitment, admissions and the syllabus. However, what concerns many Labour MPs is the issue of selection. Schools outwith local authority control might reintroduce academic selection through the back door.

Conservatives

Blair's drive to increase choice and accountability within the state sector and his introduction of city academies made it difficult for the Conservatives to create "clear water" between the two parties. Significantly, David Cameron dropped the proposal to provide free private school places. His strategy has been to declare that he is "Blair's Heir" and that he will provide a "Blair plus" approach to further educational reforms.

Cameron's announcement that if he wins the next general election there will not be a return to grammar schools (schools based on academic selection) on the grounds that they do little to benefit children from poor backgrounds has infuriated the right wing of the Conservative Party. While there are only 164 such schools left in England they are of symbolic importance to many Conservatives. Cameron's strategy depended on Gordon Brown moving to the left thus enabling Cameron to inherit some of Blair's flagship educational reforms. Unfortunately for the Conservatives this has not happened. Brown has endorsed city academies and has gone further to state that every secondary and primary school should have a business partner to provide funding and advice.

Liberal Democrats

The Liberal Democrats wish to reduce external testing and call for national tests in primary schools to be scrapped. At the 2005 Liberal Democrat Conference, Sarah Teather stated that "we need assessment for learning, not assessment for targets." The Liberal Democrats disagree with Labour's approach to educational funding in deprived areas. The Liberal Democrats wish to target money towards the individual child who underachieves. This could help "to break the link between poverty and poor achievement at school." The "pupil premium" could encourage good schools to take challenging pupils rather than leaving them to go to "sunk schools."

The Liberal Democrats also oppose the higher education policies of Labour. They would abolish tuition fees and widen grants. They argue that this would encourage more working-class children to enter higher education.

THE SCOTTISH DIMENSION

Scotland has always had a distinctive education system and there tends to be far greater consensus over education policies among the Scottish parties. All parties in Scotland are committed to the comprehensive system and the controversy over grammar schools is a distinctive English issue.

The education policies of the respective parties are outlined on page 61. Below is a brief summary of some of the key differences.

Conservatives

Head teachers would gain more control over the curriculum and school budgets and would be able to apply directly to the Scottish

UK Politics Today

government for funding specific projects. The Conservatives would introduce a pilot scheme for a city academy in Glasgow (a Labour initiative in England), which if successful would be expanded. In higher education, they would implement a 'root and branch' review of university funding and student debt. Students would be allowed to borrow as much as they needed to complete their courses.

Liberal Democrats

As members of the Scottish Executive before the 2007 election the Liberal Democrats claim credit for the introduction of the graduate endowment instead of tuition fees which are used in England and Wales. They also claim credit for the reduction of class sizes in primary and secondary schools. A 'Future of Scotland' bill would give young people new rights, starting with a pupils' council in every school.

Labour

The Labour Party highlighted the massive investment made in education in terms of staffing and resources. The McCrone agreement has brought stability and greater professionalism to the teaching workforce. Under a new education bill, 16- and 17-year-olds would only leave school if they had employment, training or further or higher education opportunities. Labour would also extend free nursery education provision to the 10,000 two-year-olds "who need it the most."

SNP

The two most significant proposals by the SNP are scrapping of the graduate endowment payment and Public-Private Partnership school building schemes which would be replaced by the Scottish Futures Trust using bonds for finance. As with the other parties, the SNP sees investment in early years education as a key to improving attainment in later years. Children would receive free fruit in schools, health and fitness checks and free school meals from primary one to primary three.

EUROPE

In December 2006 Sir Menzies Campbell, leader of the Liberal Democrat Party, stated: "and everyone knows that Europe is a fault line that runs right the way through the Conservative Party." David Cameron, the leader of the Conservative Party, would agree with this statement in private. Tony Blair, in an address to the European Parliament in June 2005, highlighted Labour's former hostility to the European Union. He stated: "I am a passionate pro-European. I always have been. In 1983 when my party had a policy of withdrawing from Europe, I told the selection panel (of Labour parliamentary candidates) that I disagreed with the policy. Some thought I had lost the selection. Some perhaps wish I had. I then helped change our policy in the 1980s and was proud of that change." Page 62 outlines the 2005 general election policies on Europe for the major parties including the SNP, and it clearly highlights the difference between the Conservatives and Labour.

Conservatives

David Cameron was aware that Euroscepticism made the party look insular, xenophobic and obsessive. John Major's Conservative government and his leadership of the party had been weakened by the in-fighting between Europhiles such as Kenneth Clarke and Eurosceptics such as Iain Duncan Smith. William Hague moved the party to the Eurosceptic viewpoint when he pledged to renegotiate the Nice Treaty of 2000 and to oppose British membership of the Eurozone. The fault line in the party continued through the leadership of Iain Duncan Smith and Michael Howard.

Cameron set out to deprioritise Europe. At the 2006 Party Conference, his first as leader, he stated: "while voters worried about public services, job security and mortgage repayments we were banging on about Europe." Cameron has endorsed the Eurosceptic viewpoint of being against further EU integration and complete opposition to the single European currency. He is also critical of the new EU treaty agreed in June 2007 by the Labour government.

Labour

Blair declared that he wanted "Britain to be at the heart of Europe" while at the same time defending British interests. It was clear that Blair was more enthusiastic than Brown for the UK joining the Eurozone. However, he accepted Brown's five economic tests being met before the government would recommend to Parliament and to the people in a referendum that the UK should join.

Blair displayed a very positive attitude towards an EU constitution in 2004. Having accepted the draft treaty establishing a constitution for Europe, he agreed to the demands of the Conservatives and the Liberal Democrats to hold a referendum on the issue. However, after the resounding defeat of the constitutional treaty in France and the Netherlands, Blair dropped this commitment. The 2005 Labour general election manifesto included a commitment to a referendum if the constitutional reforms re-emerged on the EU's agenda.

In one of his last acts as Prime Minister Blair signed the 'new' treaty aimed at changing the European Union to cope with its larger membership of twenty seven. Experts state it is a constitution in all but name. The treaty will establish an EU President voted for by national leaders and there will also be an EU Foreign Minister. The treaty will also involve a transfer of powers from Britain to Europe. Open Europe, the think tank, states that Britain will lose the powers to veto or stop actions by Europe in nearly seventy areas such as energy policy.

The Conservatives and Liberal Democrats are furious that Labour, despite its election pledge, does not intend to hold a referendum. William Hague, the Shadow Foreign Secretary, said: "given their manifesto commitment, the government has absolutely no democratic mandate to introduce those major changes without letting the British people have the final decision in a referendum."

Liberal Democrats

The Liberal Democrats are highly critical of the Conservatives' negative attitude towards the European Union. However, Menzies Campbell also implied that Labour was less than enthusiastic when he stated "and everyone knows how reluctant Gordon Brown is to deal with it." The Liberal Democrats wish the UK to be at the heart of Europe but support reform to accommodate the increase from fifteen to twenty seven countries over a three-year period. They support the implementation of a new Treaty/Constitution and would campaign for a 'yes vote' if a referendum were to take place. The Liberal Democrats also believe that "Europe should take a greater role in promoting its values through its common foreign and security policy, with the full and active participation of the UK." Britain should distance itself from the USA.

The SNP

The SNP's policy on Europe has been a consistent one. It wants an independent Scotland to "take our place at the top tables of the EU and the UN." The SNP states that an independent Scotland would automatically become a member of the EU and would not have to seek permission. The Labour and Conservative Parties disagree with this viewpoint. The SNP has been highly critical of the UK government's ability to defend the interests of the Scottish fishing industry. The new SNP Scottish Government would like the Scottish Fisheries Minister to lead the British delegation in discussions. They argue that Flanders is allowed to lead the Belgian delegation regarding Common Fisheries Policy (CFP) discussions.

TAXATION

In the past this was an area which showed a clear division between the two major parties: Labour was the party of high taxation and high public expenditure and the Conservatives the party of low taxes and low public spending. According to *The Guardian's* Michael White, the 2005 general election manifestos embedded a "Thatcherite consensus" among the parties (he included the Liberal Democrats). All the parties placed low inflation before full employment and all accepted the need for high public spending.

Conservatives

The Conservatives pledged to save £35 billion by cutting "wasteful spending." Only £4 billion of this windfall would be spent on tax cuts while the rest would be spent on "more productive investment" in public expenditure. The Conservatives accepted greater public spending and even stated that they would match Labour's plans. (See extract from Conservative Manifesto.) The Conservatives would reduce the basic rate of income tax from 22% to 20%.

> **The Conservative Manifesto 2005**
>
> "We will spend the same as Labour would on the NHS, schools, transport and educational development and more than Labour on police, defence and pensions ... Over the period for 2011–12 we will increase government spending by 4% a year, compared to Labour's plan to increase spending by 5% a year."

Labour

In his ten years as Chancellor, Gordon Brown kept within the income tax levels established by the previous Tory government. Brown announced that the basic tax rate will be reduced from 22 pence in the pound to 20 pence from April 2008. (The 10p tax rate will be abolished.) This announcement enabled Brown to outmanoeuvre the Conservatives who had promised modest tax cuts. Labour has been criticised for increasing the tax burden by 4% since 1997 thanks to a series of other tax reforms (referred to as 'stealth taxes'). Gordon Brown gave Britain a decade of economic stability, with consistent growth and low inflation. Brown stuck to the Tories' tight spending plans for the first two years of Labour's rule, then he increased public spending significantly, favouring health and education and transferring resources to the poorest families through tax credits. Brown raised the extra cash by increasing national insurance rates and using fiscal drag—leaving tax thresholds unchanged so that more people pay higher tax rates. GDP is £1.18 trillion, making the UK economy the fifth largest in the world. Government debt has fallen from 44% of GDP to 36%.

Liberal Democrats

During the 2005 general election campaign, the Liberal Democrats claimed that the two main parties were indistinguishable, hence their manifesto's title 'The Real Alternative.' The Liberal Democrats were the only party prepared to introduce higher taxes—a new higher rate of income tax of 50% for those earning over £100,000 a year. The Liberal Democrats (and the Tories) also promised to restore the link between earnings and the state pension.

At the September 2006 Liberal Democrat Party Conference the new leader won a crunch vote on his plans to drop the 50% top tax rate. The leadership's tax plans had dominated the debate at the Conference. Liberal Democrat campaign chief Ed Davey stated that the debate had been mature and good natured. "This was not a party tearing itself apart," he said. The decision did highlight the tension within the party. Liberal Democrat MP Phil Willis stated that the leadership's tax plan could start the party on "a slippery slope towards more right-wing draconian policies." At the Conference delegates approved new taxes on 'gas guzzling' cars and aviation fuel to pay for income tax cuts (a 2% cut in the basic income tax rate).

LAW AND ORDER

Labour

The traditional view of the Conservatives being the party of law and order compared to Labour's soft option image no longer exists. Tony Blair's 1994 sound bite of "tough on crime, tough on the causes of crime" became the watchword of Labour's handling of law and order issues. Despite the 2005 and 2007 terrorist attacks and the public's mistaken belief that crime levels have risen, Tony Blair left Britain a safer place. Crime fell 35% between 1997 and 2007 (serious crime rose) and the police service was significantly increased.

In his ten years as Prime Minister thirty three criminal justice bills, including the one which created ASBOs, were passed. The police were given extensive new powers and longer sentences were introduced. The outcome was a record number of 80,000 prisoners and accusations that Britain had become a "surveillance society and that civil liberties have been reduced." Tony Blair makes no apology for placing the security of law-abiding people ahead of the rights of the offender. 1960s Liberalism had gone too far. "Law and order policy had become focused on offenders' rights and preventing miscarriages of justice and the era had spawned a group of young people without parental discipline or a sense of responsibility." Blair's 'respect' campaign and his crusade against anti-social behaviour led to 10,000 ASBOs and 300,000 on the spot fines being issued. Anti-social behaviour orders, which limit the rights of individuals, are seen as an effective way to protect neighbourhoods from the behaviour of anti-social people. Labour favours the introduction of Identity Cards which are opposed by the other major parties.

Conservatives

The Conservatives, while supporting Labour in the campaign against terrorism, opposed the Labour bill that would make the incitement to religious hatred an offence. They attacked Labour's early release schemes for offenders as an insult to the "law-abiding majority." David Cameron distanced himself from the traditional Tory assumption that individuals, not the environment, cause crime. Cameron developed a more "sociological" way of looking at law and order thus adopting New Labour's strategy that the causes of crime, poverty and dysfunctional families and cultures must be tackled. Cameron's new approach was unfairly mocked by the media and other political parties—"Cameron wants to hug a hoodie" or "love a lout"—were the comments made. Many who hold traditional Tory views were also dismayed by this approach and would have preferred the 2005 Manifesto line of "tough on young offenders" to be have been the party's mantra.

Liberal Democrats

The Liberal Democrats criticised Tony Blair for reducing the debate over law and order to a dispute about what is 'tough' or 'soft'. Liberal Democrat Home Affairs spokesperson Nick Clegg (now party Leader) stated: "I want to rid everyone of the notion that our liberal values give comfort to terrorists and criminals. On the contrary, I believe strong self-confident liberalism goes hand in hand with the reassurance that the state can, must and will protect its citizens." In 2007 the Liberal Democrat leader, Sir Menzies Campbell, outlined the party's five-point plan for a safer Britain. (See below.) He stated that "Labour's record on law and order is one of abysmal failure. Tony Blair's legacy on law and order is one of tough talk and spectacular failure."

Five Point Plan for a Safer Britain

Point One — We will put more police officers on the beat

Point Two — We will take control of our town centres

Point Three — We will have honesty in sentencing. Life will mean life, only those whom judges believe should stay in prison for ever will be given a life sentence

Point Four — We will make prisons work, we will treble the number of prisoners working, and make education and training compulsory

Point Five — We will introduce an entirely new approach to compensating victims of crimes

---

SCOTTISH DIMENSION

Scotland has always had its own legal system, for example the Children's Hearing system is unique to Scotland. Security and Terrorism are reserved issues.

Labour was the senior partner in the Labour/Liberal Democrat coalition which ruled Scotland from 1999 until the May 2007 elections when a minority SNP administration gained control. The Labour/Liberal Democrat administration adopted Blair's "tough on crime, tough on the causes of crime" approach. Scotland faces the same problems as the rest of UK society, an increase in the number of dysfunctional families, the abuse of alcohol and drugs and, especially in Scotland, the existence of a 'blade culture.' This is reflected in Scotland proportionally having one of the highest prison populations in Western Europe and the highest murder rate.

Labour claims that it took tough action to tackle anti-social behaviour. It introduced ASBOs, recruited 1,500 more police officers since 1999 and introduced 550 new Community wardens. It also introduced tough laws against those who carry weapons. Labour proposed to give the police powers to issue 'instant ASBOs' without having to go through the courts. Jack McConnell stated that the Tories "talked tough but voted soft" and that "David Cameron would rather hug a hoodie than back tough action on anti-social behaviour."

The Conservatives

As expected the Conservatives criticised both the Labour/ Liberal Democrat pact and Tony Blair. The Conservatives claimed that the Scottish public had not been protected from violent crime, vandalism and theft. Their campaign slogan was "delivering real justice" and centred around five key principles:

Victims First – Victims deserve better; they and their families will always come first under the Conservatives

Safer Streets – Conservatives expect the police to show zero tolerance towards vandalism, anti-social behaviour and underage drinking

Stronger sentences – "for eight years we have been the lone voice in the Scottish Parliament for the end of the practice of automatic early release and we will continue the fight to achieve this"

More effective prisons – Conservatives accept that stronger sentencing policies will require an extra prison in the short term

Defeating drugs – Conservatives pledge massive resources to go towards expanding rehabilitation facilities for drug addicts in Scotland

Liberal Democrats

Although part of the Scottish Executive at the time of the election, the Liberal Democrats emphasised their distinctiveness from Labour. They said they would carry out a root and branch review of the legal aid system, would set up a National Drug Free Lives Unit to drive policy and would tackle anti-social behaviour. The Liberal Democrats would recruit 1,000 more police officers and increase accountability by making the police publish community crime statistics.

They would reform the Children's Hearing system to deal more effectively with persistent offenders and would expand the use of electronic tagging for more serious cases. Liberal Democrat's Scottish leader, Nicol Stephen, stated: "Across Scotland, people tell me they want more action to cut crime and make their communities safe."

SNP

In the summary of its policy, *Fresh Thinking for Scotland,* the section on law and order had as its headline "It's time for more police on the streets." While Labour would reform the overworked Children's Hearing System, the SNP pledged to clamp down on underage drinking and reinstate the Airborne 'boot camp' initiative. The SNP pledged to release the names and photographs of dangerous sex offenders who go underground. Now in office, the SNP minority administration must work in partnership with the other parties to have its manifesto policies implemented. The SNP has found common ground with the Conservatives on issues such as the treatment of sex offenders. In July 2007 the SNP announced a range of measures to focus on reducing the volume, frequency and seriousness of youth offenders.

SELECTED PARTY POLICIES IN THE SCOTTISH PARLIAMENT ELECTIONS 2007

CONSERVATIVES	LABOUR	LIBERAL DEMOCRATS	SNP
LAW AND ORDER POLICIES • Employ 1,500 more police officers. • Police board conveners will have to stand for election. • A 'three strikes and you're out' policy would hand extra jail time to those about to receive their third custodial sentence. • End Scotland's 'double jeopardy' law to allow suspects to be tried more than once for the same crime. • Give sheriffs and judges powers to deduct fines from salaries and benefits to keep fine defaulters from being jailed. • Require released sex offenders to undergo lie detector (polygraph) tests and monitor their movements through satellite tracking	• Justice centre to allow criminals to carry out 'pay back' duties in communities. • New court powers to place restrictions on violent offenders. • Powers allowing public bodies to share information with anti-fraud organisations. • New investigation powers for cross-border surveillance operations. • Powers of arrest for immigration officers working at Scottish points of entry. • Double the number of community wardens to more than 1,000 and expand environmental wardens. • 'Name and shame' neighbourhood troublemakers.	• 1,000 extra community police officers. • Tougher community sentences to make offenders work to repay their crimes and cut reoffending. • Knife crime crackdown, with seven-year maximum custody and community combined sentences. • Youth justice board and youth panels to cut youth crime. • Pilot 'dual sentencing', where offenders return to court after a period in custody to have a community part of their sentence set. • Licensing on the sale of airguns. • Double funding for drug and alcohol treatment.	• 1,000 more police on local streets. • More information for communities on dangerous paedophiles in their area. • Tougher controls on the sale of alcohol to those under the legal age to drink. • Taskforce to tackle organised crime. • Emphasis on tough community punishments to end short-term prison sentences.
EDUCATION. • Pledge to reform the nursery system to increase choice, flexibility and support for working families – for example, through the expansion of workplace nurseries. • Restore choice by abolishing the graduate endowment and replacing it with a Saltire scholarship. • Headteachers and school boards to have final say on pupil expulsions.	• Build on the introduction of free nursery places for three and four-year-olds. • Increase funding for universities by 23%. • First national policy on discipline, piloting restorative justice in schools.	• Build on free nursery places for three and four-year-olds; offer flexible, affordable childcare over the whole school day. • Claim credit for abolition of tuition fees, replacing them with graduate endowment. • An extra £35 million to improve discipline in schools.	• Extend free nursery education hours by 50%, providing a full half-day for every three and four-year-old. • Abolish student loans and replace them with grants. • Smaller class sizes and a strong school ethos will tackle discipline problems.
ECONOMIC POLICIES • Half-price council tax for older pensioners. • Reduce the number of MSPs from 129 to 108 and save taxpayers about £3 million. • Reduce the size of the public sector.	• Support for small independent shops. • An innovation and investment agency with resources of £20 million to deliver threefold increase in business research and development. • Grow Scottish tourism by half by 2015.	• Lower business rates to 0.4p below the rest of the UK. • Replace council tax with a 'fairer' local income tax based on the ability to pay. • Double the value of the small business rates relief scheme by increasing the Scottish Executive's contribution by £23 million.	• Remove business rates from 120,000 Scottish small businesses and cuts for a further 30,000. • Replace council tax with a local income tax. • Cut red tape and widen access to public sector contracts for small businesses. • £10 million scheme for new entrants to farming.

Source: *Scotsman*, April 2007.

GENERAL ELECTION 2005: PARTY POLICIES

Labour

TAXATION
Promise not to raise the basic or top rate of income tax. No extension of VAT to food, children's clothes, books, newspapers or public transport fares. New Deal bolstered. Minimum wage up to £5.35 in 2006. Aim to support wealth creators.

EDUCATION*
Will allow primaries to opt for foundation status. Wants all secondaries to become specialist schools. Business-funded 'academies' up to at least 200 by 2010. Encourage state boarding schools. Expansion of sixth-form college and apprenticeship places. Promises university top-up fees won't exceed £3,000 (plus inflation).

EUROPE
Core message: proud of EU membership. Will campaign for a 'yes' vote in a promised referendum on the new EU treaty. Back EU defence capabilities. Would back euro entry only if "five tests" met. Euro referendum promised before joining.

LAW & ORDER*
Increase number of police officers. Tougher sentences for persistent offenders. Anti social behaviour laws. On-the-spot fines for 'yobs'. Victims to have better support.

Conservative

TAXATION
Promise lower taxes. Claim they will use £4 billion of identified £12 billion expenditure savings to cut taxes in first Budget. Promise to avoid Labour 'stealth taxes'. Reduced government borrowing, they say, will avoid tax rises that otherwise would be needed. Will retain Labour's minimum wage policy, with proposed increases.

EDUCATION
Extra £15 billion for schools by 2009/10. To improve discipline, heads and governors given powers over admissions and expulsions. Slimmer curriculum, 300,000 vocational grants for 14 to 16-year-olds. Free private school places if same cost as a state-funded school. New 'Super-Colleges' allowed self-management. Scrap tuition fees.

EUROPE
Oppose the new EU constitution and would offer referendum. Would not join the euro. Would negotiate to restore former opt-out on the Social Chapter. Want EU agriculture reform and would negotiate to restore national control over fishing grounds. Say relations with EU 'mismanaged' and now threaten Britain's future interests.

LAW & ORDER
Increase number of police officers. Tough on young offenders. Criminals to serve full sentences. Tougher measures on drugs and drug offenders.

SNP

TAXATION
Lower corporation tax to 25%: business rates set below English levels. Push for economic growth. Would abolish council tax and replace it with local income tax. Want future share of oil revenue — worth £6000 billion — to establish Scottish Oil Fund with positive knock-on effect throughout future taxation and spending.

EDUCATION
Would develop a national apprentice scheme and replace student loans with a university grants system whose aim would be to remove financial barriers to higher education. Promise to increase free nursery provision by 50%. Would set up a national early education and childcare system.

EUROPE
Want an independent Scotland to "take our place at the top tables of the EU and the UN". Presuming there is a referendum on the European constitution, the party will join the 'No' camp until such time as the removal of a clause which gives exclusive competence over the fishing industry to Brussels.

LAW & ORDER
More police officers to be employed: target extra 1,000. Scrap private pensions. Reduce youth crime and all crime by tackling poverty.

Liberal Democrat

TAXATION
One proposed tax rise: 50% on the proportion of incomes over £100,000. Claim it will affect 1% of taxpayers. Revenue to be spread across education, and state care, and would contribute towards lower local taxes. Income would be the base for a new local tax to replace council tax. Greater independence for National Audit Office to scrutinise budget figures.

EDUCATION
Abolish tuition fees and widen grants. Scrap the child trust fund, adding 20,000 teachers. Lower primary class sizes. Extend school care between 8.00am and 6.00pm. Promise 3,500 children's centres set up by 2010. Reduce external testing, begin national 'sampling'. All 14+ pupils can combine vocational and academic learning. Free school transport.

EUROPE
Core message: EU membership "hugely important" on economic, environmental and legal grounds. Want Britain to be "at the heart of Europe" but say reform is needed. Claim new constitution will help. Will support 'yes' vote in referendum. Back new ways of sharing military burden, working through NATO and the EU.

LAW & ORDER
Increase number of police officers. Campaign to target drug dealing. Tackle 'yob' culture. Communities to be involved in sentences for minor crimes.

(*Devolved power in Scotland so elements of UK manifesto won't necessarily apply)

Chapter 4
Parliament

What you will learn.
1. The effectiveness of the House of Commons in scrutinising the Executive.
2. The composition and the role of the House of Lords.
3. The role of backbench MPs in the House of Commons.

Parliament is the centrepiece of the British political system. It is in Parliament that the policies proposed by Her Majesty's Government are debated and then transformed into the law of the land. It is in Parliament that Ministers of the Crown carry out their democratic responsibilities to the elected representatives of the British people. In other words, the British system of government is first and foremost a parliamentary system.

To most people the British 'Parliament' means the elected House of Commons. This is where we see the major party leaders in action. This is where the major legislative powers are located. The MPs we elect sit in the Commons as do most government Ministers. Nonetheless, 'Parliament' goes beyond the Commons; it also includes the House of Lords and the Monarch. Indeed the full formal title of the British legislature is the 'Queen in Parliament'. Under the formal legal provisions of the Constitution, the Monarch and the House of Lords are required to assent to the legislative proposals passed by the Commons before they become the law of the land as Acts of Parliament. The formal powers of the Monarch and the Lords have been gradually deprived of much of their political significance over the centuries. Their use is now governed by conventions of the Constitution although many of the formal powers remain.

The process of parliamentary change is not yet complete. Both the Monarchy and the House of Lords have been subjected to calls for further reform, though for different reasons. The cost of the Monarchy (for example, the controversy in January 1997 about whether to finance a replacement for the royal yacht Britannia) and the behaviour of the present Queen's children and their spouses have, on occasion, put the Monarchy on the front pages of the tabloids. Questions have been raised about the suitability of Prince Charles to succeed

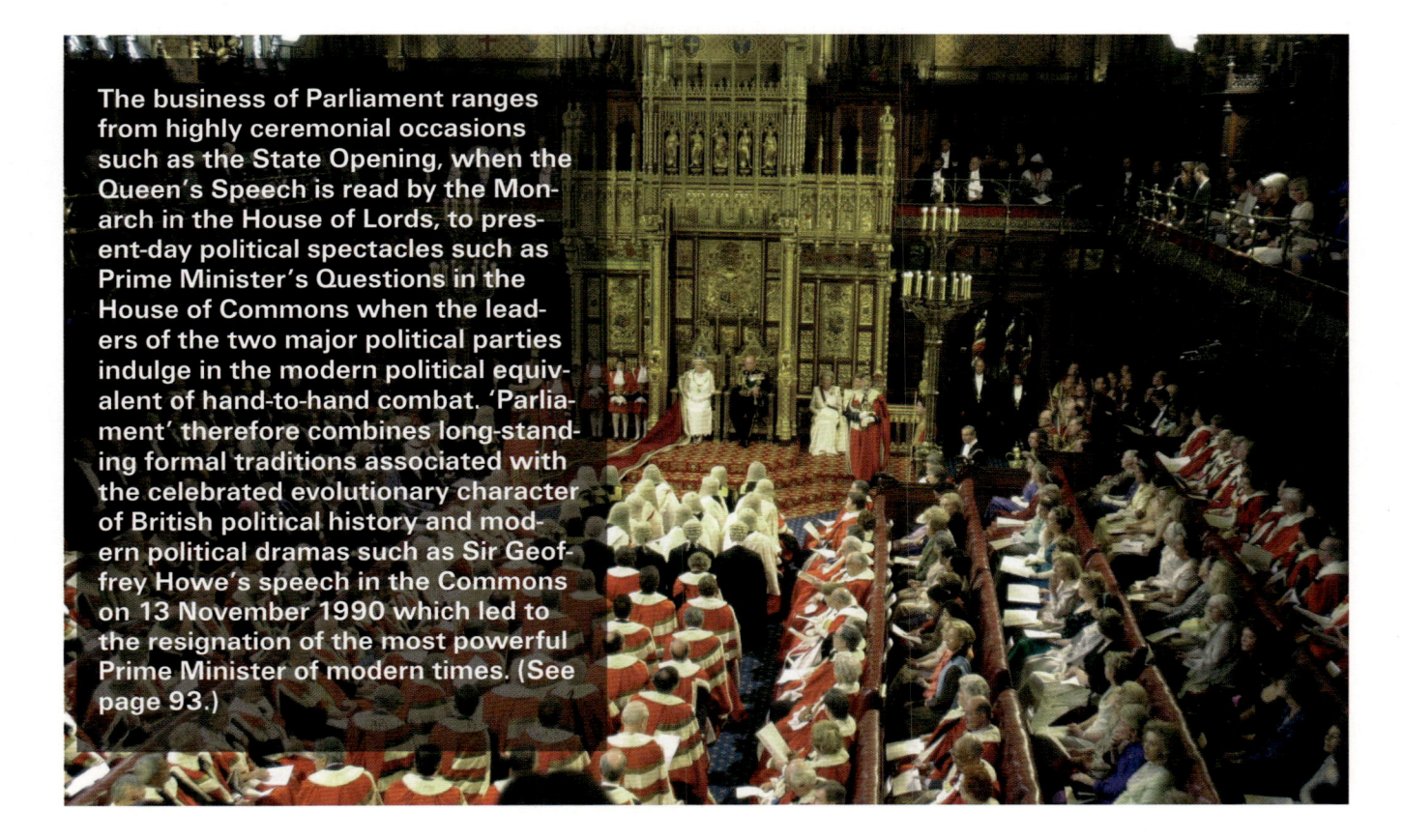

The business of Parliament ranges from highly ceremonial occasions such as the State Opening, when the Queen's Speech is read by the Monarch in the House of Lords, to present-day political spectacles such as Prime Minister's Questions in the House of Commons when the leaders of the two major political parties indulge in the modern political equivalent of hand-to-hand combat. 'Parliament' therefore combines long-standing formal traditions associated with the celebrated evolutionary character of British political history and modern political dramas such as Sir Geoffrey Howe's speech in the Commons on 13 November 1990 which led to the resignation of the most powerful Prime Minister of modern times. (See page 93.)

to the throne. The Labour government elected in 1997 reformed the composition of the House of Lords, drastically reducing the number of hereditary peers who are allowed to sit in the Upper House. Reform of the Lords is not yet complete.

THE BRITISH CONSTITUTION

A 'Constitution' is a set of rules which lay down the powers and duties of the institutions of government and establish the rights and liberties of citizens.

It is frequently claimed that the British Constitution is unwritten but this is misleading. What is true is that the British Constitution, unlike the American, does not consist of one comprehensive document most of which was laid down at one historical moment and subsequently amended to meet changing circumstances. The American Constitution is to be found at the back of every textbook on American politics. It is impossible to produce a copy of the British Constitution because it has 'evolved' over many centuries. Nevertheless, one can describe its major sources which are

▲ parliamentary statutes,
▲ the common law and
▲ 'conventions'.

Parliamentary Statutes

Acts of Parliament which are 'constitutional' in nature include the *Act of Settlement* of 1700 which requires that the Monarch is a member of the Church of England and the *Parliament Act* of 1911 which limited the legislative powers of the House of Lords. Various *Representation of the People Acts* lay down the law relating to who has and who does not have the right to vote.

Common Law

Many principles of the Constitution lie in the common law and not in parliamentary statutes. The 'common law' is to be found in judicial decisions, many of which are centuries old. The formal powers of the Monarch are common law powers. Individual rights often exist in the common law.

Conventions

Conventions are accepted constitutional rules which do not have legal status (they are not enforceable by the courts) but which are obeyed because most people believe that they should be obeyed. The best way to explain 'conventions' is to give an example. It is an accepted constitutional convention that the Prime Minister must be a member of the House of Commons. The reason is that in a democratic age the chief executive politician should be accountable to the people's elected representatives.

Some of the most important constitutional rules in Britain take the form of conventions such as the convention of ministerial responsibility. (See page 88.)

THE MONARCHY

The British parliamentary system includes a Constitutional Monarchy which has no effective political power. The royal prerogatives—personal powers which the Monarch still holds such as the power to dissolve Parliament—are, by convention, held by others such as the Prime Minister and other Ministers of the Crown. (See page 65.) They in turn are responsible to an elected House of Commons. Therefore, although he or she carries out certain prerogative functions which suggest some royal influence over political decisions, there is, in practice, no choice available to the Monarch.

In spite of its lack of real political power, the Monarchy's proper role in the British political system has become an emotive and widely debated issue in recent years. Often, people hold strong opinions about the Monarchy, either feeling that it is doing a wonderful job or else questioning the need for it at all in a democratic society in the twenty first century. Some critics even questioned the fitness of Prince Charles as the heir apparent due to him 'going public' over his marital problems with Princess Diana.

DO WE NEED THE MONARCHY?

Many people feel that the Monarchy should claim its place in history. Since we live in a democratic society where political power lies with our elected representatives rather than with the Monarch, the whole extended Royal Family is seen by many as a drain on the nation's resources.

In September 2000, Demos, a Labour think tank, set out a programme to 'modernise' the Monarchy. Three central reforms were proposed.

☞ The removal of all the Monarch's constitutional powers, such as the power to dissolve Parliament and to appoint the Prime Minister.

☞ The introduction of a referendum at times of succession to the throne for the public to decide who should be the Monarch (and, by definition, whether there should be a Monarchy).

☞ The disestablishment of the Church of England as the State's official religion, and the removal of the Monarch's role as head of that Church.

In December 2000, *The Guardian* newspaper added its voice when it called for a referendum to be held on whether the Head of State should be elected after the present Queen's death. The newspaper also backed a legal challenge of the *Act of Settlement* in the High Court in London on the grounds that the Act clashes with the European Human Rights Act. The Act institutionalises religious discrimination as it states that a Roman Catholic cannot become the Monarch of the United Kingdom. Michael Forsyth, the former Tory Scottish Secretary, described the 300-year-old *Act of Settlement* as "the grubby little secret of the British Constitution". The Scottish Parliament called for this section

(continued on page 66)

CONSTITUTIONAL MONARCHY

PREROGATIVE FUNCTIONS

The British Monarch still holds some long-standing common law powers known as royal prerogatives. These play a very visible part in British politics even though the Monarch no longer wields such powers personally but must exercise them on the advice of the government.

Opening Parliament

The parliamentary year runs from the date when the Queen 'summons' (opens) Parliament until the date when it is 'prorogued' (closed). Parliament actually chooses these dates, the Monarchy simply having a ceremonial function. The reading of the 'Queen's Speech', containing the government's major policy proposals, marks the beginning of the parliamentary year.

Dissolution of Parliament

The maximum term of any Parliament is five years, at the end of which the Monarch declares that Parliament has terminated and gives the date of the general election which has been decided by the Prime Minister. When the Prime Minister decides to go to the country before the five years are up, s/he must request the Monarch to dissolve Parliament before a general election can be held. The Monarch also dissolves Parliament when a government resigns after losing a vote of confidence in the Commons.

Appointing the PM

The Monarch still 'appoints' Ministers of the Crown, including the Prime Minister. By convention all Ministers are effectively appointed by the Prime Minister who 'advises' the Monarch of his/her choices as Chancellor of the Exchequer, Foreign Secretary, Home Secretary etc. The Prime Minister is responsible for these appointments. However, a Prime Minister cannot choose his/her successor because s/he cannot be held responsible after leaving office. The possibility that the Monarch might have a real say in the appointment of the Prime Minister forced the Conservative Party in the 1960s to change its method of selecting its leader to an election by its MPs.

The Monarch's choice of Prime Minister after an election and when the existing Prime Minister resigns or else dies in office is automatic provided that one party in the House of Commons has a majority. In such circumstances the Monarch 'appoints' the leader of the majority party. However, if there was no majority party in the Commons, the Monarch's choice of a new Prime Minister could be a difficult one. Should proportional representation (PR) be introduced at some future date, elections might routinely fail to produce a majority party in the Commons. In such circumstances the selection of a Prime Minister supported by a Commons majority could become more difficult and a much more political process. It would be harder to abide by the constitutional principle that the Monarch must not be involved in politics.

The Royal Assent

A Bill which has passed through the required legislative process in the Houses of Parliament must still receive the Royal Assent before it becomes an Act of Parliament. By convention the Monarch grants such assent. The Royal Assent has not been refused since the reign of Queen Anne at the beginning of the eighteenth century.

SYMBOLIC FUNCTIONS

Head of State

It is the Monarch rather than the Prime Minister who is the Head of State. Unlike France and the USA, the British Head of State is above party politics.

Head of the Commonwealth

The Monarch heads this multi-racial 'Family of Nations' and in this capacity usually opens Commonwealth Conferences.

The Crown

The Monarch's role as Head of State is reinforced by the fact that Ambassadors, Judges, government Ministers and so on all carry out their normal functions in the name of the Crown.

Awarding Honours

The Monarch can only personally award a few Honours, for example the Orders of Merit, the Garter and the Thistle. All other Honours awarded by the Monarch are, in fact, decided by the government.

of the Act to be repealed. The diocese of Cardinal Keith O'Brien lies in Gordon Brown's Fife constituency. Press reports suggested that Cardinal O'Brien would raise the matter with the new Prime Minister "when the pair next meet." (*The Guardian*, 5 July 2007).

There are those who argue that the Monarch's constitutional role is a more effective safeguard of British democracy than any replacement, such as an elected president, could be. The Monarch's reserve powers may encourage politicians to abide by the constitutional rules of the game. In future, if the first-past-the-post system is replaced by a more proportional system, then the power to appoint Prime Ministers in the event of a hung Parliament will become more important. If this power was taken from the Monarch and given to the Speaker it could lead to partisan decision making in the selection of the Prime Minister. Part of the reason why the Monarch is popular is that the Queen is not a politician and is an independent arbitrator in any political crisis.

THE HOUSE OF LORDS

The House of Lords, like the Monarchy, has survived the transition to democracy because its powers have been cut back and its composition modified to meet democratic expectations. The powers and composition of the House of Lords were reformed in the nineteenth century by constitutional convention and in the twentieth century by statute. (See page 68.)

In its 1997 Manifesto, the Labour Party declared that "The House of Lords must be reformed" and promised as a "first stage of reform" to end by statute "the right of hereditary peers to sit and vote in the House of Lords". This was duly achieved with the passage of the 1999 *House of Lords Act*.

The constitutional debate over reform of the Lords focuses on two key questions:
1 Does Britain still need a second legislative chamber?
2 If the answer is Yes, what should be the powers, functions and composition of the second chamber in a modern democracy?

There are a few countries, for example New Zealand and Sweden, with unicameral legislatures—only one legislative chamber. Most countries have bicameral legislatures although the relationship between the two legislative chambers varies. The Upper House in the USA, the Senate, is as powerful as the House of Representatives because both are directly elected. As a result the process of making new laws in the American Congress is more difficult.

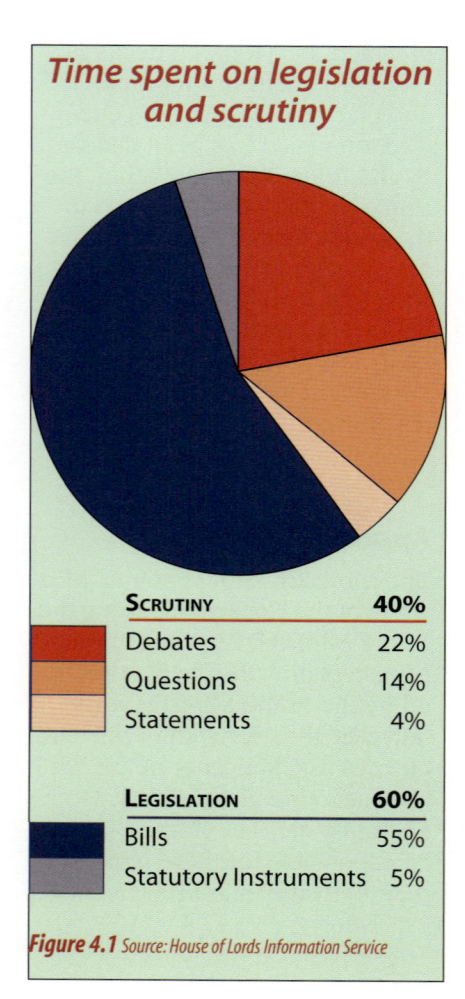

Time spent on legislation and scrutiny

SCRUTINY	**40%**
Debates	22%
Questions	14%
Statements	4%
LEGISLATION	**60%**
Bills	55%
Statutory Instruments	5%

Figure 4.1 Source: House of Lords Information Service

Government defeats in the House of Lords

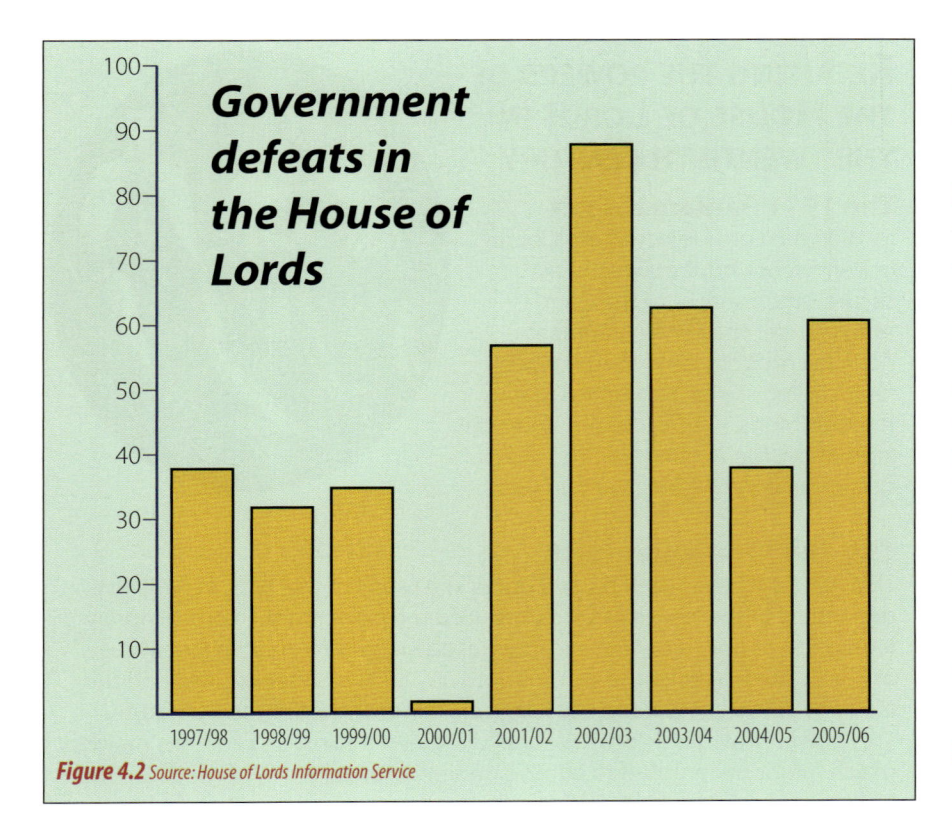

Figure 4.2 Source: House of Lords Information Service

In most countries the Lower House is stronger than the Upper House. The fact that almost every country in the world has a bicameral legislature explains why most commentators answer 'Yes' to the first question above. Upper chambers, however they are set up, are useful for three main reasons.

- Firstly, they can carry out essential tasks which the Lower House does not have the time to perform fully.
- Secondly, they can both debate themes of public interest and give representation to sections of public opinion.
- A third, more controversial, reason for an upper chamber is that it can act as a constitutional 'fail safe' device against a lower chamber which might be taken over by political extremists.

FUNCTIONS OF THE HOUSE OF LORDS

Although the House of Lords usually gives way to the will of the House of Commons, many believe that it carries out a number of useful and indispensable functions which are listed below.

Legislation

Most Bills are passed by the Lords before becoming law. However Money Bills, like the Finance Bill which contains the Budget, cannot be rejected by the House of Lords and other Bills may only be held up for about one year. If the House of Lords rejects a Bill which has been passed by the Commons in two consecutive parliamentary sessions, it automatically becomes law even if the Upper House rejects it for a second time.

The bulk of the government's legislative programme is introduced in the Commons. Consequently, the legislative business of the Lords has to await the passage of Bills in the Lower House. The government does introduce a few Bills in the Lords, usually, though not exclusively, of the non-controversial variety. In session 1990–91, eighteen of the sixty eight Acts of Parliament passed began life in the Upper House. The Lords acts as a cleaning up agency for the government which often introduces amendments in the Lords in response to improvements suggested as Bills pass through the legislative processes in the Commons. In session 2004–05 the House of Lords tabled over 3,000 amendments. Figure 4.1 highlights the time spent on legislation and scrutiny.

Public Debate

The more leisurely, less confrontational style of the Upper Chamber allows it to function as a debating chamber for issues which are of public interest. The Lords has the time to devote to such debates unlike the Commons. This also applies to the 'tidying up' function of the Lords in respect of government legislation. Consequently, the very existence of the Lords is often said to depend on its ability to perform useful tasks which cannot be fitted into the current organisation and timetable of the Commons.

Scrutiny

The Lords possesses the various scrutiny procedures available to the Commons such as Question Time, Select Committees and debate. The Lords makes a special contribution through Select Committees in two areas: European Communities and Science and Technology. The Select Committees on these two topics in the Lords are acknowledged to be more expert than their parallel Committees in the Commons.

The House of Lords has played an active role in challenging government legislation. The Lords has proved to be a considerable obstacle to New Labour over issues as diverse as hunting, terrorism, ID cards and education reform. Figure 4.2 highlights the number of government defeats in the period 1997 to 2006.

Judicial Reform

The highest court of appeal in Britain is located in the House of Lords, although this function is performed by only the small band of Law Lords. About five to ten of the Law Lords form a judicial committee which considers appeals. Following the *Constitutional Reform Act* of 2005, from October 2009 Law Lords will no longer sit in the Upper House. Instead, the highest court will be an independent Supreme Court separate from both the executive and the legislature.

THE HOUSE OF LORDS ACT

It was not until Labour was elected in 1997 with a massive working majority in the Commons that it could set about radically reforming the membership of the Lords, an aim which the party had tried but failed to achieve in the late 1960s. Labour's Manifesto commitment to abolish the hereditary principle as the major qualification for membership was achieved with the passage of the 1999 *House of Lords Act*. The government prevented a major conflict between Lords and Commons by allowing ninety two hereditary peers to sit in the Lords until it could come up with a scheme for deciding membership of the Lords on a permanent basis. A Royal Commission under Lord Wakeham was established to make recommendations. The impact of the 1999 *House of Lords Act* is illustrated in Table 4.1.

The 1999 Act left the 'spiritual' and judicial membership of the Lords untouched. The Lords Spiritual are the two Archbishops (Canterbury and York) and twenty four Bishops of the Church of England who represent the relationship between Church and State. The Lords Spiritual are entitled to attend the House of Lords only when they hold Church office. The Law Lords, twenty six in 2007, enter the Lords by virtue of their appointment to high judicial office. The Law Lords retain their seats until death so there are more Law Lords than are required to perform the judicial function of acting as the highest court of appeal in Britain.

Table 4.1 confirms the elimination of the hereditary majority in the Lords—the proportion of hereditary peers fell from 63% in 1996 to 12% in 2007. The decline in hereditary membership and a significant rise in the appointment of women as Life Peers accounts for the rise in the proportion of women in the Lords from 6.7% in 1996 to 24% in 2007. In 2007 there was one woman Law Lord.

Table 4.2 illustrates the decline in Conservative support in the Upper House. In 2000 there were still more Conservative than Labour or Liberal Democrat peers but the margin of superiority had been drastically reduced. Neither in 1996 nor in 2000 did the Conservatives enjoy an overall majority in the Lords, partly because of the large numbers of crossbenchers who do not admit to any party allegiance. By 2007 there were slightly more Labour than Conservative supporters in the Lords. The Conservative majority within the group of ninety two hereditary peers still in the Lords (forty eight Conservatives, four Labour, five Liberal Democrats, and thirty five crossbenchers) was offset by a Labour lead, 207 to 156, among Life Peers. The current membership of the Lords is much more in accord with Labour's 1997 Manifesto claim that "No one political party should seek a majority in the House of Lords".

REDUCING THE POWERS OF THE HOUSE OF LORDS IN THE TWENTIETH CENTURY

The 1911 Parliament Act
In 1909 the Lords rejected the Liberal government's budget which had secured the consent of the Commons. Under the 1911 *Parliament Act*, the Lords could no longer reject financial legislation submitted to it by the Commons. In terms of non-financial legislation, the Act limited the Lords to a delaying power of just over two years.

The 1949 Parliament Act
This Act, which was itself passed under the terms of the 1911 Act against the wishes of the House of Lords, reduced the power of the Lords to delay legislation to one year. One exceptional power was retained by the House of Lords. The Upper House can still veto any Bill which seeks to extend the life of a Parliament beyond the five years currently permitted by statute. This power provides a constitutional safeguard against a Commons majority which might be tempted to behave undemocratically.

The Life Peerages Act 1958
This Act, introduced by a Conservative government, gave prime ministers the power to create peers whose titles die with them. The impact of life peerages has been to reduce Conservative domination of the Lords and to widen its social representation.

The Peerages and Renunciation of Titles Act 1963
This Act gave hereditary peers, who were not allowed to be members of the Commons, the right to renounce their peerage and stand for election to the Lower House. This enabled hereditary peers such as Labour's Tony Benn and Conservative leader and Prime Minister Alex Douglas Home to become MPs.

The 1999 House of Lords Act
The Act changed the composition of the House of Lords.
- 92 hereditary peers were retained
- the transitional chamber consists of 92 hereditary peers, 603 life peers, 26 bishops and 26 current and former law lords.

COMPOSITION OF THE LORDS *before and after* THE 1999 HOUSE OF LORDS ACT

	1996	(Women)	2007	(Women)
Lords Spiritual	26	(0)	26	(0)
Law Lords	21	(0)	26	(1)
Life Peers	398	(16)	603	(139)
Hereditary Peers	762	(65)	92	(3)
Total	1207	(81)	747	(143)

Table 4.1

POLITICAL COMPOSITION of the House of Lords: 1996 & 2007

	1996	2007
Conservative	481	204
Labour	116	211
Liberal Democrat	57	77
Crossbenchers	320	205

Table 4.2 Source: House of Lords website November 2007

The 1999 Act did not bring the process of House of Lords reform to a conclusion because it did not establish a permanent alternative in terms of either the membership or the appropriate powers of the second chamber. In the short term, membership consists of life peers, spiritual and law lords and ninety two hereditary peers who are elected by their aristocratic colleagues on a party basis. Many people object to the hereditary principle as the basis of even a small minority of the Lords' membership and this keeps the issue of Lords reform alive.

There have been a number of developments since the 1999 Act to find a solution to the conundrum of how to structure a final reform of the House of Lords which would remove the issue from the political and constitutional agenda. There are two principal but related areas of conflict: membership and powers. The membership issue is about how to determine the composition of the 'Upper House' or second chamber: selection or election or a 'hybrid' mixture of the two. The question of powers focuses on opinion about what the functions of the Lords should be and to what extent, if at all, it should be able to challenge the authority and decisions of the House of Commons. Direct election of even a limited proportion of the Upper House carries with it the possibility of such members taking any dispute they might have with a majority in the Lower House to the electorate. This is why the simple solution of directly electing the entire House of Lords is not attractive to party leaders in the Commons. On the other hand, an entirely appointed Upper House might command little public respect because it would be regarded as the creature of those who appoint it—the Prime Minister and party leaders in the Commons at present.

The government appointed a Royal Commission on Reform of Britain's Upper House chaired by Lord Wakeham which reported in January 2000. The Commission recommended that:

- membership of the Upper House should include a broad range of experience and expertise.
- the House should be more representative of contemporary British society.
- the nations and regions of the United Kingdom should have a formal voice in the Lords.
- the two Houses of Parliament should work together to hold the executive more effectively to account.

To achieve these ends the Royal Commission recommended a 'hybrid' system of appointment and election with the emphasis on appointment by a Commission rather than by the Prime Minister. Nevertheless, like opinion overall the Commission was divided. Some members wanted a wholly elected second chamber. Others shared the view of senior Labour Cabinet Ministers, including the Prime Minister, that the reformed chamber should be by appointment only. Frontbenchers did not relish the prospect of an elected Lords

2001 White Paper on reform of the House of Lords
MAIN PROPOSALS

- The ninety two hereditary peers to be removed. Members of the Lords will no longer be called peers, but will have ML after their name.
- 30% of the new members will be women and there will be more representatives from ethnic minorities.
- 120 directly elected members to represent the nation and regions.
- 120 independent members appointed by the Appointments Commission.
- A balance of not more than 332 members nominated by the political parties (in proportion to their share of votes in the general election). The final number to be decided by the Appointments Commission.
- Number of Bishops to be reduced to sixteen. Rejection of the Wakeham Commission's proposal to include other Christian denominations.
- At least twelve Law Lords will remain in the Lords.
- Size will be capped at 600, with an interim House of about 750.

opposing the will of the lower but more powerful House of Commons. Appointment as the mode of selection was receiving a bad press because the life peers who were appointed in 2000, nominated by the three largest political parties, did not meet the second representative criterion listed above. Instead the main criterion for appointment was characterised by some commentators as rewarding individuals who had contributed to party funds. Appointment led to talk of 'Blair's Backwoodsmen' because it was the Prime Minister who formally held the power of appointment under the 1999 Act.

In November 2001 the government published a White Paper containing its proposals for reform of the Lords. The proposals (summarised in the box below) included the final abolition of the hereditary principle as a route into the Upper House. However, the proposals were still dominated by frontbench concerns about conflict between the two Houses. Appointment, albeit not by the Prime Minister, was to be more prominent than election in determining the membership, thus ensuring that patronage and party rather than the electorate would be the major influences on the membership of the reformed Upper House. Nothing came of the White Paper proposals. The next step was the appointment of a joint committee of MPs and peers to recommend reform options to be put to free votes in both Houses of Parliament. The government would then base its legislation for reform of the Lords on the opinions expressed by MPs and peers. In 2003 the Lords proceeded to reject all options except a completely appointed chamber and the Commons failed to agree on any option, although an 80% elected House was only three votes short of acceptance. That ended the matter until the 2005 election campaign.

The three main British parties all promised reform of the House of Lords in their 2005 Election Manifestos. Labour promised to "remove the remaining hereditary peers and allow a free vote on the composition of the House". The Manifesto also declared that "a reformed Upper Chamber must be effective, legitimate and more representative without challenging the primacy of the House of Commons".

How these aims were to be achieved was not spelt out. The much shorter Conservative Manifesto merely promised to "seek a cross-party consensus for a substantially elected House of Lords". The Liberal Democrat Manifesto declared that "Reform of the House of Lords has been botched by Labour, leaving it unelected and even more in the patronage of the Prime Minister. We will replace it with a predominantly elected second chamber". The Conservatives and the Liberal Democrats appeared to be more reconciled than the Labour leadership to the prospect of a "substantially" or "predominantly" elected second chamber.

The "loans for peerages scandal" (see page 55) encouraged the Labour government to discuss further reforms of the House of Lords.

In March 2007 the House of Commons held a two-day debate on reform options put forward by the government for its consideration. The debate was led by Jack Straw as Leader of the House of Commons. The various options presented and how the House voted on them are listed in Table 4.3.

The retention of two chambers (bi-cameral legislature) and a 100% elected Upper House received absolute majority support. Nonetheless, many conflicting views were expressed in the debate. Jack Straw argued for an equal measure of appointment and election (a view shared by Prime Minister Blair). This was to ensure fair representation for ethnic minorities which he believed could not be achieved by election alone. Appointment as well as election would also ensure the introduction of members whose experience and expertise would enhance debate and decision making in the second chamber. Straw emphasised that the reform should achieve "an effective, revising second Chamber, subordinate to but complementary to the House of Commons." Straw's frontbench views were

Voting on Proposals for Reform of the Lords: 7 March 2007

Reform Option	For	Against
Retain 2 chambers	416	163
Fully appointed	196	375
50% elected + 50% appointed	155	418
60% elected + 40% appointed	178	392
80% elected + 20% appointed	305	267
100% elected	337	224

Table 4.3 Source: *Hansard, 7-8 March 2007*

The 'People's' Peers

They were hailed as a breakthrough, which would pave the way towards a more workmanlike and truly representative House of Lords. But, six years on, the 'people's peers' created by Tony Blair, amid great fanfare, have the poorest attendance rate in the House of Lords and do a fraction of the work of the hereditary peers. An analysis by *The Sunday Telegraph* has revealed an astonishingly low average turnout of just 13% for the thirty six non-party political peers appointed since May 2000 [compared with] 35% for all 725 peers as a whole, and almost 40% for hereditary peers.'

Source: *The Sunday Telegraph*, May 2006

echoed by Chris Mullin (Sunderland South), who had been a Parliamentary Undersecretary at the Foreign and Commonwealth Office, but who was now a prominent backbencher. Mullin argued that "an elected House of Lords or a part elected House would be used to undermine the legitimacy of ... " the Commons.

Readers of The Times on 8 March 2007 were greeted with the headline "Farewell to the House of Lords". They were assured that MPs had decided "by a huge majority to end over 700 years of parliamentary history" and that "Decades of deadlock end with vote for a wholly elected second chamber". However, the votes do not end the story. The government, now led by Gordon Brown, has at the time of writing, still to introduce the Bill which will turn the free votes of the Commons into political reality.

THE HOUSE OF COMMONS

The House of Commons consists of 646 Members of Parliament, each representing a single constituency. England has 529 MPs, Scotland fifty nine, Wales forty and Northern Ireland eighteen.

Support or oppose the government

The reality of British politics is that the most significant function of the Commons is not to legislate but to sustain the government. While it is true that the British Constitution assumes that the executive is responsible to the House of Commons (see Chapter 5), the impact of elections and party discipline has been to give the executive more power over the Commons rather than the other way round. The executive only enjoys this power if the electorate returns a government with a comfortable working majority. Thus the first function of the Labour majority returned in the May 2005 general election was to maintain the government of Prime Minister Tony Blair. When Blair was succeeded by Gordon Brown as Prime Minister in June 2007, the new Prime Minister became the beneficiary of the strong party discipline supporting executive control of the Commons.

While Labour MPs were characterised by some as being Blair's 'poodles' there were occasional backbench revolts during Labour's first term. In December 1997 the cut in lone parent benefits led to forty seven Labour MPs voting against the government and to Malcolm Chisholm, a Scottish Office Minister, resigning his office. A large rebellion took place in May 1999, when sixty seven Labour MPs voted against the government over cuts in incapacity benefits. One of the largest backbench revolts ever took place during Labour's second term in March 2003 when over 100 Labour MPs voted against going to war against Saddam Hussain's Iraq. Labour rebellions accelerated after the 2005 election reduced the party's parliamentary majority from 167 to 66.

THE MAJOR FUNCTIONS OF THE HOUSE OF COMMONS

1. Supporting or opposing Her Majesty's Government.
2. Legislating—passing Bills sponsored by the government or by backbench MPs.
3. Scrutinising and publicising the work of the government thereby influencing what the government does.
4. Representing constituents and expressing the views of the country.

Supporting the executive is, of course, the primary function of MPs of the majority party. The first function of MPs of other parties is to oppose the government. Unless there is a government with a very small majority or no majority at all, there are severe limits on what the opposition parties can achieve. Nevertheless, proceedings in the House of Commons are vital to democracy by providing the public with often dramatic information about the behaviour of government and opposition.

SCRUTINISING THE WORK OF GOVERNMENT

As long as the government has a majority it will succeed in getting its legislative proposals and other policy decisions accepted. It is often argued that even more important than legislation is subjecting the actions of the government to close examination so that the business of government is in the open. Scrutiny also allows interested voters to judge the performance of the government on the basis of fact rather than guesswork. Such close study gives the House, in spite of its partisan framework, opportunities to 'influence' what the government does. Some commentators use the phrase 'control of the executive' to describe the impact of various scrutiny procedures though that may be going too far except when a government loses its majority or comes close to doing so.

The main scrutiny procedures are debates on the floor of the House, Select Committees and Question Time.

Debates

Debates include the second reading stage of the legislative process, adjournment debates, and substantive motions. Most debates involve the government having to explain, defend and justify both its actions and its policies. The executive is forced to account for its actions to Parliament.

THE LEGISLATIVE PROCESS

Legislative proposals (Bills) may be introduced in either the Commons or the Lords. However, the government introduces most of its legislation in the Commons. Government Bills expressing its policies take up most of the legislative timetable. A limited time is made available for Private Members' legislation. There are six main stages in the legislative process.

1 White Paper
A legislative proposal may begin as a 'White Paper' which contains the government's thinking on an issue. White Papers are really written to allow consultation. The government will consider comments from interested parties before firming up its policy by drafting a Bill.

2 First Reading
The Bill is introduced by its title being read. There is no debate. The Bill is then printed in full and distributed to MPs.

3 Second Reading
A debate is held on the floor of the House on the general principles of the Bill. The debate commences with the government Minister responsible for the Bill explaining and defending its contents. The opposition 'shadow' frontbencher then gives what is usually the case against the Bill. The critical moment is the vote at the end of the debate. If it is rejected, the Bill is withdrawn. Usually the two major parties impose a 'three line Whip' to ensure maximum turnout and therefore victory for the majority governing party. (See the Whip system, page 77.)

4 Committee Stage
The Bill is now referred to a standing legislative committee for a detailed clause-by-clause examination. The committee stage of Bills of constitutional significance, such as the European Communities (Amendment) Bill which led to acceptance of the Maastricht Treaty, may be taken on the floor of the Commons. This is also where the committee stage of money Bills such as the Finance Bill (the budget) takes place, thus allowing all MPs to examine them in detail. Standing committees are made up for each Bill, with usually about twenty MPs sitting on the committee. The parties are represented according to their strength in the Commons, so the government normally has a majority. Amendments are made, many of which the government accepts because they will improve the Bill.

5 Report Stage
The Bill as amended by the committee is 'reported' back to the House when further amendments, often introduced by the government, are debated and put to the vote.

6 Third Reading
Once again the principles of the Bill, now as amended, are debated. Usually the debate is shorter than it was on the second reading.

If the Bill is approved by the Commons it then goes through a similar process in the Lords (unless it is a Finance Bill) before receiving the Royal Assent. (The Monarch has not given the Royal Assent personally since the middle of the nineteenth century.) The Bill is now an Act of Parliament and enters the Statute Book as part of the law of the land.

The legislative process takes up about one-third of the time of the Commons, most of it on government Bills. In 2005–06, fifty four Acts of Parliament were passed.

Adjournment Debates in the House of Commons: Week of 16 July 2007

At the end of each parliamentary day a motion is put that 'this House do now adjourn'. A backbencher then speaks on an issue which he/she has chosen and a government Minister replies. Backbenchers frequently select topics which are significant to their constituents, perhaps pointing out problems which their constituents believe are in need of attention. The range of topics which come up in Adjournment Debates is illustrated below.

	Backbench Sponsor	Topic of Debate
Monday 16 July	David Kennedy (Stafford) Labour	Future of MOD establishment in the MP's constituency given that certain functions had been moved elsewhere.
Tuesday 17 July	Adam Price (Carmarthen East and Dinefwr) Plaid Cymru	Concern about a constituent subject to a detention and removal order. Case to be reviewed.
Wednesday 18 July	Gordon Marsden (Blackpool South) Labour	Concerns about disabled access following transfer of some Crown Post Offices to within WH Smiths' premises.
Thursday 19 July	John Mann (Bassetlaw) Labour	Anti-Semitism

Formally the executive is accountable to Parliament. However, party politics and the electorate usually ensure that the government controls Parliament rather than the other way round. For this reason debates do not normally end up with the government being defeated. In the last three months of the Major government, when it lost its overall Commons majority, the opposition parties attempted to force a general election by bringing motions of confidence before the House. The government survived all of these motions because the opposition parties could not unite. The Ulster Unionist parties frequently came to the government's rescue.

The opposition parties are allowed twenty days per session (seventeen for the major opposition party and three for the third largest party) when they can choose the issues to be debated. Labour selected the BSE crisis as the topic to be debated on 17 February 1997 in the hope of moving a vote of no confidence against the Agriculture Minister Douglas Hogg. This tactic failed, even though the government no longer had a majority in the House, because Ulster Unionist MPs refused to join the attempt to bring down the government.

Backbench MPs are given the opportunity to force the government to explain and defend its policies through the procedure of adjournment debates which are held at the close of each parliamentary day. The speaker holds a weekly ballot in order to decide which backbench member will get to choose the subject for each daily debate.

Question Time

Question Time begins the business of the Commons four days a week. It lasts for about thirty minutes and now plays a dramatic part (proceedings are often televised) in securing the redress of constituents' grievances, representing the people and ensuring the responsibility of the executive to Parliament.

Question Time allows MPs to 'grill' Ministers about their policies and actions. MPs must put questions (of which Ministers are informed in advance); they must not attempt to debate. Questions may be designed to elicit information to embarrass the government (if the question is put by an Opposition MP), or to allow a government Minister to release a particularly favourable piece of information (if the question is put by a government backbencher). Ministerial reputations can be made or lost at Question Time.

One of the first parliamentary actions of the new Labour government in 1997 was to reform 'Prime Minister's Questions'. The Prime Minister had, since 1960, been present to answer questions for fifteen minutes on Tuesdays and Thursdays. Labour decided to schedule 'Prime Minister's Questions' on Wednesdays for the full thirty minutes. Such a move was justified on the grounds that it would permit more in-depth questioning of the Prime Minister and that it would thus improve the ability of the Commons to hold the country's most powerful politician responsible for his/her own actions and also his/her government's actions. Others argued that the reform merely added to the cult of the personality and to the forces making for 'Prime Ministerial government' at the expense of 'Cabinet government'.

Select Committees

Debates on the floor of the House of Commons are grand occasions which, through television and the press may catch the public eye and influence public opinion. A less dramatic but more detailed scrutiny of the government is provided by a comprehensive Select Committee system covering the major government departments. This system has been in place in its present form since 1979. These committees have an investigative or supervisory function, which means that they were set up "to examine the expenditure, administration and policy of individual departments". They can look into how public policy is worked out or formulated and also how such policy is implemented or put into practice. The committees have the power to request the presence of both government Ministers and civil servants for questioning and representatives of outside bodies may also be asked to give evidence.

The purpose of the scrutiny function of the Select Committees is twofold: to keep government departments on their toes and to make sure that government is open to the public eye. The parties are represented according to their strength in the House as a whole. Each Committee has about eleven members.

There are currently seventeen departmental Select Committees including one each for Scottish, Welsh and Northern Ireland Affairs. When the Select Committee on Northern Ireland Affairs was established in 1994, it was claimed that the decision was influenced by the government's need to retain the votes of Ulster Unionist MPs when it was in danger of losing the support of Eurosceptic Conservative MPs. The occasional dramatic role of Select Committees was highlighted in September 2007 in the wake of a banking and financial crisis occasioned by a run on Northern Rock Bank by its depositors who feared a collapse of the one-time building society. The Commons Treasury Select Committee questioned the Governor of the Bank of England, Mervyn King, and a Deputy Governor over the Bank's handling of the crisis. The Chairperson of the Treasury Select Committee, John McFall (West Dunbartonshire), accused the Bank of England of being "asleep at the wheel" as the crisis unfolded. In the eyes of most Committee members the Bank of England should have seen the crisis coming and should have acted to prevent it. The publicity given to what the Committee said turned attention to whether steps should be taken to hold Bank of England personnel responsible for an alleged decline in the reputation of financial management in Britain.

Criticisms of Select Committees

The adjacent example supports the viewpoint that Committees have improved the scrutiny of government. The requirement of government Ministers and their officials to give evidence has often resulted in changes of policy.

Nevertheless, criticism has been made of the Select Committees. A report in May 2000 by the Liaison Committee, which coordinates the work of Select Committees, highlighted their shortcomings. The Liaison Committee stated that the government "has been too ready and has found it too easy to thwart the work of the Select Committees in holding Ministers to account". The Liaison Committee highlighted two major areas of concern, namely the influence of the party Whips and lack of resources.

● Party Whips play a crucial role in the appointments to the Select Committees and can veto any MP whose opinions do not suit. Frank Field, an independent-minded MP and a former Labour Minister, was unable to get a place on the Public Accounts Committee, and Anne McIntosh, a Conservative MP and a former member of the European Parliament, was denied membership of the European Scrutiny Committee.

The Liaison Committee's proposal to introduce a new method of selection which would ensure that Whips do not interfere in appointments to Select Committees was welcomed by Parliament. A Commons motion calling for greater independent scrutiny of the executive attracted more than 200 signatures, including 127 from Labour backbenchers.

● With the exception of the Public Accounts Committee, Select Committees suffer from a lack of resources. There are only 107 staff, assisted by 145 part-time specialist advisers, to service twenty five committees.

Membership of Select Committees may lead to friction between the government and its backbench supporters. In July 2001, the new Chief Whip, Hilary Armstrong, removed two Labour colleagues,

---

The deployment of British armed forces in Iraq and Afghanistan in recent years raises controversial political issues which often hit the media headlines and attract the attention of the House of Commons Select Committee on Defence. This Committee, which is chaired by an Opposition Conservative MP (currently J Arbuthnot MP, NE Hampshire), plays an important role in ensuring that the executive is held accountable for its policies and actions. The Committee published more than a dozen Reports in the 2006–2007 parliamentary session.

One of the more controversial conclusions of the Defence Select Committee was the 7th Report (May 2007) *Army's Requirements for Armoured Vehicles (HC 159)*. One of the more damning allegations about UK military operations in active warzones is that the frontline troops have not been adequately equipped. This report investigated the problems encountered in an attempt to provide the armed forces with a satisfactory medium-weight armoured vehicle. The Committee concluded that "The MoD's attempt to provide a medium-weight vehicle requirement has been a sorry story of indecision, changing requirements and delay. It is high time the MoD decided where its priorities lie".

Donald Anderson and Gwyneth Dunwoody, from their posts as chairpersons of two House of Commons Select Committees. As respective chairpersons of the Foreign Affairs and Transport Committees they had been occasionally 'troublesome' to the government. Tony Blair's 'poodles' decided to bite and MPs voted to reinstate Donald Anderson and Gwyneth Dunwoody. This was an embarrassment to Tony Blair and reinforced the 'control freakery' allegations against his government. Robin Cook, the Leader of the House, accepted that the government had made a mistake and that the action of the MPs was correct. A Conservative MP, Sir George Young, declared that the Leader of the House, the Cabinet Minister responsible for getting the government's business through, should not be the chairperson of the Commons 'modernisation' Committee. the Labour government ignored this suggestion

FRUSTRATING THE EXECUTIVE

The various parliamentary procedures described above provide opportunities for backbenchers of the governing party and also Opposition MPs to frustrate and occasionally defeat the government, even one with a 'comfortable working majority'.

Labour backbenchers were largely loyal to the party leadership during Labour's first term in office after the Thatcher–Major years. A large parliamentary majority did not stimulate revolts. However, the 2001–2005 Parliament has been described as one of the most rebellious since the Second World War. Furthermore, the Labour government returned in 2005 has received several setbacks to its legislative programme on issues related to the war against terrorism and its consequences.

One of the most spectacular rebellions against the Labour leadership took place in March 2003 during a debate on a government motion when 139 Labour MPs voted, along with the Liberal Democrats and the Nationalist parties, against the decision to go to war against Saddam Hussein's Iraq. However, the government was not defeated on this issue because the Conservatives supported the decision. More Labour MPs supported than opposed the government's decision, but Conservative abstentions would have severely embarrassed Blair and his government colleagues. This was the largest rebellion by Labour MPs during Blair's premiership. There were few other alarms for the Labour government during its second term, 2001–2005. Even so, one authority on backbench behaviour has described that term as "noteworthy for both the frequency and size of the backbench rebellions that took place". (Philip Cowley *Making Parliament Matter?* in Dunleavy et al *Developments in British Politics 8*, Palgrave, 2006) Parliamentary parties have been less rather than more cohesive and disciplined in recent decades, including the Major years. It has to be emphasised that more rebellions on the backbenches do not often lead to defeats for governments on the floor of the House of Commons, although these have not been unknown in recent years.

Labour backbenchers became even more rebellious early on in Labour's third term. The 2005 election reduced the government's majority to sixty six. Labour suffered two defeats during the passage of the Terrorism Bill in November 2005 and another two defeats over the Racial and Religious Hatred Bill in January 2006. The government was also 'rescued' by the Conservative Opposition during the passage of the Education and Inspections Bill in March 2006.

The Terrorism Bill included provision for a ninety day detention period during which suspects could be held and questioned without being charged. This was defeated by 322 votes to 291 due to forty nine Labour MPs voting against it and another fourteen not voting. This was the Labour government's first defeat in the Commons since the party was returned to power in 1997. Three Scottish Labour MPs voted against the government: Katy Clark (Ayrshire North and Arran), David Hamilton (Midlothian) and Mark Lazarowicz (Edinburgh North and Leith). Another three Scottish Labour MPs did not vote. An Opposition proposal for a twenty eight day detention period was then passed by 323 votes to 290. The Commons action was welcomed by the Muslim Council of Britain and Liberty, a civil rights pressure group, and criticised by the Police Federation of England and Wales and the Association of Chief Police Officers. These defeats were attributed to leadership failures. A compromise of less than ninety days' detention but more than twenty eight days could have been reached if backbenchers had been consulted.

Two more defeats came during the passage of the Racial and Religious Hatred Bill. The government's objective was to reduce social tensions based on religious differences and to protect minorities subjected to abuse. The intention was to give religious groups such as Muslims the same protection under the law as Jews and Sikhs already possessed. The fundamental issue arising out of the government's proposals concerned striking a proper balance between protecting those threatened and not significantly infringing the right to freedom of speech. Protection was to be achieved by defining an offence of "inciting religious hatred" in terms of threatening words and behaviour including insults and abuse. The Lords tabled amendments requiring that the undesirable behaviour leading to prosecution had to be "threatening" rather than merely "abusive and insulting" before it could be deemed to be an offence under the Act. The burden of proof would be on the prosecution to prove a criminal intent rather than establishing what could be described as "reckless" behaviour.

Two government motions to overturn the Lords' amendments, which were unacceptable to the government, were defeated by the narrow margins of ten votes and one vote respectively. These amendments were seen by some as watering down the efforts to bring to trial those accused of inciting racial and religious hatred and by others as a necessary defence of the right of freedom of speech. Rowan Atkinson, the comedy actor, was a critic of the government's proposals on the grounds that members of his profession would be deprived of the right to make social comment. A Home Office Minister promoting the Bill claimed that it "will not rule out criticism of religion or outlaw the telling of religious jokes".

The votes were strongly partisan, even though the majority party lost. Conservative and Liberal Democrat MPs, along with the Scottish and Welsh Nationalist MPs, voted without exception in favour of protecting freedom of speech. The government lost because twenty six Labour MPs rebelled on the first amendment and twenty one on the second. These defeats were attributed to the Labour Whips getting their calculations wrong by giving too many backbenchers leave to be absent to campaign in the Dunfermline and West Fife by-election. The defeat by a solitary vote on the second amendment was not without a humorous side. The Prime Minister had been present in the House to vote on the first amendment but had been allowed to leave to attend to other business before the second vote took place. If he had stayed the result would have been a tie and the Speaker could have exercised his casting vote on behalf of the government. The issue hit the headlines in November 2006 when the leader of the British National Party was found not guilty of inciting racial hatred in his political speeches. Those who had voted against the Lords' amendments earlier in the year now argued that the Act had been watered down too much.

There have been bigger rebellions which did not lead to the defeat of the government. The long-standing divisions within the Labour Party over the issue of Britain's independent nuclear deterrent produced a massive revolt against, but not defeat for, the Blair government in March 2007. Ninety five Labour MPs voted for a motion to defer a decision on whether to renew the Trident nuclear missile programme. This happened during a debate on a government motion to renew it. Eighty five MPs then opposed the government motion to renew in principle the Trident nuclear missile programme. Nigel Griffiths, MP for Edinburgh South, Deputy Leader of the House of Commons, resigned from this position a few days before the vote in which he voted against the renewal. Another three parliamentary private secretaries, including Robin Cook's successor as MP for Livingston, Jim Devine, resigned their posts because of their opposition to the government's policy on Trident. Charles Clarke, a former Home Secretary, voted against the government.

The Trident issue gave the Conservatives the opportunity to remind voters of Labour's internal conflicts between the 'old' Left and the 'New' Labour which surfaced under Blair's leadership both in opposition and in government. Their defence spokesman, Liam Fox, referred to the dangers posed to an effective defence policy by "unreconstructed old Labour".

MEMBERS OF PARLIAMENT

MPs are expected to represent both their constituents and the nation, but there are strict limits on how far they may go as constituency representatives. (See 'The viewpoint of an MP' on page 82.) MPs of the governing party are expected to support their party leaders in government so that their common objectives may be achieved. Opposition MPs are expected to unite behind their leaders who form an alternative government in waiting. Perceptions of party loyalty and unity may play a decisive role in determining general election results.

THE ROLES OF THE BACKBENCHER

Members of Parliament are not equal in status in spite of their common representative function. There are two types of MP—frontbenchers and backbenchers. The seating arrangements in the Commons emphasise its partisan nature as does the presence within the legislature of the political executive—Prime Minister and Cabinet—which is a central feature of the parliamentary system. The two major parties sit confronting one another. Members of Her Majesty's Government and of Her Majesty's Opposition sit at the front (the front benches) and their supporters who do not hold office

Rowan Atkinson was a critic of the government's Racial and Religious Hatred Bill on the grounds that members of his profession would be deprived of the right to make social comment.

THE WHIP SYSTEM

The task of maintaining discipline among MPs lies with the Party Whip. Each party has a Chief Whip and a number of assistant Whips. The Chief Whip also plays an important part in communicating the mood of MPs to the leadership of the party.

Each week the Whips issue MPs with notices giving the order of business for the following week. Each item to be discussed will be underlined once, twice or three times according to its importance. A debate underlined once indicates no division (vote) is expected; one underlined twice indicates there will be a division which MPs are expected to attend unless they have organised to 'pair' with a member of the other major party; a three-line whip indicates that the division is of vital importance and all members are requested to attend. The Whips are responsible for 'getting the votes out' in the division lobbies. Occasionally the Whips do not succeed; a Labour government defeat on part of the Religious and Racial Hatred Bill in 2006 was attributed to 'poor whipping'.

Whips have an important say in the appointment of party members to Select Committees, and to the post of Junior Minister. If an MP defies the Whips, he/she will be warned and if he/she persistently fails to support the party the Whip can be withdrawn. This means that the party disowns the MP and he/she serves the rest of that term as an Independent. At the next election the party will select a new candidate to fight the seat leaving the 'rebel' to contest the seat as an Independent. George Galloway was deprived of the Labour Whip in 2003.

George Galloway lost the Labour Whip in 2003 and formed the Respect Party.

Whips also act as tellers when a vote takes place. At least one Whip is always present at the debate, keeping an eye open for trouble. Whips seldom speak in the House and are discouraged from expressing any political opinions outside it.

Parliamentary (House of Commons) Timetable 2003–2004

Procedure	Percentage of Commons Timetable
Government legislation	38.7
Government motions (debates)	2.6
Financial business (e.g. Budget)	2.7
Opposition motions	9
Question Time	9.3
Private Members' Bills	5.8
Adjournment debates (backbench)	6.4
Adjournment debates (government)	8.4
Addresses (e.g. Queen's Speech)	2.7
Other business	14.4

Table 4.4

sit behind them (backbenchers). Thus each party has its frontbench leadership and its supporting backbenchers. Backbenchers are also known as Private Members.

The 'record breaking' 1997 general election returned 419 Labour MPs, including the Speaker, to Westminster. The new government, the Labour frontbench, comprised seventy three MPs (fourteen women), and fifteen members of the House of Lords (five women). A further sixteen MPs (two women) were appointed as Whips, and another forty one were appointed as Parliamentary Private Secretaries (PPSs) to Ministers. The PPSs are on the fringe of the government, hoping for promotion to ministerial status when the Prime Minister decides to reshuffle her/his government team. For example, when Martin Chisolm resigned as Undersecretary of State at the Scottish Office in protest at his government's proposed cuts in welfare benefits, he was replaced by Calum MacDonald who was serving as PPS to the Secretary of State for Scotland, Donald Dewar. These government appointments left 290 Labour MPs on the back benches. After the 2005 election the number of Labour backbenchers had dropped to just over 200 due to election losses and a rise in the number of government posts. (See Table 4.7.) The Conservative frontbench in the Commons comprised forty MPs; another ten Conservatives were appointed as Whips. This left just over 100 Conservative backbenchers. This chapter looks primarily at the role of backbenchers. Chapter 5, The Executive, examines the role of frontbenchers.

The backbench 'class of '97' included 260 MPs new to the House of Commons, a post-war record. This was due to Labour's larger than expected majority and to a large number of retirements (117) prior to the election. New MPs made up 44% of the Parliamentary Labour Party (PLP) and a majority (twenty nine out of forty six) of the Liberal Democrats' parliamentary representation. The size of the Labour majority and the large proportion of 'fresher' MPs stimulated speculation about how disciplined the new intake would be. Large majorities are sometimes thought to encourage indiscipline because the government is very unlikely to be defeated if a few of its backbenchers defect or abstain on issues about which they feel strongly.

Representation, which is one of the central functions of the British Parliament and its members, may be looked at from two distinct viewpoints.

- MPs 'represent' both their constituents and their constituencies.
- MPs are also representative of some sections of British society.

To what extent are they representative of society as a whole? In other words, we are interested in what our Members of Parliament do and in who they are.

Backbenchers and voting

The first duty of the MP is observed in the division lobbies of the Commons. MPs have little option but to toe the party line, especially if they are politically ambitious and hope one day to be part of the leadership of their party and be a member of the government. British parliamentary parties are strongly centralised and disciplined. Thus MPs have frequently been scornfully described as 'lobby fodder'—as mere supporters of their frontbench leaders who are expected to be like good children 'seen and not heard'. A government with a comfortable working parliamentary majority controls the business and the timetable of the Commons. It allocates the majority of the parliamentary timetable to enacting its own legislative policies and debating issues of its choosing. Studies of MPs' behaviour suggest that in recent years there has been an increase in the incidence of backbench rebellion. (As discussed on pages 75–76.)

Table 4.4 indicates the relative shares of frontbench (including Opposition frontbench) and backbench time in the 2003–2004 parliamentary timetable. Backbenchers are allocated about 12% of the timetable for their two major contributions to the work of the Commons: Private Members' legislation and Adjournment Debates on topical issues which they select. Backbenchers also play a leading role at Question Time, although the focus is more on how Ministers perform under the pressures of interrogation and the televising of parliamentary proceedings. MPs do participate in debates on government legislation and on issues selected by both front benches, although such debates are led by government and Opposition spokespersons.

The most significant parliamentary procedures from the backbench viewpoint are adjournment debates, questions both oral and written, and Private Members' legislation. These procedures permit backbenchers to represent their constituents, to introduce Bills of their own, and to compete for promotion to the front benches.

Backbenchers in the legislative process

Although the primary function of a legislature might appear to be to legislate, the legislative process in the Commons is dominated by the government of the day. Backbench MPs have very few opportunities to introduce legislation. Rather, they are expected to support or oppose the government's legislative programme which dominates the parliamentary timetable.

Backbenchers are given two procedures by which they may introduce Bills which they have initiated themselves or are putting forward on behalf of the interests of their constituents or pressure groups to which they are sympathetic—the Private Members' ballot and the 'ten minute' rule. Every parliamentary session a ballot is held which awards twenty backbenchers the opportunity to introduce Bills for which time is allocated on Fridays. The lucky MPs have a fair chance of seeing their proposals enacted—on average eight to ten of the Bills introduced in this way reach the statute book.

Age of MPs by Party (%)

Age	Labour	Conservative	Liberal Democrat	Others	All
Under 40	10.5	15.7	29	12.9	13.9
40-60	70.3	66.2	61.3	41.9	68.3
60+	19.2	18.2	9.7	12.9	17.7
Average age	52.7 yrs	49.9 yrs	46.4 yrs		51.8 yrs

Table 4.5: Source: DODs Parliamentary Companion 2007

Ethnic Representation

The number of candidates from an ethnic minority background almost doubled between 1992 (twenty three) and 1997 (forty two). Labour's ethnic minority representation increased from five in 1992 to nine in 1997 when Glasgow Govan elected the first Muslim MP, Mohammed Sarwar (pictured left). In 2005 the three main parties put forward 117 ethnic minority candidates: forty two Liberal Democrats, forty one Conservatives and thirty four Labour. Fifteen were elected, thirteen Labour and two Conservative.

Number of Women MPs: Selected Elections 1945–2005

Election	Number of Women Candidates	Number Elected	% of House of Commons	Conservative	Labour	Liberal	Other
1945	87	24	3.8	1	21	1	1
1964	89	28	4.4	11	17	0	0
1979	206	19	3.0	8	11	0	0
1983	276	23	3.5	13	10	0	0
1987	327	41	6.3	17	21	2	1
1992	568	60	9.2	20	37	2	1
1997	NA	120	18.2	13	102	3	2
2001	NA	118	17.9	14	95	5	4
2005	NA	128	19.8	17	98	10	3

Table 4.6 Source: Times Guide to the House of Commons

MPs may also introduce Bills under the ten minute rule which permits an MP to explain the purpose of a Bill without any guarantee that space will be available in the parliamentary timetable to take the Bill through the full legislative process.

HOW REPRESENTATIVE ARE OUR MPs?

MPs represent, but how representative are they? Who are the MPs we elect in terms of their social characteristics? The conventional wisdom has long been that MPs have been predominantly 'male, middle class and white'. Nonetheless, there have been changes over the years and the 1997 general election may have been a significant landmark in gender representation. Compared with the Commons elected in 1945, the Conservative Party in Parliament has become less elitist in educational terms and the Labour Party has become less working class and more middle class.

Middle-aged MPs

The average age of MPs elected in 2005 was 51.8, ranging from 46.4 for the sixty two Liberal Democrats to 52.7 for Labour's 335 members. Only two MPs were under 30, both women and both Liberal Democrats. Fifteen MPs were over 70, ten of them Labour. Sixty per cent of Liberal Democrat MPs were under 50 in 2005. One of their older MPs, Menzies Campbell, was elected as leader of the party at the age of 65 in 2006—but his resignation in 2007 was the result of persistent questioning by the media about his fitness for leadership due to his age.

Recent electoral fortunes explain the age differences by party. The run of Labour victories has meant that Labour MPs have been growing older since first entering Parliament before or in 1997. Candidates tend to be younger than sitting or outgoing MPs. The large electoral defeat in 1997 meant that the Conservatives had an involuntary clear-out. Almost one-third of the Liberal Democrats elected in 2005 were first time MPs which lowered the average age considerably.

Educational background

MPs are highly educated individuals; just over two-thirds of those elected in 2005 had been to university. The figures for the main political parties were Labour 64%, Conservatives 81%, and Liberal Democrats 79%. The Conservatives have the highest proportion of their MPs educated at public school (60%); Labour had 18% and the Liberal Democrats 39%.

Gender Representation

As noted earlier the 1997 general election marked an important breakthrough in the representation of women in Parliament. The first woman to sit in the Commons was Nancy Astor in 1919. However, female representation at Westminster remained under 5% of the total membership of the Commons until the 1980s when it started to rise from a low point of only nineteen women out of 639 MPs in 1979.

Trends in the number of women candidates and women MPs are illustrated in Table 4.6. There was

(Continued on page 81)

Women in British Government 1997 – 2007

	1997		2001		2007	
	Total	No. of Women	Total	No. of Women	Total	No. of Women
Cabinet	22	5	23	7	23	5
Ministers of State	31	6	33	11	35	11
Junior Ministers	35	8	34	10	35	10
PPSs	41	8	53	17	52	21
Totals	129	27	143	45	145	47

Table 4.7

The disappointment of the failure to advance the representation of women in Parliament in 2001 was compensated to some extent by the Prime Minister's appointment of more women to all levels of executive office. (See Table 4.7.) Following the 2001 election 30% of Cabinet members and of government posts overall were women. The proportion of women in frontbench positions had risen to 37% when Gordon Brown appointed his first government in 2007. The rise was concentrated in the fourth tier of government, PPSs.

Notes: The Labour, Conservative and Liberal Democrat Parties each put up fifty eight candidates in 2005, not fifty nine. This is because the Speaker of the House of Commons since 2000, David Martin, is elected from Glasgow North East where he stands as "the Speaker". It is customary for the major parties not to oppose the Speaker. The SNP and the SSP did not respect this tradition.

Nine women, eight Labour and one Liberal Democrat, were elected out of the fifty nine Scottish seats at Westminster in 2005. This meant that 15% of Scottish MPs were women compared to almost 20% for the House of Commons as a whole. This compares with 37% in the Scottish Parliament and almost 50% in the Welsh Assembly. The Conservatives selected the fewest women candidates. The SSP and the Greens selected the highest proportion of women candidates but won no seats. Although Labour selected fewer women candidates than some other parties, Labour was the most successful by far at getting them elected. The boundary changes accompanying the reduction of Scottish seats from seventy two to fifty nine cost the SNP's Annabelle Ewing her seat at Westminster. The Liberal Democrats' Jo Swinson was an unexpected winner in Dunbartonshire East.

GENDER REPRESENTATION IN SCOTLAND
Scotland's Women at Westminster, 2005

Party	No. of Women Candidates	Percentage of Women Candidates	No. of Women Elected	Success Rate (%)	Percentage of Women MPs in Scottish Party (H of C)
Labour	10	17.3	8	80	18.2
Conservative	4	6.9	0	0	0
Liberal Democrat	14	24.1	1	7	8.3
SNP	12	20.3	0	0	0
SSP	16	27.6	0	0	0
Total			9		15.2

Table 4.8 Source: 2005 General Election Results reported in the press

Women Candidates and MPs by Party, 1997 & 2005

Party	No of Women Candidates 1997	No of Women Candidates 2005	No of Women Elected 1997	No of Women Elected 2005	Success Rate (%) 1997	Success Rate (%) 2005	% of Party in Commons 1997	% of Party in Commons 2005
Labour	159	166	102	98	64	59	24.4	27.6
Conservative	67	122	13	17	19.4	13.9	7.9	8.6
Liberal Democrat	142	145	3	10	2.1	6.9	6.5	16.1
Nationalist	23	16	2	0	8.7	0	20	0
Other	NA	NA	NA	*3	NA	NA	NA	NA
Total	391		120	128	30.0			19.8

Table 4.9 * Northern Ireland returned three women MPs, one each from the DUP, the UUP and Sinn Fein.

In 1997 the euphoria of entering Parliament and becoming part of the historic force to change the male atmosphere of the Commons quickly evaporated for many of the new intake. Three female MPs, Jenny Jones, Judith Church and Tess Kinghorn, announced in 2000 that they would not stand again and were leaving politics. Adjacent are the comments of some of the women MPs who made no attempt to hide their contempt for the 'archaic' traditions of the House.

Anne Campbell, MP (protested about long hours)
"The Tory view is that it's such a privilege to work here, we should put up with everything. I have been told if I can't stand the heat to get out of the kitchen – and by other women! They are always the worst."

Tess Kinghorn, MP
"The whole place is organised for men working in the city and popping into the club for dinner and a vote. We're lecturing Britain on being a modern, dynamic country and we ought to be leading from the front."
(Tess gave birth to twins during her time as an MP)
"We tell the public they have a right to up to forty weeks maternity leave and I started work four days after a Caesarean section because there were things I couldn't pass on."

Julia Brown, MP (Reprimanded by the Speaker, Betty Boothroyd, for requesting permission to breastfeed in the committee rooms.)
"This is … a terrible place to work. Women aren't as good at tub-thumping, dispatch box speeches and it's childish. I don't want to be like that."
"For parents of young children, the late hours are a problem because you can't get twenty four hour childcare. Westminster needs to let us give our children all the time and love they deserve while working to make the world a better place for them."

very little change in the number of women candidates and women MPs between 1945 and 1970, with fewer than 100 candidates and thirty MPs throughout this period. Then the number of women candidates doubled between 1970 and 1979. By 1992 there were over 500 women candidates with the number elected rising to sixty in 1992 and 120 in 1997. The 1997 election represented a major breakthrough in gender representation. The 2001 election saw the number of women MPs fall back by two to 118. The number of women appointed to government office did increase significantly, however. (See Table 4.7.) The number of women elected increased again slightly in 2005 to 128, 19.8% of the Commons membership, ninety eight of them Labour. The Liberal Democrats doubled their number of women MPs in 2005. In spite of the large increase in women MPs since 1979, the proportion of women in the House of Commons, just under 20% after the 2005 election, remained much lower than the proportion of women in the British population as a whole which is just over half (52%).

The considerable variation in the number of women candidates and MPs by party is illustrated in Tables 4.6 and 4.9. Labour is well ahead of the other major British parties with women MPs making up just over a quarter of the Parliamentary Labour Party in 2005. There are two reasons for this achievement. Firstly, Labour took positive measures to encourage Constituency Labour Parties (CLPs) to adopt female candidates. The 1993 Labour Party Conference set an objective of selecting women in at least half of the Labour-held seats where the sitting MP intended to retire at the next election. Labour went even further by encouraging women-only shortlists at the candidate selection stage. Many other CLPs selected women candidates without resorting to women-only shortlists. The result in 1997 was that there were 150 women in Labour's total of 628 candidates in Great Britain. (Labour, like the other major British parties, did not put up any candidates in Northern Ireland.) Secondly, Labour's landslide victory meant that no fewer than 64% of Labour's women candidates were elected.

However, some disgruntled male Labour members complained to an Industrial Relations Tribunal that such lists contravened the *Sex Discrimination Act*. They argued that being an MP constitutes employment, that the selection of candidates amounts to competing in the job market and that therefore the Act outlawing sex discrimination in employment practices should apply to the selection by parties of parliamentary candidates. The Tribunal found in their favour in August 1996. Thereafter women-only shortlists were not permitted but the candidates already selected by this method were allowed to stand in 1997. Only four of the thirty eight new Labour MPs elected in 2001 were women because the great majority of CLPs where the sitting MP stood down selected male candidates. No women-only shortlists were permitted in 2001. The number of female Labour MPs fell by seven and female SNP MPs by one; the Conservatives and Liberal Democrats added one and two women MPs respectively. The most significant advance in female representation in 2001 occurred in Northern Ireland where three women were elected—one each for the DUP, the UUP and Sinn Fein. They were the first women elected in Ulster in over quarter of a century.

The 2001 Labour Manifesto included a commitment to introduce legislation "to allow each party to make positive moves to increase the representation of women". *The Sex Discrimination (Election Candidates) Act* was passed in 2002 πallowing all-women shortlists. The 2005 general election produced a modest increase in gender representation. The three main parties each selected well over 100 women candidates in 2005 with the Conservatives in particular increasing the number of women candidates but not yet the number of women MPs.

Local Representative

I speak to the government and the country as the voice of Grimsby, articulating the needs of its people, its industries, its council, its development. I am required increasingly to be the town's public relations booster. This is a right to be heard but not to get. Normally, governments listen—and then explain why nothing can be done. Occasionally they concede, though usually only to wider causes espoused with others. Recently, helping to win belated redundancy pay and compensation for trawlermen who lost their jobs when Icelandic fishing stopped in 1976 was a rare local triumph.

Local Ombudsman

Status and the local representative role give MPs access to the top, to the chief executive officer on consumer matters, the Minister on policy or the local departmental head on individual cases. This isn't an ability to exert influence or change correct decisions but to remedy failures. An MP's complaint gets a full explanation, which often satisfies the constituent. The threat of publicity in the press or by questions and adjournment debates allows MPs to bully both private and public organisations and that occasionally helps.

Most MPs hold weekly surgeries and a minority of MPs finance offices in the constituency to serve local needs. To pay for all this, as well as telephones (rural MPs often provide one number at local rates to cover several exchanges, which is an expensive business) and staff in Westminster to service parliamentary work, MPs get a maximum allowance of £87,276.

Party Representative

Most MPs are in Parliament on a party ticket. Party is a career ladder to climb, a substitute for thought and a whirl of the obsessive. In Parliament, the party is a framework of control, ensuring that MPs tramp through the lobbies, feeding party points every day, providing yah-boo fun, and trundling them out to every by-election as unpaid door knockers. The policy role of MPs is largely gone, handed to policy forums guided by Ministers. The Parliamentary Labour Party (PLP) is seldom used by Ministers to gauge Party or public opinion. Ministers only trust focus groups and pals, so the MP's role is being reduced to campaigning and transmitting messages from on high down to the faithful.

Legislator

All-powerful in theory, MPs are impotent in practice. Laws cannot be passed without them, yet what the government wants goes through, largely unaltered—even when it should be. Legislation, which takes around 45% of parliamentary time, is the job worst done. Government gives backbenchers ammunition for the defence but prefers them to shut up so as not to consume time. In opposition, effective arguments depend on individual research and help from interested parties. Government backbenchers are on standing committees to vote, not speak.

VIEWPOINT OF A MEMBER OF PARLIAMENT

Austin Mitchell has been Labour Member of Parliament for Grimsby since 1977. Here he identifies the different roles of an MP which centre around three masters—Parliament, party and constituency. He also highlights the reforms which he believes are necessary to improve the effectiveness of MPs.

Controller of the Executive

Most members of the governing party see their role as supporting the executive, however bad its case. Many may grumble, a few may vote against their party and more may abstain. Yet the premium is on maintaining unity. Dissent is never taken to the point of endangering the government. Question Time typifies the problem. The opposition attacks everything, while the government backbenchers rally loyally, even sycophantically, particularly at Prime Minister's Question Time. Select Committees are better: they can examine the intellectual basis of government policy. They provide a forum for detailed questioning of Ministers and access to the specialised information which makes MPs influential.

Trainee Minister

Most MPs want to become Ministers, to hold power and change things, and the House of Commons is the ministerial recruiting and training ground. MPs hope to be noticed. Being in opposition trains shadow Ministers, while 150 juniors and trainees on both sides learn the techniques of the dispatch box, master specialised fields and develop the tactics of debate and giving nothing away. Apprenticeship gives no influence on policy and can be a dead-end street but it is an experience all MPs want.

Austin Mitchell's views on the reforms needed to improve the effectiveness of MPs

- Constituency and London offices with staff and sufficient money to pay for them.
- A career path other than becoming a Minister.
- A greater role in the legislative process.
- A change in the role and power of the Whips.
- Joint parliamentary committees to tap the expertise of the Commons and the Lords.
- Better television coverage to bring current affairs to a wider audience, e.g. a current affairs channel.

Chapter 5
The Executive

What you will learn.
1. *The organisation of the Executive branch.*
2. *The relative powers of the Prime Minister, Cabinet and senior civil servants.*
3. *The limits of the executive's power.*

THE TRADITIONAL VIEW

Traditional political theory assumed that there should be three institutions of government:

- a legislature to pass laws
- an executive to implement these laws
- a judiciary to interpret the meaning of the laws passed by the legislature

This traditional view of government, which puts the legislature at the beginning of the policy making process, is generally consistent with describing the British political system as a parliamentary system in which the executive is responsible to the legislature. Nevertheless, it has long been inaccurate as a description of the relative powers of the legislature and the executive. It is certainly true that the British executive, led by the Prime Minister and his or her Cabinet colleagues, has the responsibility of implementing the laws passed by Parliament. However, as in most countries today, it is the executive branch of government which is the most powerful source of the policy proposals debated in, and accepted or rejected by, Parliament. It is the executive branch which decides how much to spend on the NHS or whether to hold a referendum on the issue of a common European currency, the 'euro'. It remains true that Parliament must give its consent to executive proposals, but that consent is rarely withheld. The secret of executive dominance lies in comfortable working majorities supporting the government in the Commons, in strong party discipline and in the 'first-past-the-post' electoral system.

The radical reforms achieved by post-war Labour governments, 1945–51, and by the Thatcher governments of the 1980s, coupled with the emergence of strong prime ministers like Thatcher and Blair confirm the considerable strength of the British executive. Nonetheless, there have been significant exceptions to the normal practice of executive dominance. The Labour governments led by Harold Wilson and James Callaghan from 1974 to 1979, and the Conservative government of John Major from 1992 to 1997 were weakened by small and eroding

---

THE STRUCTURE OF GOVERNMENT 2007

Below is a description of the several layers of seniority within the Labour government appointed after Gordon Brown became Prime Minister in June 2007.

PRIME MINISTER AND CABINET (23)
(18 men; 5 women: 21 MPs; 2 Lords)
Almost all Cabinet Ministers are heads of individual government departments
e.g. Jacqui Smith MP Secretary of State for the Home Department

MINISTERS OF STATE (33)
(22 men; 11 women : 26 MPs; 7 Lords) (an increase of 5 women compared to 1997)
e.g. Two Ministers of State within the Home Department
Tom McNulty MP – Minister for Policing
Liam Byrne MP – Minister for Immigration and Asylum

LAW OFFICERS (3)
Baroness Scotland of Asthal QC – Attorney General
Vera Baird QC MP – Solicitor General
Lord Davidson of Glen Clova QC – Advocate General for Scotland

JUNIOR MINISTERS (34)
(Parliamentary Secretaries and Under-secretaries)
(24 men; 10 women: 24 MPs, 10 Lords)
e.g. 3 Under-secretaries in Home Department
Vernon Coaker MP – Crime
Meg Hiller MP – Immigration and Asylum
Admiral Sir Alan West – Counter-terrorism

PARLIAMENTARY PRIVATE SECRETARIES (52 MPs)
(Serve as personal assistants to government Ministers)
(31 men and 21 women)

GOVERNMENT WHIPS
House of Commons (18)   House of Lords (7)
Government Chief Whip   Geoff Hoon MP Parliamentary Secretary to the Treasury.
(Hoon is a Cabinet member)

[142 Labour MPs are government Ministers of various degrees of seniority or are on the fringes of government as Whips or Parliamentary Private Secretaries which leaves about 210 MPs on the Labour backbenches]

parliamentary majorities and went down to electoral defeat in 1979 and 1997 respectively. The Labour government could not 'deliver' devolution in the 1970s and the Conservative government could not enforce party unity on European Union issues in the 1990s. Even Mrs Thatcher's long tenure in the primary political office in Britain ended in tears. Tony Blair experienced some major disappointments when events and colleagues combined to deny him some of his principal policy aims after the outbreak of war against Iraq in 2003 and a drop in electoral support in 2005.

The strength of the British executive depends ultimately upon the support of the electorate expressed in comfortable parliamentary majorities. When that support weakens, the executive is weakened. The Labour governments led by Blair did not suffer defeat on any of their legislative proposals until after the 2005 election when their Commons majority was almost 100 seats less than it had been after the 1997 and 2001 elections.

There are three areas of interest in relation to the role of the executive in British politics.

- ▲ How is power organised and distributed within the executive branch itself? The main question here is whether British government should be described as prime ministerial government rather than as Cabinet government.
- ▲ What are the constitutional and political relationships between the executive and legislative branches of government? This question focuses attention on the conventions and practices of ministerial responsibility and on the role and status of the civil service.
- ▲ What changes to the executive branch have followed from the introduction of devolution for Scotland and Wales and the reintroduction of a Northern Ireland executive? Some areas of decision making have been removed from the central British executive in Whitehall and Westminster and assigned to executives in Edinburgh, Cardiff and Belfast. This aspect of executive government in Britain will be dealt with in Chapters 7 and 8 on Scotland.

The British executive branch divides into three parts:
- the Prime Minister
- the Cabinet and Junior Ministers
- the Civil Service.

The Prime Minister and Cabinet Ministers are politically partisan when they make policy decisions whereas the civil service is politically neutral and performs administrative tasks.

THE POWERS OF THE PRIME MINISTER

The modern Prime Minister derives his/her power from three principal sources:
- the powers of appointment, commonly known as 'patronage', and of dissolution.
- the position of majority party leader
- chairperson of the Cabinet.

Power of Appointment

The Prime Minister's power to appoint the members of the Cabinet and a long list of non-Cabinet Ministers is his/her most powerful personal weapon within the executive branch. The Prime Minister, in taking over the office, decides which politicians to include in the Cabinet and which subsequently to demote or promote. The power to 'hire and fire' includes the right to 'reshuffle' the membership of the Cabinet and government at any time and for whatever reason. The Prime Minister also decides the size of the Cabinet. Prime Ministers are strongly tempted to exercise such powers when their government is doing badly in the opinion polls and is believed therefore to be in need of a little 'freshening up'.

Gordon Brown made seven new Cabinet appointments when he took over as Prime Minister in June 2007, thus ensuring that the Cabinet would be seen as the Brown Cabinet and not as a continuing Blair Cabinet.

Room was made for the newcomers by the prior announcements of John Prescott, John Reid and others that they would retire when Brown took over. (Reid was appointed Celtic Football Club Chairman after leaving the government.) Brown tried to use his newly acquired appointment powers in an innovative way by offering Cabinet posts first to Menzies Campbell, the Liberal Democrats' leader, and then to Lord Paddy Ashdown, a former leader of the same party. Both refused!

The Prime Minister may decide to forgive and forget in his/her appointments. Brown appointed John Denham as Secretary of State for Innovation, Universities and Skills. Denham had resigned in 2003 as Minister of State because he could not support the government's policy on Iraq.

The power to appoint is known as 'patronage' and extends far beyond the 'hiring and firing' of members of the government. The Prime

On 8 June 2001, Robin Cook entered 10 Downing Street as the Foreign Secretary and left as the Leader of the House of Commons. He had been demoted by the Prime Minister in the Cabinet reshuffle following the general election.

UK Politics Today

Minister has the final say in the appointment of life peers, archbishops and bishops in the Church of England and members of the judiciary. In exercising these appointment powers, the Prime Minister is essentially the heir to the personal prerogative powers of the Monarch who now has no influence over appointments, although newly selected Ministers still have to go to Buckingham Palace to be formally ushered into office by the Monarch of the day.

The Power of Dissolution

The Prime Minister enjoys other powers independent of Cabinet colleagues. The Prime Minister alone decides when to ask the Monarch to dissolve Parliament and, consequently, decides the date of the general election. The Prime Minister is, by convention, exercising one of the prerogative powers of the Monarch and it can be used to hold general elections whenever opinion polls suggest that the government will be re-elected. For this reason Margaret Thatcher successfully called general elections in 1983 and 1987 with one year of the five-year Parliaments still to run. Tony Blair successfully did likewise in 2001 and 2005. John Major, in contrast, had to wait out the full five-year terms before holding elections in 1992 and 1997. James Callaghan, Labour Prime Minister from 1977 to 1979, was criticised for not calling a general election in the autumn of 1978 when Labour might have won. Instead Callaghan waited in the expectation that Labour would do even better in the spring or summer of 1979. However, the 'winter of discontent' intervened and Labour was forced into an election in June 1979 which produced the first of three Conservative election victories under the leadership of Margaret Thatcher.

The power to dissolve Parliament is regarded by some as a weapon which may be used to discipline rebellious elements within the ranks of the governing party. However, the threat to call an election may not be credible if the government is behind in the opinion polls. Not long after the 1992 election, when the Conservative Party was trailing behind Labour in the opinion polls, John Major threatened to call a general election if the Tories did not back his stance on the Maastricht Treaty. This threat could obviously not be carried out and merely served to make Mr Major look weak, especially when he had to withdraw the threat, stating that he had been misunderstood.

The last two years of Mr Major's reign as Prime Minister and Tory leader were plagued by internal party dissension and criticism of his leadership. In 1995, in an effort to reassert his control over his party, Major resigned as party leader but not as Prime Minister. He could not call an election because the polls suggested that the Conservative government would have been badly defeated. Major was opposed by John Redwood, who had been Secretary of State for Wales until he resigned to fight for the leadership of the Conservative Party. Major won the election by 218 votes to 89. This result was interpreted as both a vote of confidence in Major and as an indication that the right wing of the party was unhappy with Major's leadership and his stance on European Union issues.

Majority Party Leader

The first-past-the-post electoral system usually returns one party with a comfortable overall majority to the House of Commons. The leader of that party becomes Prime Minister. Parties elect their leaders and the House of Commons formally confirms the majority party leader as Prime Minister. Tony Blair stood down as Labour leader several weeks before resigning as Prime Minister to allow Gordon Brown to stand for the party leadership before being asked by the Queen to form an administration. Brown's almost unique status as the long-term 'Prime Minister in waiting' accounts for the unusual absence of any rival candidate in the leadership election which should have followed Blair's resignation as Labour Party leader. Brown, the only candidate, was declared party leader at a special party conference on 24 June 2007. This action sent a clear signal to Buckingham Palace that Brown should be asked to form a government which the Queen duly did on 27 June, minutes after Blair had submitted his resignation to the Monarch.

The significance of party was emphasised when Brown appointed Harriet Harman as Leader of the House of Commons, bringing her back into the Cabinet after a lengthy absence. Harman's elevation from Minister of State under Blair to Cabinet Minister was the result of her being elected, surprisingly according to most commentators, deputy leader of the Labour Party in succession to the departing John Prescott. Harman was elected on the fifth count of the Labour Party's electoral college, beating the favourite, Alan Johnson, who took over the politically sensitive position of Secretary of State for Health.

As chairperson of the Cabinet, the Prime Minister decides what is to be discussed and how often the Cabinet will meet. He/She also summarises the view of the Cabinet which all government members then have to support in public.

The power of dissolution may turn out to be a doubtful advantage for a Prime Minister. It was widely expected in the autumn of 2007 that Gordon Brown, having taken over as Prime Minister three months previously, just over two years into Labour's third term since 1997, would call a general election. Labour was ahead in the polls; economic forecasts were expected to be less favourable for the former Chancellor of the Exchequer in the coming months; a new mandate would emphasise that Brown was a vote winner and would reinforce his control of his party; and he could then expect at least another four years to achieve his aims for the country. The timing of the speculation was unfortunate for the Prime Minister. The approach of winter meant that a decision had to be taken soon after the Conservative Party Conference in Blackpool in the first week of October. It is considered unwise to hold an election in the depths of winter because bad weather can reduce turnout, especially of Labour supporters. Party conferences are frequently followed by a rise in the party's poll standings. Several polls at the end of the week of the Conservative conference indicated a significant decline in Labour's lead over the Conservatives. Brown was taunted by both the Conservative leader, David Cameron, and the SNP leader, Alex Salmond, to call an election. Brown's decision NOT to go the polls resulted in a bad press for the Prime Minister personally, partly because many felt that the electoral speculation had been encouraged, or at least not discouraged, by Labour. Salmond, bolstered by the SNP's strong performance in the May 2007 Scottish Parliament elections, called Brown a "feartie".

Cabinet Chairperson

The Prime Minister chairs Cabinet meetings and is the political head of the civil service. The Prime Minister usually controls the agenda, leads the discussion and sums up the 'sense' of the meeting. As Chairperson of the Cabinet the Prime Minister may, in practice, dominate Cabinet meetings. Attlee and Thatcher were adept at this form of control. The Prime Minister is the one member of the Cabinet with a 'global' view of the business of government. Cabinet Ministers who are in charge of large government Departments are too busy with their own Departmental responsibilities to be concerned with the work of other departments. This partly explains the move away from collective decision making in Cabinet to a more bilateral style of decision making which has taken place under strong Prime Ministers such as Thatcher and Blair. The role of Cabinet chairperson persists in the role of the Prime Minister as the almost ever-present link in the series of bilateral meetings with Cabinet Ministers which dominate the executive decision making process. References were made to 'government by sofa' because Blair met his government colleagues in his small Downing Street office.

The Prime Minister's position may also be affected by the emergence of an 'Inner Cabinet' which may be formal or informal. This 'Inner Cabinet' may be no more than the leading Departmental Ministers among whom there is an acknowledged 'pecking order'. The Foreign Secretary and the Chancellor of the Exchequer hold the two most prestigious offices after the Prime Minister. The Deputy Prime Minister may or may not be significant. Mrs Thatcher reluctantly appointed Geoffrey Howe as Leader of the House of Commons and

THE PRIME MINISTER'S POWER BASE

There is no Prime Minister's department as the Prime Minister does not have a ministry to run. There is a Prime Minister's office which includes political advisers as well as permanent civil servants. Over the years the number of staff employed in the Prime Minister's office has increased.

The Cabinet Office has traditionally provided support to the Prime Minister. However, under Tony Blair it developed an even closer relationship with the Prime Minister's office, to the extent that the Cabinet Office is now an extension of the Prime Minister's office.

In an answer to a question in 1998 on the future of the Cabinet Office, the Prime Minister gave the following reply: "The role of the Cabinet Office has traditionally been to help the Prime Minister and the government as a whole to reach collective decisions on government policy. Since the election, the three principal parts of the centre—my own office, the Cabinet Office and the Treasury—have worked closely and effectively together, and with other Departments, to take forward the government's comprehensive and ambitious policy agenda."

Deputy Prime Minister in 1989 but 'froze' him out of important decision making because they disagreed on the European issue. John Major appointed Michael Heseltine as Deputy Prime Minister in 1995 in order to secure the support of a senior Cabinet member in difficult circumstances. Michael Heseltine and Kenneth Clarke were in a pro-European Union minority in the Cabinet towards the end of the Major administration when they limited the Prime Minister's options in this policy area which was tearing the Conservative Party apart. John Prescott, the Deputy Prime Minister under Blair, represented the 'soul' of the Labour Party as a link to its traditional working-class roots which have been in decline in the age of 'New Labour'.

There may be other powerful Cabinet members who on occasion limit the power of the Prime Minister. It was widely believed that the Chancellor of the Exchequer, Kenneth Clarke, a supporter of monetary union within the European Union, prevented John Major adopting a more 'Eurosceptic' position in discussions about whether and when, if ever, Britain should accept a common European currency. The classic case of a Cabinet Minister limiting the Prime Minister's political freedom of action was Gordon Brown as Chancellor of the Exchequer during the Blair premiership. The Prime Minister could 'demote' Robin Cook from Foreign Secretary to Leader of the House of Commons in 2001 but he never felt strong enough to demote Brown to a less powerful ministry.

Cabinet Committees

Before the full Cabinet meets to discuss the most significant issues facing the government, preliminary decisions will have been reached in Cabinet committees. The Cabinet often can do little other than formally approve the decisions of these committees which are composed of the departmental Ministers who are the 'experts' on the subject matter dealt with in committee. In 2006 there were twenty three standing (permanent) and seven ad hoc (temporary) Cabinet committees. The Prime Minister is a member of the most important Cabinet committees which do much of the work of the Cabinet. Of the twenty three standing committees, the Prime Minister and the Chancellor of the Exchequer (Gordon Brown) each chaired five, the Deputy Prime Minister (John Prescott) and the Lord Chancellor (Lord Irvine) each chaired four. The Prime Minister chaired committees dealing with sensitive political and constitutional issues such as Northern Ireland, Constitutional Reform, consultation with the Liberal Democrats, and Defence and Overseas themes. The Chancellor chaired committees dealing with economic issues such as welfare to work, productivity and competitiveness, energy and public expenditure.

THE CABINET: A REVISED VIEW

The term 'Cabinet government' used to be used along with 'Parliamentary System' as principal features of the British constitutional system. In recent decades the role of the Cabinet seems to have diminished as both the frequency and the length of its meetings have been reduced. There is a question mark against the contemporary accuracy of 'Cabinet government' as an essential element of the British political system. The frequency of Cabinet meetings reached a peak in the early 1950s with over 100 meetings annually; the Cabinet met twice a week and for two hours at a time. By the 1970s the number of meetings was down to sixty annually. Thatcher and Blair further reduced the time Ministers spend in Cabinet. Blair held about forty meetings per year, many of which lasted for an hour or less. Fewer and fewer decisions appear to have been taken by the Cabinet. One commentator alleges that the only decision truly made by the Cabinet since 1997 was the one to back the bid for the 2012 Olympics to be held in London. Nevertheless, the Cabinet does still meet and remains the arena within which opposition to the Prime

(Continued on page 89)

MINISTERIAL RESPONSIBILITY

Ministers are, by convention, individually and collectively responsible to Parliament for personal and departmental policy and administrative actions. The conventions of ministerial responsibility are among the most important rules of the British Constitution.

The convention of collective responsibility which governs relations between the political executive—the Prime Minister, Cabinet and junior Ministers—and the legislature, especially the House of Commons, has two elements.

- The first element relates to the links between the executive and the legislature by requiring that the executive resigns if it is defeated on a motion of confidence in the House of Commons.

- The second element relates to the executive branch. Members of the government, no matter how low they are in the pecking order, for instance Parliamentary Private Secretaries who are on the borderline outer limits of government, must support publicly the policies arrived at in Cabinet or else they must resign. A Prime Minister may dismiss a colleague who refuses to toe the collective line.

There are always great shouts of 'resign' when a government loses an important vote in the Commons. The government may accept the judgement of the House as it did when the ninety day detention period in the Terrorism Bill was reduced to twenty eight days by both the Lords and the Commons in December 2005. (See Chapter 4.) Alternatively, the government may ask for a vote of confidence which it usually wins.

Only three votes of confidence have been lost in over a century. The last occurred in 1979 when the Labour government, which no longer enjoyed a majority in the Commons, was defeated on the issue of Scottish devolution and resigned, only to lose the ensuing election.

Cabinet Ministers and all other members of the government not of Cabinet rank are bound by collective responsibility to support government policies in public, even if they spoke against the decision or have misgivings. Every Minister is considered to have agreed to Cabinet decisions, even those which are not unanimous. If they publicly disagree with the decision, they must resign. It is rare for the Prime Minister to dismiss a colleague for publicly disregarding the convention of collective responsibility.

There have been over forty resignations since 1945 by Ministers refusing accept collective responsibility for government decisions. In 1986 Michael Heseltine, then Secretary of State for Defence in the Thatcher administration, resigned when he dis-agreed with the government's policy on the 'Westland Affair'. Mrs Thatcher refused to allow a decision reached by a Cabinet Committee to be discussed in the full Cabinet, a move which incensed Heseltine. Heseltine resigned because he would not support the decision in public and because he objected to the Prime Minister's handling of the matter in Cabinet. Robin Cook resigned in 2003 because he could not support the decision to go to war against Iraq. Clare Short, Secretary of State for International Development and a member of the war Cabinet on the conduct of the war and its aftermath, followed Cook onto the backbenches several weeks later. Short had remained 'on board' reluctantly for a time because her ministerial position was relevant to the task of developing a post-war recovery programme for Iraq.

Ministers are also responsible to Parliament for their own actions and for the work of their departments. This means giving Parliament full information about the policies and actions of the executive branch on occasions like Question Time and during debates. Over the years the extent of individual responsibility has been narrowed as it has become clear that Ministers are personally acquainted with only a small proportion of departmental decisions and actions. Ministers remain responsible for the major policies of their departments, although collective responsibility may take over in order to shield Ministers who are under attack. When Lord Carrington resigned as Foreign Secretary over the events leading up to the Falklands War, Mrs Thatcher tried to persuade him to carry on. The Prime Minister was prepared to protect her Foreign Secretary by, in effect, assuming that the entire Cabinet was responsible for those events.

The conventions of ministerial responsibility have had a crucial impact on British politics by encouraging the development of centralised, disciplined political parties. Because a government could be forced to resign if defeated on a vote of confidence in the House of Commons, or because the government would be severely embarrassed if it frequently lost major votes such as those lost on the 2005 Terrorism Bill, usually enough of the government's backbenchers will be loyal to ensure victory when the House of Commons 'divides'—MPs vote on the issues at stake. Similarly, opposition MPs usually toe the party line in order to put maximum pressure on the government. The two-party system stimulates intense rivalry between the main protagonists, further increasing party loyalty; government backbenchers do not wish to put their own positions at risk.

Minister and other powerful senior Ministers may be expressed. There was no concerted effort by the Cabinet to resist the critical decisions leading to the Iraq War in 2003 which means that all of its members had to accept responsibility for what subsequently transpired. Ministerial responsibility remains a vital element in the British political system.

THE BLAIR PREMIERSHIP 1997–2007

Assessments of Blair's premiership have concentrated on his alleged 'presidential' style, his relationship with Gordon Brown and his responsibility for the Iraq War. It is significant that Blair regarded Major as a weak Prime Minister who failed to give leadership or to control his own party. His administration 'hit the ground running' in 1997 as Parliament passed the Bills granting devolution to Scotland and Wales. Blair's decision in 2007 to give up the premiership and to leave the Commons meant that he was the first PM since Harold Wilson not to be forced out of office by party colleagues (Thatcher) or by the electorate (Callaghan and Major).

Control from the Centre

Blair came to office with a total lack of experience of government but with a huge parliamentary majority. A major feature of his office was his determination to bypass the traditional sources of influence such as senior civil servants in Whitehall. This was achieved through the appointment of special advisers, who doubled in number to seventy four over the 1997–99 period. Half the increase took place in 10 Downing Street where the number of special advisers rose from eight to twenty five. (See Senior Civil Servants and Special Advisers, page 91.)

Much was made, especially in Parliament, of an order in council allowing special advisers Jonathan Powell, Chief of Staff, and Alastair Campbell, Chief Press Secretary, to 'manage' career civil servants in the No. 10 private office and press office respectively. Sir Richard Wilson, Cabinet Secretary, denied that this was harmful to the 'independence' of senior civil servants: "I do not think that the senior civil service of 3,700 people is in danger of being swamped by seventy-odd special advisers."

While much is made of Tony Blair's personal ascendancy within the Cabinet, his premiership was based in part on a power sharing agreement with Gordon Brown, his Chancellor of the Exchequer. The Blair-Brown alliance, through the triennial comprehensive spending review (CSR), tightly controlled the direction of spending of all Departments. As David Lipsey puts it in his book *The Secret Treasury*,

> "The CSR was a triumph for a strong Prime Minister and a strong Chancellor working together. Nothing illustrates this more clearly than the brutality of its execution. The two just called in Ministers and told them how much they were getting. There was no appeal."

The Cabinet under Blair

Blair's practice as Prime Minister continued and strengthened a longer term transition from collective to bilateral decision making within the executive. Senior Ministers privately complained about feeling that they were on the outside and not involved in collective decision making. The diminishing role of the Cabinet was made clear in the first week of the Blair government when the crucial decision to transfer responsibility for setting interest rates from the Chancellor/Prime Minister to the Bank of England was made before the Cabinet had even met for the first time.

Instead of conducting business at Cabinet meetings or even in Cabinet Committees, Blair preferred 'Bilaterals'—two-sided meetings—with his Secretaries of State. While this gave Ministers direct access to 10 Downing Street in matters relating to their own Departments, it ensured that they would not have an overview of strategic government policy or an insight into other Department policies and performance.

Cabinet meetings seldom last longer than an hour; a thirty minute meeting just before the 1997 recess may well have been a postwar record. The agenda tended to be informal, merely standing items grouped under domestic, foreign and parliamentary decisions. It was not surprising, therefore, that the Cabinet seldom engaged in challenging debate over policy. The postponement of joining the eurozone, the reduction of the lone parent benefit and the future of hereditary peers were not decided at Cabinet meetings. The Millenium Dome was discussed at Cabinet but a decision was pushed through despite the misgivings of the majority of Cabinet members.

Revised Ministerial Code 1997

The publication of the Revised Ministerial Code and its paragraph 88 order (see box) reinforced Blair's centralisation of power and his control over Cabinet colleagues. For Peter Preston of *The Guardian*, adherence to 'Paragraph 88' would reduce any Minister to a "diminished drivelling figure" and Peter Riddell in *The Times*, declared: "Goodbye Cabinet Government, Welcome Blair Presidency".

MINISTERIAL CODE PARAGRAPH 88

In order to ensure the effective presentation of government policy, all major interviews and media appearances, both print and broadcast, should be agreed with the Nº 10 press office before any commitments are entered into. The policy content of all major speeches, press releases and new policy initiatives should be cleared in good time with the Nº 10 private office.

POLITICISATION OF THE CIVIL SERVICE

MOORE v SIXSMITH

Clear evidence of the tension between special advisers and senior civil servants was provided in the crisis which engulfed the Department of Transport, Local Government and the Regions (DTLR) in February/March 2002. Sir Richard Mottram, Permanent Secretary of the DTLR, had had excellent relations with John Prescott when he was the Minister in charge in Blair's first administration. However, in 2001 Stephen Byers became the new Minister and brought with him his special adviser Jo Moore.

Jo Moore's loyalty was to Stephen Byers and to the Labour Party, taking the view that the concept of public service belonged to a different age. In September 2001 Stephen Byers came under pressure to dismiss his 'spin doctor' when it became known that she had advised 'burying' bad news by issuing departmental press releases immediately after the 9/11 terrorist attacks. Byers resisted this pressure, but Moore was forced to offer a public apology for her behaviour.

In November 2001 Martin Sixsmith, a former BBC Foreign Correspondent and now a senior civil servant, was appointed director of the DTLR's ninety-strong communications department. His predecessor had been transferred after he had refused to sanction an alleged Jo Moore-inspired smear campaign against Bob Kiley, the London transport commissioner. Relations between the special advisers and permanent civil servants were strained and hostile. In February 2002 more allegations against Jo Moore were leaked and she agreed to resign after Byers promised that Sixsmith would also resign from the civil service. Byers announced to the House (and later repeated his statement on television) that he had accepted Sixsmith's resignation. This was untrue as Sixsmith had not resigned, nor had he been sacked. An agreed compromise between Sixsmith, Mottram and Alastair Campbell whereby Sixsmith would resign from the DTLR and would be found an alternative senior civil servant post, seemed the obvious solution to this crisis. However, Byers was furious that only his loyal assistant Jo Moore had resigned. He felt that the civil service was conspiring against him and so refused. The consequences were fatal for Byers. A smear campaign was launched by Downing Street to discredit Sixsmith, saying that he was disloyal to the government and 'loyal journalists' in Labour-supporting newspapers such as the *Daily Mirror* attacked Sixsmith's integrity and investigated his private life.

Martin Sixsmith, above, found himself in conflict with his political masters.

Sixsmith retaliated by going to the press and an article in *The Sunday Times* in February 2002 set off the explosion which would destroy Byers. He was forced to admit that he had falsely announced Sixsmith's resignation. He also admitted that he had told officials he did not want Sixsmith to be compensated with another job in the civil service. He had denied this in a television interview.

Tony Blair and Stephen Byers tried to ride out the media and parliamentary storm. However, in the end Byers was forced to resign as he had told the House a direct lie.

As *The Sunday Times* stated, the whole affair highlighted "a ministry in chaos and a government staffed by apparatchiks who had lost contact with the truth ... their obsession with powerful spin doctors marshalling a fictitious 'line to take' on an incident or policy, while trampling on the civil service's commitment to impartial truth had got the government into deep water."

THE CIVIL SERVICE

The executive branch in Britain comprises a political element, who are the elected politicians, and a non-political or neutral administrative element, the civil servants. Theoretically, government Ministers make the policy decisions and civil servants administer those decisions. Constitutionally, Ministers are responsible to Parliament for the policies and administration of their Departments. Politicians are elected on the basis of policy promises which should determine their aims and their approach to the policy issues and problems arising during their term in political office. Civil servants, who are permanent appointees, are expected to be anonymous, being neither 'named nor blamed' in public for departmental successes and failures. They provide Ministers with the advice they need to formulate and supervise the administration of policy decisions.

The dividing line between Ministers and civil servants is difficult to maintain in practice. Civil servants may remain in the same department for many years whereas Ministers, on average, rarely serve more than two years in one department. Accordingly, civil servants acquire an expertise in the types of problems likely to confront the Minister which may give the bureaucrat considerable influence in the departmental decision making process.

Historically, fears have been expressed that the civil service could frustrate the will of both individual Ministers and entire governments. Senior civil servants are likely to have been educated at Oxford or Cambridge, and they constitute a social elite in strategic positions within the government. However, such fears have not been realised. The radical policy reforms introduced by the 1945–51 Labour government and by the Conservative governments of the 1980s suggest strongly that a determined government should have little difficulty in bending the civil service to its will. The same is true of many individual Ministers.

Senior Civil Servants and Special Advisers

In July 2001 the government published a list of its seventy one special advisers who provide political and strategic advice to Ministers. Ten Downing Street had the services of twenty six special advisers and most Cabinet Ministers had two. Significantly the Treasury, the power base of Gordon Brown when he was Chancellor, had the greatest number of special advisers after the Prime Minister's office. Brown's chief special adviser until 2004, when he left to seek a parliamentary seat, was Ed Balls who was accused of trying to direct the government's policy on entry into the Eurozone. Balls was elected to Parliament in 2005 and joined Brown's first Cabinet as Secretary of State for Children, Schools and Families. Brown's appointments included the former Metropolitan Police Commissioner Lord Stevens as a senior adviser on international security issues attached to the Prime Minister's Office.

The main decisions on the conduct of the Iraq War were made by as many advisers as elected politicians. The politicians were Tony Blair, the Foreign Secretary Jack Straw, the Defence Secretary Geoff Hoon, and the Secretary of State for International Development Clare Short (until she resigned). The advisers were the Chief of Staff Jonathan Powell, the Director of Communications Alistair Campbell, the Director of Political Relations Sally Morgan, and the Foreign Policy Adviser David Manning. This ad hoc arrangement has been described as a Prime Ministerial Committee rather than a Cabinet Committee and contrasts with the War Committee of Cabinet Ministers under Margaret Thatcher which ran the 1982 Falklands War.

Andrew Tyrie a Tory MP (and former special adviser) claimed that "they (advisers) are effectively unelected Ministers. They are the people who are really running the country and I don't think that is acceptable."

There is unease in the senior civil service over the role and influence of special advisers. All ministerial departments have one or more special advisers who are personal appointees of the Secretary of State but who are employed as temporary civil servants. The activity and behaviour of special advisers has attracted much attention and criticism, especially the infamous 2004 Byers, Moore and Sixsmith affair which provided an insight into the secret world of Ministers and senior civil servants. (See opposite.)

Critics accuse Labour of undermining the independence and integrity of senior civil servants. They cite the following developments since 1997 to support this viewpoint.

1. The decision that up to three special advisers in the Prime Minister's office should be able to act as line managers of and give instructions to civil servants. Only two were appointed and one of these, Alastair Campbell, resigned in 2003. The second was Jonathan Powell the Prime Minster's Chief of Staff.

2. The opening up of many senior appointments to competition outwith the system so that a number of permanent secretaries and others have been recruited from outside Whitehall. Martin Sixsmith, who was previously a BBC foreign correspondent, falls into this category.

3. In September 2003 the government widened the role of special advisers. They could now "on behalf of their Minister, convey instructions and commission work from civil servants." Special advisers now share a role previously held exclusively by Ministers' private secretaries.

4. In 2003 the Blair government attempted to give Ministers the final say in the appointment of senior civil servants within their department. Such a move would have ended the

independence of the civil service commissioners in the appointment of staff. This was firmly opposed by the Civil Service Union and by the Public Standards Committee of the House of Commons and in the event the government backed down.

Civil Service Reforms

Before the 1997 general election both the major political parties committed to introduce a Civil Service Bill if they were elected. Once in power Labour accepted the recommendations of the Committee on Standards in Public Life that there should be a Civil Service Act. However, no progress had been made by July 2002. Cabinet Office Minister Douglas Alexander stated that although the government remained committed to legislation, it had higher priorities. In November 2004 the government finally published a draft bill or consultation document. The proposed Act would have ensured by law that the civil service would be impartial and would prevent government Ministers breaking the civil service code, the code of conduct for special advisers and the ministerial code. However, there was no indication of a Civil Service bill in the May 2005 Queen's speech which outlined the parliamentary programme for the third administration led by Prime Minister Blair.

It was therefore something of a surprise that one of Gordon Brown's first announcements in July 2007 was that he intended to introduce a Civil Service Bill. It is hoped that legislation would:

- enshrine the principles of the civil service
- lead to the appointment of civil servants on merit following fair and open competition. Parliament would now have a role to ensure the independence and integrity of the civil service
- clarify the legitimate and constructive role of special advisers within government departments

The Prime Minister commands attention from the media and so can talk to a mass audience. No other Minister can gain such media attention.

The Power of the Media

Media coverage may strengthen or weaken the Prime Minister's position. The Prime Minister's personal popularity often protects him/her from his/her leading rivals. In spite of critical press comment, John Major remained more popular in the opinion polls than his party as a whole. Media comments suggested that his most dangerous rival was Kenneth Clarke, the Chancellor of the Exchequer. However, Clarke was even more unpopular than Major with the Tory right wing because the Chancellor was perceived as being a Europhile rather than a Eurosceptic.

LIMITING THE PRIME MINISTER'S POWER

During the twentieth century, Prime Ministers gradually acquired more influence over the decisions which are made by the government, leading to claims that we have Prime Ministerial rather than Cabinet government. However, the Prime Minister's powers are limited in various ways.

Powerful Colleagues

The Prime Minister's power in the Cabinet is limited by certain considerations. Theoretically a Prime Minister can promote to ministerial rank whichever MPs he/she

When Gordon Brown was Chancellor of the Exchequer he had very strong support within the Labour Party. This made it very difficult for the Prime Minister to sack him.

THE resignation of Mrs Thatcher on 28 November 1990 after more than eleven years in office indicates that there can be limits to the tenure of even the most powerful of Prime Ministers. Her downfall was caused by a combination of factors:
- She had made enemies in the Conservative Party, particularly Sir Geoffrey Howe and Michael Heseltine.
- The provision of a constitutional mechanism for challenging party leaders.
- The belief of many Conservative MPs that they would not be re-elected if Mrs Thatcher remained as leader.
- The highly emotive influence of the European issue within the Conservative Party.

Leadership Contest

The first ballot was held on 19 November. The Prime Minister, who was in Paris, 'won' by 204 votes to 152 with sixteen Conservative MPs not voting. The margin of victory was fifty two—two votes short of an outright victory.

In the second ballot an overall majority was required. Heseltine was certainly going to stand. The Prime Minister immediately announced her intention to stand. On 22 November came the dramatic announcement that Mrs Thatcher was withdrawing from the contest. Why did she take the decision which brought her 'reign' to an end?

Mrs Thatcher consulted with her Cabinet colleagues. If they had been unanimous in encouraging her to contest the second ballot she would have done so, but most of them told her she would lose to Heseltine. This advice proved to be crucial. Ironically, the collective decision making model of Cabinet government prevailed; the Prime Minister gave way to the majority view. She stood down, releasing Major and Hurd to take part in the contest. On 2 December Major won by 185 votes to Heseltine's 131 and Hurd's 56 votes.

Mrs Thatcher leaves Downing Street for the last time. Although she was a very successful Prime Minister, she was removed by her party's MPs when they felt that she had become a liability.

chooses. However, those who display the greatest ability really must be included in the government, even though some of them may represent views to the right or the left of the Prime Minister's own position. Senior party members are more or less guaranteed a Cabinet place, although the Prime Minister may not always give them the government post each desires. It is generally assumed that it is safer for the Prime Minister to include potential rivals in the Cabinet than to leave them on the back benches where they could become the focus of opposition if and when public opinion turns against the government. The convention of collective responsibility forces Cabinet Ministers to support all government policies in public and prohibits the voicing of dissent.

Party Support

Without party backing, the Prime Minister would not be party leader and therefore would not be Prime Minister. Party leaders are subject to re-election annually, although challengers have been rare. Mrs Thatcher became Conservative leader by challenging and defeating Edward Heath in 1975 after the Party had lost the October 1974 general election. She was challenged on two occasions during her almost sixteen years as Conservative Party leader. The first challenge in 1988 did not pose a serious threat to her leadership, but the second challenge in 1990 led to her stepping down as leader and as Prime Minister. (See above.) Blair was never challenged and Gordon Brown was elected unopposed to follow him as party leader.

The Power of the Electorate/ Public Opinion

The electorate also exercises some control over the Prime Minister whose party must seek re-election at least every five years. An unpopular party will not be re-elected. Prime Ministers who lose general elections may resign as party leader shortly afterwards (Home in 1964, Callaghan in 1979 and Major in 1997) or they might, like Heath after the 1974 elections, lose a party leadership election. Wilson, on the other hand, survived Labour's loss in the 1970 general election. Most commentators believe that Mrs Thatcher, first elected to 10 Downing Street in 1979, grew more powerful after her re-election in both 1983 and 1987. Her failure to retain the Conservative Party leadership in the 1990 contest was widely attributed to a belief among Tory MPs that the party would not win the next election if she remained as leader.

Prime Ministers may also be prevented from achieving major aims by lack of support in the general public. It was widely believed that Blair wished to take Britain into the euro-based European Monetary System. He was not able to do so because of lack of public enthusiasm for the project. Instead, Blair had to be content with a declaration that, in principle, Britain would join once five economic tests, laid down by Gordon Brown's sceptical Treasury, were satisfied. This had not happened by the time Blair left office.

Events

The biggest limitation on Blair's powers and achievements can now be seen to have come from the political fallout from the September 11th 2001 attack on the twin towers of the World Trade Centre in New York. The issue of how to respond to that attack and how to cope with the threat of international terrorism decided the political agenda for much of Blair's second term, which had begun promisingly with the May 2001 Labour landslide. (See Chapter 2.) The subsequent decision to ally Britain closely with the United States in the fight against terrorism led to participation in hostilities against Iraq and in Afghanistan. The political and economic costs of intervention in Iraq and Afghanistan weakened the chances of success of the Prime Minister's major priorities on the domestic front which included reform of public services and relations with the EU. These problems and the fall in Labour's support in the 2005 election probably persuaded Blair to hand over the premiership to Gordon Brown much earlier in his third term than he would have liked or had intended. Blair has been described by many as the strongest British Prime Minister apart from Thatcher in the post-1945 era but that did not ensure that he achieved all his goals.

The Opposition

The second largest party in Parliament is officially recognised as 'Her Majesty's Loyal Opposition'. Assuming the government has a healthy majority, the opposition has little chance of outvoting it in the House. In terms of providing a check on the government's actions, its powers are very restricted and, in fact, the House of Lords (Chapter 4) and pressure group activity (Chapter 6) have far greater influence.

The role of the opposition parties is a frustrating one. All that they can really do is emphasise the worth of their own policies, attempt to discredit government policies and actions, and 'score points' in the Commons. The main opposition party offers an alternative range of policies and can embark on a long-term campaign of swaying the electorate. The most recent example of an opposition party displacing the incumbent government electorally was Labour's 1997 victory. This was partly based on a long-drawn-out campaign by its leaders, particularly Blair and Brown, to persuade business leaders that the Labour Party should no longer be regarded by the business community as the natural enemy of capitalism, the market or the middle classes. How much of Labour's 1997 triumph should be attributed to the charm offensive by Blair and Brown and how much to the Conservatives shooting themselves in the foot over Black Wednesday remains a debatable issue.

FROM CABINET TO PRIME MINISTERIAL GOVERNMENT?

The essence of British government used to be considered to be 'Cabinet government', a form of collective leadership. The Prime Minister's position relative to the Cabinet was described by a famous phrase 'primus inter pares'—first among equals. This suggested that in spite of the Prime Minister enjoying powers denied to other Cabinet Ministers, such as the power of patronage and appointment, the Cabinet reached its decisions collectively on a majority basis, even though the Prime Minister summed up the sense of the meeting. The phrase suggested that the Prime Minister's status as the Minister at the head of government was of a formal nature with little extra power attached. During the course of the twentieth century, however, the Prime Minister became more powerful so the holder of this office is no longer just 'first among equals'. Indeed, many commentators claim that British government should now be labelled 'Prime Ministerial government' to indicate where the decisive policy making power usually lies. Some go further by saying that prime ministers like Thatcher and Blair accumulated so much personal power over the political process that the system has effectively become 'presidential' in character.

Presidential System?

An occasional claim that the transition from Cabinet government to Prime Ministerial government has gone even further by transforming the British system into a presidential system needs careful examination. The two offices have to be compared according to two institutional dimensions: relationships within the executive branch and relationships between the executive and legislative branches of government.

The American President is directly elected which makes him/her separate from and almost entirely independent of the legislature. Along with the Vice President, who owes his/her position to being selected as the President's running mate, the President is the only elected member of the executive branch which makes him/her more powerful than the British PM within the political executive. Unless something drastic occurs, as happened to President Nixon, the American President is guaranteed at least four years in office. S/He will not be driven out of office like Thatcher or 'persuaded' to move

President Bush and Prime Minister Blair address the media at the end of a summit meeting. Did Mr Blair encourage a shift to a more powerful Prime Minister's office?

on like Blair. In relation to the rest of the executive branch the American President is more powerful than the British Prime Minister. There has seldom been any approximation to the Blair-Brown relationship within the American executive. When things go wrong a prominent American Cabinet member falls on his/her sword, e.g. Donald Rumsfeld, the powerful Defence Secretary who had a major input into the development of American policy towards Iraq. The American chief executive is usually more powerful than the Prime Minister within the executive branch. Presidents are more likely than Prime Ministers to be restricted by the legislature. The American Congress is independent of the President because it is separately elected. Congress has often frustrated the domestic policy initiatives of Presidents as Bill Clinton quickly found out.

In sharp contrast, the British Prime Minister is elected from one parliamentary constituency only and sits in the House of Commons along with 645 other MPs. The Prime Minister owes his/her position in the first instance to his/her political party and not to voters in primary elections. The collective executive which he/she leads is responsible to the House of Commons but this constitutional condition has, via the agency of disciplined political parties, made the British executive much more powerful than the American President vis-à-vis the legislature.

To describe the British political system as 'presidential' underestimates the executive's ability to get its policies through the legislature. The British executive, Cabinet or Prime Minister, is usually more powerful than the American President because of its almost habitual control of the legislature—especially in relation to domestic policy. It is only when that control is weakened by election results which give the government a small or no overall majority such as those in 1974 (February and October) and 1992 that the British Prime Minister and Cabinet run into serious difficulties in their efforts to enact their policy programme. Prime Ministers have had a variable relationship with the rest of the British executive branch. Some have indeed enjoyed sufficient power over their colleagues to merit the accolade of 'prime ministerial government'. Thatcher is the most recent obvious example. Blair in his first term was often compared with Thatcher as evidence of a transition to prime ministerial government in Britain. However, the Blair-Brown relationship complicates this discussion. Some commentators talk of a 'dual monarchy' to describe Brown's role in relation to domestic policy, especially after Labour's second term began in 2001 and Blair quickly got entangled in foreign problems, most obviously Iraq. Brown is said to have 'thwarted' Blair's wishes regarding joining the Eurozone and also NHS Reform.

THE LIMITS OF EXECUTIVE ACCOUNTABILITY

The evaluation of executive accountability is considered in the following case study of controversies relating to Britain's participation in the American-led and controlled attack on Iraq in March 2003 which led to the downfall of the Iraqi President, Saddam Hussein, and the longer term occupation deemed necessary to prosecute the war on terror and to establish democracy in Iraq. The Iraq War has had a profound impact upon British politics in the first decade of the twenty first century. It contributed to a significant, though limited, decline in Labour support in the 2005 election (see Chapter 2), to Tony Blair cutting short his tenure of 10 Downing Street sooner into his third term than expected, and to conflicting evaluations of his achievements as Prime Minister.

The Hutton Inquiry

Allegations of governmental improprieties reached a peak in 2003 with the appointment of Appeal Court Justice Hutton to inquire into the circumstances of the death of Dr David Kelly, a biological weapons expert who had been a member of a UN Inspection team in Iraq in the 1990s. Kelly was an employee of the Ministry of Defence. He discussed the Iraq War with a BBC journalist who made controversial claims critical of the government in a Today programme which was broadcast on the basis of his conversations with Kelly. Kelly thus became embroiled in a conflict between the government and the BBC over the truthfulness and accuracy of the government's version of the intelligence or 'facts' used to justify Britain's military actions against Iraq. Kelly's subsequent suicide heightened the highly controversial debate about whether Britain should ever have participated in the war and stimulated several levels of inquiry which may have been seen as attempts to render the Labour government accountable for its policies.

The Hutton Inquiry was established on 18 July 2003 immediately after Kelly's death. The government wanted it "urgently to conduct an investigation into the circumstances surrounding the death of Dr Kelly." The questions raised by the war against Iraq were wide-ranging. The main al-

CHRONOLOGY of the 'IRAQ' ISSUE

11 September 2001	Attack on the World Trade Centre, New York.
January 2002	Bush brands Iraq, Iran and North Korea as the "axis of evil".
September 2002	Blair government publishes 'dossier' of evidence of Iraq's weaponry including weapons of mass destruction (WMD) which could be deployed within 45 minutes.
7 March 2003	UN Inspection Team (UNMOVIC) led by Hans Blix reports that there is no evidence of underground or mobile nuclear weapons manufacturing facilities in Iraq.
18 March 2003	House of Commons passes motion supporting the use of "all means necessary to ensure the disarmament of Iraq's weapons of mass destruction". The Liberal Democrats and 139 Labour MPs vote for a motion claiming that the case for armed intervention had not yet been made.
20 March 2003	Invasion of Iraq commences.
9 April 2003	Fall of Baghad.
29 May 2003	BBC journalist Andrew Gilligan claims on the Today programme that he has information suggesting the government had 'sexed up' the case for intervention, especially in relation to WMD.
15 July 2003	Dr David Kelly, thought to be Gilligan's source, appears before Commons Select Committee on Foreign Affairs. Subjected to hostile questioning.
17 July 2003	Death of Dr David Kelly, thought to be Gilligan's source.
18 July 2003	Appointment of Justice Hutton to conduct inquiry into Dr Kelly's death.
	Report of Foreign Affairs Select Committee.
September 2003	Report of Intelligence and Security Select Committee.
28 January 2004	Publication of Hutton Report.
29/30 January	Resignations of BBC Director General (Greg Dyke), Chairman of Board of Governors (Gavyn Davies) and Gilligan.
3 February 2004	PM orders the institution of a committee of Privy Councillors chaired by Lord Butler to investigate the accuracy of intelligence on Iraq's weapons of mass destruction up to March 2003.
July 2004	Report of Butler Inquiry.

legation against the government was that it had knowingly published false information or exaggerated intelligence to justify going to war. This information was allegedly contained in the government's September 2002 'dossier', particularly a claim that Iraq could deploy weapons of mass destruction (WMD), probably chemical and biological weapons, at forty five minutes' notice. This claim was based on unattributable 'intelligence' received by the government concerning Iraq's military capabilities including WMD. The government had various motives for going to war against Saddam but Iraq's possible possession of WMD seemed to many to be the clinching argument in favour of the government's actions.

What exactly was Hutton going to investigate? Opponents of the war wanted him to consider whether the charge of falsifying or exaggerating the intelligence was true. Hutton had to decide how far he should go in his possibly more limited inquiry into the circumstances surrounding the death of Dr Kelly. How would he define 'circumstances'? Hutton first of all dismissed consideration of whether the intelligence contained in the dossier was strong enough to justify the belief that Iraq's armed capability posed such a threat to British interests that military action against Iraq was required. Furthermore, he did not propose to investigate whether the intelligence was unreliable. Instead Hutton decided to concentrate on Gilligan's two claims. Firstly, Gilligan alleged that the government knew that it was not true that Iraq could deploy WMD within forty five minutes. His second assertion was that the government demanded, mainly through the agency of Alastair Campbell, the Director of Communications in the Downing Street Press Office, that the information in the dossier be 'sexed up' in order to strengthen the case for war.

Hutton's was not the only inquiry into the government's behaviour. The House of Commons provided a more immediate and more partisan scrutiny of government actions. The sensational nature of Gilligan's claims in the Today programme and the subsequent naming of Dr Kelly as his source drew the attention of the House of Commons Select Committee on Foreign Affairs which subjected Kelly to intense questioning. The Committee's report cleared Campbell of inserting the forty five minutes claim into the September 2002 dossier but only on the casting vote of the chairperson, who at the time was a Labour MP. Opposition MPs did not vote to clear Campbell because of a lack of evidence.

The House of Commons Select Committee on Intelligence and Security also passed judgement on these events. Its September 2003 Report agreed with the Labour majority on the Foreign Affairs committee that Campbell had not 'sexed up' the dossier. Geoff Hoon, the Defence Minister, was criticised for not informing the Commons that two members of the MoD's Intelligence Staff had expressed concern that the September 2003 dossier had exaggerated the threat posed by Iraq. Nevertheless, the Select Committee did pass judgement on the issue of the quality of the presentation of the government's case:

"The language of the dossier may have left with readers the impression that there was fuller and firmer intelligence behind the judgement (to go to war) than was the case. Our view … is that judgements went to (although not beyond) the outer limits of the intelligence available." In the language of the street, the government was pushing its luck but got away with it.

Hutton's conclusions were largely favourable to the government and critical of the BBC. Hutton concluded that Gilligan's allegation that the government was aware of a falsity in the 'forty five minutes' claim was unfounded. On the 'sexing up' issue, Hutton attempted to define the meaning of the phrase which had been picked up and given prominence by the media. In Hutton's words: "The term 'sexed-up' is a slang expression, the meaning of which lacks clarity in the context of the discussion of the dossier". It could mean a claim that the dossier did actually contain intelligence which the government had inserted knowing it to be false. Alternatively, it could mean merely that the government believed the intelligence to be reliable and wanted the strongest possible interpretation placed on it to make the case against Iraq as convincing as possible.

The Hutton Report decided that it was not possible to know exactly what Kelly had said to Gilligan although it seemed unlikely that Kelly would have told the BBC journalist that the government knew its forty five minutes claim was wrong. The forty five minutes claim, the 'sexing up' action, was not added at Alastair Campbell's request.

Hutton was critical of the BBC's role in the affair, saying that more editorial control should have been exercised over Gilligan's broadcast. No checks were made by the Today programme editors regarding the reliability of the claims made against the government. Hutton further criticised the BBC for not investigating properly the government's subsequent complaint that the Today claims against it were wrong.

THE BUTLER REPORT

Immediately after the publication of the Hutton Report on 28 January 2004 the Prime Minister ordered another inquiry to answer questions not tackled by Hutton. Five Privy Councillors led by Lord Butler, who had been Cabinet Secretary and Head of the Home Civil Service, were asked among other tasks to investigate the accuracy of intelligence on Iraqi weapons of mass destruction up to March 2003 and to highlight any "discrepancies between intelligence before the conflict and what has been learned since the end of the conflict". The other members of the Inquiry comprised one Labour

MP, formerly government Chief Whip, one Conservative MP, once a Minister in the Northern Ireland Office, a Field Marshall, and a Chairman of the Police Federation. The Butler Inquiry was regarded as being clearly an Establishment body.

The Butler Report concluded that the intelligence which the government had relied on in going to war in Iraq was "indeed seriously flawed". The Report commented in general on the shortcomings of intelligence, particularly its "incompleteness", as a source of information on which crucial policy decisions, such as going to war, might be made: "In fact, it (intelligence) is often, when first acquired, sporadic and patchy, and even after analysis may still be at best inferential." The September 2002 'dossier', which was issued in an unprecedented fashion, at a time when the likelihood of war against Iraq was being widely discussed in the media and elsewhere, was said to have omitted warnings from the government's own Intelligence Services about the "limited intelligence base" on which policy judgements were being made. However, no blame was attributed to any individual and Blair was explicitly exonerated of knowingly making false claims about the threat posed by Iraq. The Prime Minister declared in the Commons that "no one made up the intelligence". The forty five minutes claim was criticised for a lack of clarity as to what it meant. There were also doubts about the reliability of the intelligence on which the claim was based. Indeed the Butler Report concluded that Iraq "did not have significant—if any—stocks of chemical or biological weapons in a state fit for deployment, or developed plans for using them." On a possible motive for attacking Iraq as part of a war against international terrorism the Report concluded that there was no evidence of cooperation between the Iraqi regime and al-Qaeda.

Conclusions

The government was 'held to account' in that its actions were examined closely in the public eye. No Ministers resigned over the events leading to and described in the Hutton Report although the Defence Minister, Geoff Hoon, received much media criticism. Nevertheless, he continued as Defence Minister until the 2005 election after which he was moved to the position of Leader of the House of Commons and was still in the Cabinet. Ministers did resign over the Iraq War—Robin Cook before it started and Clare Short after it had begun. Both resigned because they would not accept collective responsibility for the war. The Cabinet could have 'rebelled' against the Prime Minister's wishes which seemed to be based in part on his relationship with the American President, George Bush, but the Cabinet did not rebel. When Gordon Brown succeeded Blair as Prime Minister in June 2007 he quickly made clear his support for his predecessor's policy of maintaining British troops in Iraq as part of the attempt to establish democracy, reduce conflict between warring factions within Iraq and to eliminate Iraq as a base for international terrorism. Brown visited both Washington and Iraq in the first four months of his tenure.

The resignations of Greg Dyke and Gavyn Davies in the wake of the Hutton Report signified a comprehensive defeat for the BBC in its ongoing conflict with the New Labour government. They were held accountable in that they paid a price for the indiscretions, according to Hutton, of BBC employees. The acting Chairman of the Board of Governors, Lord Ryder, apologised unreservedly to the government for the BBC's errors. Greg Dyke accused the government of systematic bullying of the BBC over coverage of the war.

There was some political fallout for the government. The electorate was much less favourable to Labour in 2005 (See Chapter 2) and did reward the Liberal Democrats who had opposed the war. Historians will eventually judge Blair's conduct of British policy towards Iraq and the problems of international terrorism.

The Butler and Hutton Inquiries did not tackle the issue of whether the government should have gone to war against Iraq. Rather they focused on the government's behaviour: did anyone lie? did anyone falsify the evidence? was the evidence compelling? did the decision makers on Iraq realise that the intelligence was weak and possibly unreliable? That judgement was left to politicians and to voters. Robin Cook gave his answer by resigning as the war began. Clare Short did likewise some months after him. MPs voted on the issue of going to war with about one-quarter of the PLP joining the Liberal Democrats in opposition. The Select Committees of the Commons passed their judgements on aspects of the controversy about intelligence in the government's case for going to war. The electorate issued a mild rebuke in the 2005 election when other issues were more pressing for most voters.

Chapter 6
Pressure Groups

What you will learn.
1. The role of pressure groups in a democracy.
2. The effectiveness of pressure groups on the decision making process.
3. The influence of the media on the decision making process.

The emphasis so far in *UK Politics Today* has been on 'top down' government and politics: the Monarchy, Parliament, the Prime Minister and Cabinet, party leaders, and constitutional rules such as the electoral system. Ordinary men and women have entered our account of politics in Britain by way of elections and voting which may occasionally change the direction of policy making by returning to office the main opposition party at the expense of the government which may have been in office for five years (Labour in 1979) or eighteen years (the Conservatives in 1997). More often, voters confirm the tenure of the government of the day. In this chapter we focus more directly on 'governance from below' or 'bottom up governance' by extending our definition of 'representation' to include pressure groups and public opinion. The 'representative' function of social groups is assuming greater significance because of the questions marks raised against the quality of British representative democracy by falls in electoral turnout and in political party membership.

Parties are blunt political instruments. The wide range of political opinions in any country cannot be represented fully by a few political parties which combine interests in the search for common ground. Party leaders cannot satisfy all sections of their parties all of the time. The government is not too concerned about satisfying the policy aims of the people who did not vote for it, and opposition parties cannot achieve much for their supporters until they get back into high office. People who have little interest in party politics will sometimes be provoked into political action by an issue which affects them intimately. Many people have pressing interests or political objectives which may be threatened by or are unlikely to be satisfied by the government of the day. For these reasons, individuals seeking to achieve political objectives often have to go beyond party politics and the occasional election to have any hope of achieving their aims.

Society provides ready-made alternatives to parties as vehicles of partisan political interests. One of the most ancient of famous political sayings is Aristotle's dictum: "Man is by nature a social animal". Society breeds organisations. There has been an acceleration in the formation of social organisations, most of which have been established for reasons which have nothing to do with politics. Sport, religion, work, hobbies, leisure, 'good causes', 'social problems' and personal problems have stimulated the creation of organisations such as the Scottish Football Association, the Church of Scotland and the Roman Catholic Church, Trade Unions, the Ram-

Many groups combine 'interests' and 'cause'. In December 1997 there were rumours that Labour's review of the welfare system would result in cuts in various types of benefit and in some benefits being made conditional on going to work. Several groups receiving benefit reacted by protesting outside the gates of Downing Street, throwing paint on the gates and chaining themselves to the railings. In February 1998 one protest was organised by the Disabled People's Direct Action Network which feared that disabled people would lose benefits which in some cases paid for goods or medicine "which they could not otherwise afford". Other disabled groups such as Radar (Royal Association for Disability and Rehabilitation) supported the action. These groups see the fight to safeguard the economic interests and benefits of disabled people as a 'cause' since the disabled need special protection.

blers Association, the Salvation Army, the Howard League for Penal Reform, Alcoholics Anonymous, Fathers 4 Justice, the Animal Liberation Front, the World Wildlife Fund, the Scottish Beaver network and so on. The list seems endless.

All social organisations are potential pressure groups. Social organisations will enter the political process to advance or protect the interests of their members when they want something from the government or when government decisions seem likely to affect their members adversely. Some organisations are explicitly political and are permanent, while others are established to promote a view on a single issue and may be only temporary in duration.

Religion provides examples of occasional pressure group activity by organisations whose principal reasons for existence lie beyond the political sphere. In the 1997 election campaign one of the few adverse moments for the Labour Party in Scotland occurred when Archbishop Winning reprimanded it for its refusal to take a pro-life stand on the abortion issue. The General Assembly of the Church of Scotland may also be 'political' on occasion, making known its views on a wide range of issues. Legislative proposals either by the government or by backbenchers often stimulate pressure group responses. After the 1997 election a Private Members' Bill to introduce a ban on fox hunting stimulated many organisations to campaign for or against the proposed legislation—the League Against Cruel Sports supported the Bill while the Countryside Alliance opposed it.

There has been considerable public debate about a worrying decline in the classic forms of democratic participation: voting and membership of political parties. Only 60% of voters turned out in 2005. There are fewer than one million members of political parties in Britain. The National Trust, on the other hand, has 2.7 million members. The Royal Society for the Protection of Birds (RSPB) has over one million members. Almost 30% of adults are members of motoring organisations. Public opinion, often organised by pressure groups, may seek to influence government decisions by holding protest demonstrations on issues such as the poll tax, the Iraq War and fox hunting. A less active role for public opinion is to be found in the polls which are published weekly in the media on every imaginable political issue.

TYPES OF PRESSURE GROUP

There are two basic types of pressure groups according to the characteristics of membership:
1. Interest groups—so called because they represent the sectional economic interests of their members, e.g. the interests of the 'working man' or the interests of 'big business'. Their distinguishing feature is who they represent. Membership is closed.
2. Promotional or 'cause' groups. Promotional groups are defined by the cause they represent—by what they stand for. The Howard League for Penal Reform promotes a particular view of prison policy (what prison should be for; conditions of inmates). Membership of promotional groups is open-ended; anyone who believes in the cause can join. The 'cause' is usually non-economic.

Some groups may pursue both an interest and a cause. The BMA and the EIS support the economic interests of their members and the causes of 'good health' and 'good education' respectively. Fathers 4 Justice, set up to represent separated or divorced fathers who complain about lack of access to their children, may also have a dual identity. The group is sectional in that it represents a limited, easily defined set of individuals, but it may also be claimed to be promoting the cause of 'responsible shared parenting'.

Groups may also be distinguished according to the extent of access to government which they enjoy: insider and outsider groups. Insider groups are regularly consulted by the government because their expertise, such as the medical expertise of the British Medical Association (BMA), is useful when policies are being formulated. Such policies are then implemented by BMA members (the medical profession). Outsider groups enjoy little access to the corridors of power because their views are shared by few in government circles irrespective of party. The Campaign for Nuclear Disarmament (CND), while it might be supported by some individual MPs, espouses views on nuclear defence which are unacceptable to major party hierarchies. Outsider groups indulge in public campaigns in the hope of influencing public opinion which might make the government think again, although CND has not been successful despite following such a strategy.

Trade Unions

The best known, and biggest, interest groups are trade unions and employers' federations. Trade unions were created and still exist primarily to defend and improve the wages and working conditions of their members. Their principal adversaries are the firms employing their members and whose main activity is to compete in the marketplace and make profits. Interest groups have closed memberships. In other words, individuals have to work in a particular industry or possess a particular skill in order to join the general or craft union which represents workers in that industry or with that particular skill.

The two sides of industry are represented by the most powerful pressure groups in Britain. Trade unions individually and collectively represent millions of workers. By the end of the 1970s there were over 13 million trade unionists, although the number had fallen to 7.3 million by 2000 (almost 30% of the British workforce). Membership numbers have since stabilised at that figure. In 2006 the biggest union was UNISON which had over 944,356 women amongst its 1.343 million members. On 1 May 2007 the Transport and General Workers Union (TGWU) and Amicus, a major engineering union, merged to form UNITE. The new union has over two million members, becoming the biggest union in Britain. Collectively, unions are organised into the Trades Union Congress (TUC) which acts as an 'umbrella' organisation for the trade union movement with fifty nine unions affiliated. The EIS (Educational Institute of Scotland), with 58,829 members, is affiliated to the TUC. Not all unions are TUC affiliated. The Police Federation is not permitted by law to affiliate. TUC leaders and the leaders of individual unions are frequently consulted by the government because their approval may make the difference between success and failure in respect of many economic and industrial policies.

The political role of British trade unions has been a central issue in recent decades for two reasons. Firstly, the status of unions within the Labour Party has raised questions about their political power. (See Chapter 3.) Many people believed that the unions possessed too much power. Secondly, trade union power and organisation was one of the major targets of 'Thatcherism' in the 1980s. There was much trade union reform which has, for the most part, been accepted by New Labour.

Trade Union leaders may progress from high office at union level to a leading position in the Labour Party or in government. Alan Johnson, General Secretary of the Communication Workers Union, 1995–97, entered Parliament in 1997 and joined the Cabinet in 2004 as Secretary of State for Work and Pensions. Johnson has been described as "a genuinely working-class MP in an increasingly middle-class party."

Employers' Organisations

The links between the 'other side' of industry—companies who are the employers—and the Conservative Party are much less formal than the links between Labour and the unions. There is no equivalent of trade union affiliation to the Labour Party. The most obvious connection between business interests and the Conservative Party is financial. Many companies contribute large sums of money to the Conservatives. Industries form their own federations to make representations to the government when necessary, for instance the Engineering Employers Federation. The top business pressure group is the Confederation of British Industry (the CBI) which is the TUC's counterpart. The CBI represents over 200,000 businesses: 80% of Footsie (FTSE—Financial Times Stock Exchange) Top 100 firms are CBI members. Its political role as a pressure group is clearly stated on its website: "We are the premier lobbying organisation for UK business on national and international issues." Other umbrella associations on the business side are the British Chambers of Commerce, the Small Business Association and the Institute of Directors.

Promotional Groups

Promotional or 'cause' groups have a long history. William Wilberforce MP founded two organisations in his fight to abolish slavery: the Society for the Abolition of the Slave Trade in 1787 and the Antislavery Society in 1823. The modern equivalents pursuing a humanitarian principle or cause would include Oxfam, Christian Aid, the RSPCC, the World Wildlife Fund and many others. Environmental groups have flourished in recent decades in response to the realisation that mankind was endangering not only the quality of life of many of Earth's inhabitants but also, in the worst case scenario, the survival of the planet and the human race. Greenpeace and Friends of the Earth are now among the best known pressure groups. Protesters against poverty and disease in developing countries have converged in great numbers in cities hosting the G8 meetings of the world's richest nations, attracting massive publicity in the process.

When relations between employers and employees break down a strike may occur. When the government is the employer its popularity can be affected by the dispute.

DIFFERENCES BETWEEN POLITICAL PARTIES & PRESSURE GROUPS

	POLITICAL PARTIES	**PRESSURE GROUPS**
Principal Objectives	Winning elections Forming government Implementation of broad policy platforms	Protecting specific economic interests or promoting a specific cause Influencing government
Membership	Open-ended: anyone may join	Interest Groups (closed): confined to members e.g. trade unions Cause Groups (open-ended): anyone may join
Methods	Putting up candidates in elections Putting MPs into government	Persuasion Protest Campaigns to influence public opinion Sponsoring parliamentary candidates

PRESSURE GROUP TARGETS

Pressure groups 'target' elements of the political system which will help them to achieve their objectives. The most obvious targets are:

1. The executive branch (Ministers and civil servants).
2. The legislature (backbench MPs).
3. Party factions (left, centre and right wings of the major parties) sympathetic to specific pressure group interests or causes.
4. Public opinion and voters.

In Britain decision making is much more narrowly concentrated than it is in the USA. The focus of most pressure group activity has traditionally been Whitehall. Policy making in Britain, once the general election is over, is concentrated in government departments which means government Ministers or the civil servants advising them. A government which has just been elected, especially if it has replaced a government of the rival major party, will have certain policy objectives from which it is unlikely to be diverted. The scope for influencing policy will not be great when a government transforms its manifesto proposals, for example devolution, into legislative form. On the other hand, the government will also have to cope with problems which arise unexpectedly. In that case the government may be open to suggestions from 'interested parties'.

British MPs have long been considered to be much less useful to pressure groups than American Senators and Representatives, because voting in the legislature in Britain is determined much more by party loyalty and discipline enforced by the Whips. Most British MPs feel compelled to vote with the party majority most of the time unless they feel very strongly about an issue. For this reason, although MPs may be useful to pressure groups as far as publicity is concerned, they do not usually cross party lines to vote in accordance with these objectives when party interests clash with pressure group interests.

PRESSURE GROUPS IN ACTION

Pressure group participation in politics takes various forms. The larger economic interest groups, which are often consulted as of right when the government is formulating policy, will try to 'persuade' the government to grant their wishes or demands. Promotional groups are more likely to resort to direct action such as public demonstrations, protest marches and 'stunts' in attempts to influence government decisions.

Pressure group strategies vary according to the nature of the groups involved and the stages of the government decision making process. The principal decision making stages are:

1. Formulation of policy where the emphasis is on consultation and persuasion for insider groups who have access to the government. Groups sometimes try to find sponsors in Parliament for their own proposals for legislation or executive decisions.
2. Legislative stages where the emphasis is on the publicity generated by MPs speaking in support of group interests or causes. Backbench MPs may introduce legislative proposals on behalf of groups.
3. Implementation of policy where the emphasis may be on protest on behalf of those who lost out when decisions were taken.

Consultation

Often the government will invite groups and organisations to comment on policy proposals which have been published in the preliminary form of a White or Green Paper. At this stage the government is still open to persuasion. In the autumn of 1997 the Labour government invited the public to respond to its proposals to encourage saving which involved replacing TESSAs and PEPs with Individual Savings Allowances (ISAs).

The consultative access granted to many, but not to all, pressure groups as representative institutions has long been accepted as a necessary and legitimate part of the democratic process. Politicians and civil servants spend much time and effort listening to pressure group demands. This is done in order to persuade public opinion of the validity of the government's policy and to make implementation of that policy easier once it has entered the Statute Book. Groups, in turn, realise that they need to persuade the government to give them some of what they want. A process of consultation has therefore emerged in which representatives of groups and interests are in frequent contact with the policy makers (government Ministers and civil servants) in Whitehall. Government and insider groups need each other. The government relies on workers who are union members to implement policy. Educational policies such as the introduction of new tests or exams have to be put into practice by the teaching profession. In return the government will listen to such groups when policy is being formulated.

The process of consultation between groups and government developed much earlier and is much more pronounced in the USA where it has become known as 'lobbying'. Pressure groups are known collectively in the USA as the 'Lobby' because their representatives lie in wait for important policy makers in the corridors in the Congress buildings (Capitol Hill) and in government departments. For many years 'lobbying' and 'lobbyists' were regarded with suspicion in Britain because they were associated with giving undue influence to a limited number of groups and with corruption because it seemed that votes were for sale in Congress where party discipline is much weaker than in the House of Commons. However, in recent years the business of political consultants has developed significantly in Britain and accusations of 'sleaze' against some consultants, a few government Ministers and some MPs have hit the newspaper headlines.

(Continued on page 107)

GROUPS AS THE SOURCE OF POLICY

Intriguing news items appeared in *The Sunday Herald* and *The Times* in 2007 which illustrated the occasional role of pressure groups as sources of policy proposals. "Beaver's return to Scotland comes closer" read one headline. The sub-heading referred to "Animal groups" which might be misleading because some 'animal rights groups', usually regarded as outsiders, have been accused on occasion of using intimidation or violence to secure their aims. 'Conservationist' is more appropriate as a description of the prime movers in this example of pressure group activity.

The *Sunday Herald* article suggested that the new SNP Scottish government was, like its Labour-Liberal Democrat predecessor, sympathetic to controversial moves to secure the return of the European beaver to Scotland. Beavers had been hunted to extinction elsewhere in Britain by the nineteenth century. The groups in favour are led by the Scottish Wildlife Trust and the Royal Zoological Society of Scotland, both of which may be described as possessing insider status, and the Scottish Beavers Network, a promotional group of more recent origin. The groups proposed to introduce about twenty beavers from Norway into the Knapdale Forest in Argyll. The *Times* article pointed out that local people were being consulted and that opposition had been expressed by local farmers, by the Scottish Rural Property and Business Association and by a Conservative MSP for the Highlands and Islands. Several levels of government were involved. The United Nations has a Convention of International Trade in Endangered Species of Wild Fauna and Flora. The European Union has a directive permitting the reintroduction under licence of extinct animals. The Scottish government is the appropriate decision making body. Scottish Natural Heritage failed in an attempt to secure a licence permitting a similar scheme to get off the ground in 2005. The Scottish government has been asked to decide again on whether to grant an application for a licence to bring back the beaver.

The central political issue here is commonplace in politics: a clash between a cause and an economic interest. Reasons offered by conservation groups in favour of the project include conservation for its own sake, although conservation of this species requires its reintroduction, and resulting improvements to wetlands habitats in Scotland. An economic argument is made via links to tourism which is increasingly important to the Scottish economy. The argument against the reintroduction of beavers is based on claims that they may cause harm to trees and domestic gardens. Farmers regard beavers in much the same way as they regard foxes: as costly pests which should be eliminated or, in this instance, not introduced into the environment.

Opponents of the beavers claim that they will cause damage to trees.

THE FUEL PROTESTS OF SEPTEMBER 2000

The discontent of small businesses in the road haulage industry and in other industries dependent on using petrol and diesel fuel, such as farmers and fishermen, was at the heart of an embarrassing political crisis for the Labour government, and the Prime Minister in particular, which erupted in early September 2000. The crisis focused attention on the use of direct action against government policy in an attempt to force the government into lowering the price of fuel. Fuel prices have long been a bone of contention between the government and industries for whom fuel costs can limit profits. Groups such as the CBI, the Road Hauliers Association and the NFU routinely ask the Chancellor before every Budget to lower fuel taxes which are claimed to be higher than in other European countries.

The direct action began, apparently spontaneously, on the evening of 7 September 2000 when a number of protesters, believed to have been from the small business sector, began to picket the entrance to a large oil refinery at Stanlow in Cheshire. Within four days hardly any fuel was being delivered to petrol stations throughout Britain. The government was not immediately aware of the dangers of the direct action which was more typical of French than of British politics. By Monday 11 September it was clear that problems were escalating as fuel supplies were not getting out of the refineries, either because tanker drivers could not get out due to intimidation or because they would not cross the picket lines out of sympathy with the protesting pickets.

What was the government to do? Its major aim was not to be seen to give in to the protests. If it did give in, it would be perceived as weak and the strategy could be used by other groups enraged by government policies. The principal danger in letting the protests continue was that essential services such as the NHS would be deprived of vital supplies like blood and ambulance services as vehicles ran out of fuel.

To begin with the public, many of whom buy petrol, were sympathetic to the protesters. The media reported the protests sympathetically, portraying the pickets as supporters of the common man against an uncaring and remote government. The pickets did allow some tankers out to supply essential services such as ambulances. The Prime Minister summoned oil company bosses to 10 Downing Street on Wednesday 13 September and 'read them the riot act'. The government was supported by the TUC General Secretary who urged tanker drivers to cross the picket lines. By Friday morning the pickets had withdrawn and the tankers were supplying petrol stations once more.

What brought the direct action to an end? The government did not climb down by promising to reduce fuel prices immediately nor did it need to bring in the Army to drive the petrol tankers as had been suggested in some quarters. What persuaded the pickets to end their protests peacefully was a change in the public mood registered by the tabloid press. The *Mirror's* headline on Thursday morning was: 'Enough is Enough'. Once it was clear that essential services could be damaged, that supermarkets could run out of staple foods, and that people would not get to work on time, or indeed at all, the protesters realised that they would soon run out of public sympathy.

The Chancellor announced in his November 2000 economic statement that there would be a freeze on fuel duties until April 2002 and a package for motorists that effectively reduced the price of petrol by 4p and the price of diesel by 8p per litre. Direct action had worked to some extent on this occasion without the government of the day having to climb down in an embarrassing fashion. The key element was the attitude of the general public who began with some sympathy for the protesters which encouraged them to intensify their action. Once that sympathy had evaporated thanks to the inconveniences suffered by the public the protest came to an end. The Chancellor's decision to meet the protesters halfway by granting a temporary stay of execution on fuel tax rises may be attributed to the fact that masses of voters, motorists, were affected by the rising costs of petrol and diesel. Placating them made sound political sense in the short term with the government, in office for over three years when the fuel protests erupted, looking for a favourable opportunity to have its mandate renewed in the not too distant future. An attempt to repeat the 2000 protest and outcome fizzled out without success in 2005.

The Fight to Ban Fox Hunting

The *Hunting with Dogs Act* received the Royal Assent on 18 November 2004 and came into effect in England and Wales on 18 February 2005. This was seven years after a Private Members' Bill to ban fox hunting was introduced in the Commons by Labour backbencher Michael Foster (Worcester). The prolonged struggle to ban fox hunting illustrates several aspects of politics in Parliament:

1. the role of backbenchers and their relationship with the government
2. the involvement of pressure groups in the legislative process
3. the use of the Parliament Acts
4. the impact of devolution on the political process
5. the interaction of politics and the law

Protesters on both sides of the debate made their opinions known through public demonstrations. It is sometimes more effective to campaign quietly in the background to persuade the government of the worth of your cause.

The Bill, which received its second reading in November 1997, did not reach the Statute Book in the 1997–98 parliamentary session because the government did not allocate adequate time for the Bill to complete its parliamentary stages. In spite of a favourable Commons majority and support from public opinion there was considerable opposition from a vocal minority claiming to represent rural opinion and interests which were allegedly being overrun by an ignorant urban majority. On 1 March 1998 a massive Countryside March organised by a pressure group called the Countryside Alliance, formerly known as the British Field Sports Society, was held in London with 200,000 people attending to demonstrate their opposition to the proposed ban on fox hunting and to demand restrictions on the right to roam on private land. The Bill was 'talked out' on 13 March 1998.

The government was uneasy about the Bill for several reasons even though Labour backbenchers were solidly in favour as indeed was rural public opinion as a whole. The Home Secretary Jack Straw was unsympathetic, fearing that a ban could be difficult to implement and would lead to a breakdown in public order if rural hunts attempted to defy a statutory ban. The government did not welcome the prospect of mass arrests at a time when claims were being made that Labour was essentially an urban party looking to ride roughshod over rural interests. The supporters of the Countryside Alliance are overwhelmingly Conservative and upper middle class.

The Bill was reintroduced in the 1999–2000 session by Ken Livingstone after the Prime Minister and the Home Secretary, mindful of the overwhelming support in the PLP for the Bill, both promised that this time sufficient parliamentary time would be made available. There had been twenty two Private Members' Bills on this subject in the previous twenty years. This time the Bill lapsed in the Commons on 7 April 2000 because there was not a quorum when it came up for its second reading. A quorum of one hundred MPs is required to give a Bill its second reading; only seventy four MPs voted.

The government decided to bring matters to a head by introducing a Bill which would leave it to Parliament to decide how to solve the problem. This was an unusual piece of legislation in that it was introduced by the Home Secretary, Jack Straw, who declared that "it was not determined principally by the government." Nonetheless it was clear that this time the government would find time for the passage of the Bill through the entire legislative process. The Bill comprised three options which had been developed in discussions between the government and three opposing political factions on this emotive issue. Parliament was to choose one of the options.

The Countryside Alliance, representing those in favour of fox hunting with dogs, proposed self-regulation by Hunts by means of a newly established Independent Supervisory Authority on Hunting.

An organisation called Deadline 2000, comprising the RSPCA, the League Against Cruel Sports and the Fund for Animal Welfare, proposed a total ban on hunting with dogs. This would 'criminalise' fox hunting. The third option was proposed by the Middle Way Group, represented by three MPs, one from each of the three largest parties in the Commons. The 'middle way' would be to permit fox hunting to continue but only if consent was given by a new independent public body to be called the Hunting Authority which would issue licences to individual Hunts.

On 18 January 2001 the House of Commons voted in favour of the Deadline 2000 option. Some publicity was given to Mr Blair flying off to Belfast before the vote was taken, suggesting that the Prime Minister would have preferred the 'Middle Way' option because that would have avoided the threat of public disorder which might have been provoked by the criminalising of fox hunting.

Even this 'government' Bill did not reach the Statute Book in the 2000–2001 session. It ran into opposition in the Lords, where there were many hunt supporters who ensured that passage of the Bill would be prolonged. The Lords could have invoked its delaying powers sanctioned by the 1911 and 1949 *Parliament Acts*. (See Chapter 4.) The calling of the general election in June 2001 meant that there was not enough time to complete parliamentary scrutiny of the proposed legislation.

By now responsibility for this matter in Scotland had devolved onto the Scottish Parliament. The Labour MSP Lord (Mike) Watson (Life Peers may sit in the Scottish Parliament) introduced a Bill which, rather than focusing on the emotive issue of the rights and wrongs of bloodsports such as fox hunting and hare coursing, called

Many people in the countryside view the fox as a threat to their livelihood and hunting with dogs as a reasonable method of controlling their numbers.

for a total ban on hunting with dogs in Scotland. Watson's Bill ran foul of the Committee on Rural Affairs which refused to support the Bill because it would have outlawed all hunting with dogs, by farmers as well as by hunts. The Rural Affairs Committee, chaired by a Conservative MSP, was more favourable to 'rural interests' than the Scottish Parliament as a whole. When the Bill was reported back in September 2001, the Parliament decided by a clear majority in a free vote, eighty four to thirty four, to allow it to proceed to the next stage of the legislative process. This decision was overwhelmingly supported by Labour and SNP members while most Conservative and Liberal Democrat MSPs, representing in the main rural areas, opposed it. The *Protection of Wild Mammals (Scotland) Act* was duly passed in 2002.

Opponents of the legislation forced the issue into the courts. A call for a judicial review of the legislation by the Countryside Alliance and others was dismissed. In the process the Courts ruled that the ban on "mounted fox hunting" did not infringe the European Charter on Human Rights. Subsequently, the Master of a Borders Hunt was charged under the Act but was found not guilty by the Sheriff Court at Jedburgh on the grounds that it had not been proved that fox hunting had actually taken place. The Scottish legislation thus contained loopholes. Nevertheless, there has been a reduction in fox hunting with hounds north of the border.

In the meantime the English legislation was taking longer to reach the Statute Book. Labour had committed itself in its 2001 Election Manifesto under the heading of 'Sport' to "give the new House of Commons an early opportunity to express its view in a free vote". The same clause sought to defuse any anxieties on the part of practitioners of other rural pursuits by declaring that "we have no intention whatsoever of placing restrictions on the sports of angling and shooting." The Bill did eventually clear the Commons in the 2001–2002 session. It was then rejected by the Lords. The same action was taken in 2003 even though the government made it clear that it would invoke the *Parliament Acts* to pass the legislation without the consent of the Lords. The government duly did so and the *Hunting with Dogs Act* at last entered the Statute Book in 2004. This was only the fourth use of the *Parliament Acts* in over fifty years.

The ban on fox hunting was achieved due to the persistence of some backbench MPs backed by pressure groups outside Parliament who together overcame the reluctance of a party leadership whose radical leanings were weakened by the responsibilities of executive office. The government was sympathetic to those seeking to ban fox hunting for sport but tried to seek a compromise which would be acceptable to some rural interests.

ANTI-NUCLEAR DEMONSTRATIONS: FASLANE
Paying the price of protest

A group of 600 brightly costumed protesters gathered yesterday at Faslane base to celebrate the finale of Faslane 365. The year-long campaign included 200 protests and more than 1,000 arrests. Demonstrators believe Faslane 365 contributed to the election of the new anti-Trident SNP Scottish government by pushing the nuclear issue into the public eye. But it has cost the taxpayer an estimated £6m in policing bills and has disrupted local communities so badly that angry parents took to the streets asking the anti–nuclear protesters to stop.

Opinion polls appear to support the SNP's opposition to a replacement for Trident. According to a YouGov survey in February 66% of Scots are opposed to the government spending a capital cost of £25bn on a new nuclear missile system to replace Trident.

The original Faslane peace camp was set up in 1982 and over the years those arrested have included churchmen, Buddhist monks, politicians and an eight-week-old baby. In 2001 MP George Galloway and former SSP leader Tommy Sheridan were arrested—with Sheridan sentenced to seven days in jail.

Adapted from *The Herald*, 2 October 2007

Protest

Consultation may not give pressure groups what they want from the government. Sometimes groups want to influence the government before policy is formulated. In such cases pressure groups may feel the need to move from consultation and persuasion to protest by using more direct action.

The massacre of schoolchildren in Dunblane in March 1996 stimulated the Snowdrop Campaign which successfully called for legislation to ban the possession of handguns in private hands. Snowdrop achieved a petition of over 750,000 signatures in six weeks; shooting organisations could manage only one-tenth of that in an opposition campaign. Snowdrop was one of the first campaigns to use the Internet to distribute campaign literature. Use of the Internet has become a pressure group tactic known as cyberactivism.

Opponents of fox hunting demonstrated vigorously against it at strategic times such as the many Boxing Day Hunts up and down the country. Sometimes these demonstrations led to violent clashes between the two sides. The objective of the protesters was to generate publicity for their cause. Public opinion polls suggested that opposition to fox hunting increased because of such publicity. The eventual passage of the law banning fox hunting came about because an alliance between backbench support in Parliament and activist groups in the country overcame the reluctance of a government not prepared to sponsor the legislation. (See the case study on pages 105–106.)

Promotional groups may appear suddenly when a number of like-minded individuals decide to act in concert to right what they consider to be an injustice. Fathers4Justice was founded in December 2002 by fathers who claimed that they were experiencing unacceptable difficulties in gaining access to children after divorce or separation. The group quickly achieved publicity for its cause when it perpetrated a number of 'stunts' such as two members spending three nights on the roof of the Royal Courts of Justice dressed as Batman and Robin, and powder-bombing the Prime Minister in the House of Commons. Reactions to this behaviour ranged from sympathy for individuals in their situation to strong criticism of the 'stunts'. The serious aim of the group is to reform family law, not just on behalf of fathers but for all parents and children caught in this situation. Their 'cause' is 'responsible shared parenting'.

Protests are seldom as effective as those achieving the bans on handguns and fox hunting and the freeze on fuel tax (See page 104). Decades of CND activity have not led to Britain abandoning its nuclear defence capability because Labour leaders have agreed with the Conservatives that such a defence is required in the modern world. Faslane, the home of Britain's nuclear weapons, has witnessed decades of peaceful protests, the most recent campaign being Faslane 365 which ended in October 2007. (See extract from *The Herald*.) Anti-war groups in vain organised large STOP THE WAR demonstrations against the Iraq War. It was left to the 2005 electorate to issue a mild rebuke to the government responsible.

PRESSURE GROUPS: A LEVEL PLAYING FIELD?

On the positive side, pressure groups add to the representative and democratic dimensions of politics and government by widening participation in the decision making process of the state. The political participation of pressure groups provides the basis for a relatively new theory of politics known as 'pluralism'.

A 'pluralist' political system is one in which power is widely distributed throughout society rather than being confined to the rich, the government, MPs, or powerful groups such as large companies, the 'Establishment' and trade unions. If all sections of society are able to form groups which give them some effective influence when important decisions affecting them are being made, then a strong element of pluralism is present. Society will be that much more democratic if political participation is widespread—if no significant sections of society are excluded from political decision making. Groups may end up on opposing sides of conflicts over policy decisions. The debate over longer drinking hours found CAMRA (Campaign for Real

The increasing intrusion of the media into politics is indicated by the emergence of recent additions to the language of politics such as 'spin doctors', 'sound bites' and 'transparency'. Government and opposition parties attempt to influence what the media says about them and their opponents. They employ 'spin doctors' who interpret for the benefit of the media the meaning of political events in the hope that the media will accept their partisan point of view. Parties also rely heavily on the media during election campaigns to get their side of the story through to voters.

Alastair Campbell (left), Labour's former 'spin doctor', was said to be more powerful than most elected Ministers.

Ale) and the British Tourist Association opposed by the BMA, the Campaign against Drink Driving and various alcoholics' organisations.

The positive side of pressure group activity may be summed up as follows: pressure groups extend and improve democracy by representing the views of individuals and social organisations beyond the contributions made by voting, parliamentary representation and political parties. The negative side of pressure group politics is the claim that there is not a level playing field; that in the world of pressure groups God favours the big battalions; that some pressure groups are much more equal than others.

THE MEDIA AS 'PRESSURE AND INFLUENCE'

The media consists of newspapers, television and radio, cinema, publishing, telecommunications, music and the performing arts. Media channels inform, educate, entertain and influence those who read, watch and listen. They also convey to their readers and audiences the opinions of those who control the media and use it to advertise what they have to 'sell' which ranges from commercial goods and services to political and other opinions and values.

Media industries have grown enormously as a result of technological advances such as satellite, cable and digital television, computers and the Internet. Increasing standards of living have brought everyone within reach of the media's offerings. The advertising industry, which uses the media intensively, has become one of the leading economic sectors; the British stock market fell significantly in June 2001 when a leading advertising company announced a fall in revenues indicating an unwelcome decline in economic activity at a time when recession in the USA was threatening to repeat itself in Europe.

Controversy surrounds the subject of the media's influence on individuals and on society. Reading books and newspapers, watching television, listening to music and going to the cinema all expose individuals to the opinions and images 'communicated' by these activities. Cultural attitudes, social values, morality and political opinions are all thought to be subject to the influence of the channels of mass communication. Does behaviour described by the media affect social behaviour? Is our view of 'foreigners', such as refugees, based on media images? Does the media have a significant impact on individual voting behaviour to the extent of determining the results of general elections or referenda?

These are controversial questions which bring the media into the political spotlight not only as the means of communicating political opinion and values but also as a subject for governmental regulation to ease any undesirable aspects of the media in operation.

Newspapers and television

The media's primary role is the almost neutral-sounding one of reporting the news. However, even straight reporting can have political implications because the messages or images conveyed may favour some politicians at the expense of others. Reporting the run on the pound in September 1991 showed the Major government in a poor light but the media could hardly be expected not to report such unfavourable news.

Even more significantly, the media conveys 'opinion' as well as news, and such opinions are often clearly 'biased' in favour of particular political parties or ideologies. Many newspapers and political magazines openly proclaim their political allegiance and partisan attachments as highlighted in Chapter 2. In 2007 the Conservative and anti-EU newspapers the *Express* and the *Mail* were trying to put pressure on the Brown government to hold a referendum on the European Reform Treaty. (See Chapter 3 pages 58.) The headline in an October 2007 *Express* article on this issue was

> "Traitor (Gordon Brown) surrenders power to Europe".

The anti-EU newspaper the *Sun* also campaigned against the Treaty urging its readers to put their names to a *Sun* petition demand-

UK Politics Today

ing a Referendum. Influential radio and television programmes such as Today, Newsnight and Question Time give opportunities for journalists and the general public to question Ministers and party leaders.

Politicians and the media

The relationship between politicians and the media is ambiguous. They need each other but are suspicious and wary of each other. Politicians often complain of media bias, alleging that the press and television have misrepresented their views or emphasised events favourable to opposing political forces. At the same time politicians rely on the media to publicise their policy proposals and political views. In turn the media relies on politicians, especially those in government, to supply it with information which allows journalists to comment accurately on political matters. It is not unknown for politicians to use the media by leaking information to journalists by means of 'unattributable' briefings. The tense relationship between Blair and Brown over exactly when Blair would stand down from the premiership in favour of Brown was fed by their political friends 'leaking' bits of news designed to bolster one or the other in the ongoing conflict. Significantly, Brown made use of the media to announce in a television interview with Andrew Marr that there would be no election in 2007. Brown was criticised for not informing Parliament first before going on television.

There are some controls over what is communicated by the media and how this is done. Governments are expected to regulate the media to lessen any harmful effects it might have on society, to ensure honesty and objectivity in reporting, and so on. Yet the widespread acceptance of the need for some regulation of the media often stimulates accusations of unnecessary censorship and selfish manipulation by the government. A 'free press' has long been regarded as an essential attribute of a free, democratic society. Indeed the phrase 'the Fourth Estate' was coined many years ago, when the media was confined to the printed word, to suggest that the press should be considered along with the Monarchy, the Lords and the Commons as an essential constituent part of the democratic political system.

The role of the press, and now of the much more extensive and complex media system, is to ensure that governments do not operate in secrecy and cannot therefore act like dictators. 'Transparency' has entered the political vocabulary precisely because of widespread complaints that it was not always clear what governments were doing and why. Politicians now claim to strive for transparency, meaning that everyone should be able to see exactly what they are doing and why. 'What you see is what you get' has become one of the strident claims of many politicians.

THE MEDIA AND POLITICS

The media's political significance can be conveniently analysed under two main headings:
- Ownership, Control and Political Partisanship
- The Media and Elections (See Pages 28–30)

Ownership and Control

The media is usually divided into two main categories: print (for example daily and Sunday newspapers) and electronic (for example terrestrial and satellite television). Both have experienced massive growth in recent decades.

Television

Television and radio have been subjected to massive changes as a result of technological innovations. Until the beginning of the 1990s British television was monopolised by the terrestrial channels of the British Broadcasting Corporation (BBC) and Independent Television (ITV). The BBC is a state-owned public corporation financed by a licence fee paid by listeners and viewers. The licence fee is set by the Secretary of State for Culture, Media and Sport.

Since its origins in the 1920s, the BBC has been associated with the concept of 'public service broadcasting'. In other words the main functions of the BBC should be to educate and inform rather than to entertain. Public service broadcasting emphasises factual programmes such as documentaries rather than 'soaps'. The introduction of commercial television to Britain in the 1950s forced the BBC to compete with ITV channels which derive their revenue from selling advertising space during and between programmes. The principal defence of the BBC being financed by a licence fee is that to produce good quality public service programmes the BBC must be protected against the 'dumbing down' of programme content which would undoubtedly follow from dropping the licence fee system and subjecting the BBC to the whims of the marketplace.

Since 2007 the BBC has been governed, under a Royal Charter running to 2016, by an Executive Board led by the Director General, responsible to a BBC Trust of twelve, led by the Chairman. The new BBC Trust replaced the BBC Board of Governors whose reputation was damaged when the Chairman resigned in 2004 following publication of the Hutton Inquiry. The Charter requires the BBC to be politically neutral although it recognises its editorial independence. In recent years the appointments of both the Director General and the Chairman of the Board of Governors have aroused political controversy. In 1998 Greg Dyke was appointed as Director General by the fairly new Labour government elected in 1997. Dyke's appointment caused controversy in certain quarters because he was known to be a Labour supporter who had contributed £50,000 to p-arty funds. The Conservative leader, William Hague, declared that he could not support Dyke's appointment which went ahead regardless. The conflict in 2003–4 between the Labour government and the BBC over reporting and commenting on the conduct of the Iraq War, described in detail in Chapter 5 The Executive, led to a major shake-up in the top personnel at the BBC. This followed the resignations of both the Director General and the Chairman of the Board of Governors. The new Chairman of the BBC Trust is Sir Michael Lyons, a former local government chief executive.

Relations between the media and the government of the day may be 'touchy' because 'news' reporting is frequently seen as biased by politicians of all colours. The BBC in Scotland finds it difficult to satisfy the conflicting demands of the governments in London and Edinburgh. When Prime Minister Gordon Brown opened the BBC's new headquarters building in Glasgow in September 2007, he used the opportunity to instruct BBC personnel that they must not be too parochial in their outlook, to remember that the BBC is British. His remarks were made against a background which included a long-running debate about broadcasting a Scottish News at Six north of the border at the same time as the UK Six O'Clock News was being broadcast from London. The BBC in Scotland had gone along with the SNP leader Alex Salmond's demand that the executive branch in Scotland should now be called the Scottish government rather than the Scottish Executive which is the term used in the Scotland Act.

Independent television, including the relatively new satellite and cable channels, is subject to the authority of the Independent Television Commission (ITC) which is responsible for a code of practice ensuring quality of service, and for dealing with complaints. Its members are appointed by the government.

The position of the BBC and the quality of its programmes has been threatened by the triumph of the market and the arrival of new channels. During the Thatcher era the Conservative government, which had privatised much of the public sector, set up the Peacock Commission to investigate the BBC's status as a public corporation financed by a licence fee. It was widely assumed that the government wished to abolish the licence fee and make the BBC dependent on advertising revenue. Nevertheless, the Peacock Commission reported in favour of the BBC's existing status which was guaranteed until 2006. The BBC has been able to acquire additional revenue from its publishing interests, including the Radio Times, and by selling programmes abroad. However, there appears to be a never-ending debate about the quality of service offered by the BBC at a time when competition for viewers has intensified. Television has been generating huge revenues for sports such as football which sell access to the highest bidder. The BBC lost the televising of cricket test matches and the 2007 Rugby World Cup to the commercial channels. Should the BBC 'waste' its public revenues by spending huge amounts of money on sport in an attempt to compete for viewers with commercial television?

The Press

The British press is renowned for its massive circulation figures but its ownership is notable for being concentrated in a few hands, including multinational firms and foreign nationals. The current ownership of the major British national newspapers is shown in Table 2.16, page 29.

Britain is one of the most media-conscious societies in today's world. Circulation figures are high. About 80% of households receive a national paper. The press is usually divided into two types—tabloid, also known as the popular press, and quality broadsheet. The tabloids include the Sun, the Express, the Daily Mail, the Mirror, and the Daily Star. The quality papers are The Times, The Guardian, The Financial Times, The Independent and The Telegraph. The quality papers carry more in-depth articles and emphasise political reporting and opinion. The tabloids sell more copies daily than the broadsheets with the Sun enjoying prime position as Britain's best-selling daily paper with a circulation of 3,158,045 in August 2007. The highest selling newspaper in Britain is not one of the dailies but the News of the World, published on Sundays, which sold an average of 3,352,154 copies on Sundays in August 2007. The staunchly Conservative Telegraph is the biggest selling quality broadsheet, selling 887,289 copies.

The papers listed in Table 2.16 are British papers in that they are sold throughout the United Kingdom. In addition there are significant national/regional papers in many parts of Britain such as the Daily Record, The Herald and The Scotsman in Scotland. Almost 90% of the population read a regional or local newspaper. The Daily Record, which used to be Scotland's largest selling paper and is the sister paper of the Mirror, reaches 50% of Scottish adults. The Record sold 576,603 copies daily in May 2001 but was overtaken in July 2006 by the Sun. The Sun sold 409,034 copies daily to the Record's 375,236 in August 2007. The Herald and The Scotsman, the two Scottish papers claiming to be national in scope and quality in content, sold 69,058 and 59,981 respectively in August 2007.

News International, which owns the tabloid Sun and the 'quality' broadsheet The (London) Times, is run by the Australian born American citizen Rupert Murdoch. The Financial Times was owned by a Canadian citizen Conrad Black, but he lost control following his trial and conviction for corporate fraud in the United States. The importance of ownership was clearly illustrated when the Labour-supporting peer, Lord Hollick, took over the Express in 1999. The Express changed its political preference from Conservative to Labour in time for the 2001 election and back again to Conservative after Hollick sold it.

Freedom of Information Acts (FOIA)

Freedom of Information Acts passed in 2000 for England and Wales, and in 2002 for Scotland by the Scottish Parliament, took effect in 2005. The legislation gives individuals the right to ask any public body for all the information it possesses on any subject. In particular the legislation gives citizens the right to request any information being held on themselves. In other words citizens have a legal right to know what information about them is being held. The aim of the legislation is to provide more 'open government'. The long-term effect will be to subject public bodies to greater scrutiny. There are various exemptions to the general rule of release of information but the onus is on the public body to prove that the public interest justifies denial of the information requested. Governmental responsibility for implementing the legislation has been assigned to the newly formed Ministry of Justice, a spin off from the Home Office. There is an independent Information Commissioner responsible for the day to day running of the freedom of information scheme. The Commissioner deals with appeals against any refusals to release information.

Freedom of Information is a controversial subject. A major criticism of the delayed Bill is that it contains too many exemptions. Reports that the delay was allowing government departments to shred documents were met with the response that a rationalisation of records was taking place. The Prime Minister supported the delay on the grounds that departments would be confronted with masses of demands for the release of information and needed time to prepare for the rush. The Lord Chancellor, Blair's friend Lord Irving, and the Information Commissioner were in favour of a shorter delay.

Exemptions to the general rule of granting requests for information included:
- If the information is readily available from other sources.
- The security services: MI5, MI6 and GCHQ.
- Information covered by parliamentary privilege.
- Personal details covered by the *Data Protection Act*.

The *FOI Act* increased to seventy five years the length of time before information about the Monarch's communications with the government and information about the awards of honours could be released. The normal period is thirty years.

Most of the over 40,000 requests for information in January 2005, the first month of operation of the FOIA, were granted. One exception was the full text of the Attorney General's advice to the government that the invasion of Iraq in 2003 was legal.

One quick result of the legislation was to provide information about MPs' expenses. The House of Commons revealed that in 2000 the average expenditure claim was £118,000 for staff costs and travel. A cross-party group of MPs, supported by some Ministers, tried to make Parliament exempt from disclosure requirements on the grounds that MPs' dealings with constituents should be confidential. Opponents argue that such an exemption would bring Parliament into disrepute by enabling MPs to evade disclosing details of expenses. The Private Members' Bill containing this proposal could not find a sponsor in the House of Lords.

Chapter 7
Scottish Devolution & Electoral Systems

What you will learn.
1. The historical and electoral background to devolution.
2. The Scottish party system.
3. The effects of the electoral system on decision making in Scotland.

In May 1999 a Scottish Parliament met in Edinburgh for the first time since 1707. Its first major action was to establish a Scottish Executive (government). This Executive was drawn from Labour Party and Liberal Democrat Party MSPs who agreed to form a coalition government following the first elections to the Scottish Parliament on 6 May 1999. The creation of the Scottish Parliament and Executive, along with their Welsh counterparts, was called devolution and meant a major reform of the British Constitution. The constitutional and political consequences of these reforms will be worked out gradually in the years to come. For some, devolution paves the way for the eventual break-up of the United Kingdom. For others, devolution was a necessary step to prevent precisely such a break-up.

DEVOLUTION IN HISTORICAL PERSPECTIVE

The roots of the devolution issue which emerged in the last thirty years of the twentieth century are visible in the Treaty of Union of 1707 which eliminated Scotland's independence and its Parliament but which also recognised that 'Scotland was different'. Ever since, Scotland has demonstrated both 'British' and 'Scottish' characteristics.

For over 250 years the Scots accepted the Union characterised by parliamentary sovereignty, the Monarchy and a strong British executive (Cabinet government) without mounting any major objections. There was a certain

THE ROAD TO DEVOLUTION

The timeline below highlights the highs and lows of Scotland's struggle to establish a devolved Scottish Parliament. The low point was the failed 1979 devolution referendum, whereby a low turnout and a small majority for the Yes campaign ensured defeat for those in favour of devolution. In the same year, the Conservatives came to power and were totally opposed to devolution. The Conservative governments of Margaret Thatcher and John Major (1979–1997) were hugely unpopular in Scotland. Many of their policies, including the hated 'Poll Tax' were deeply opposed by the vast majority of Scots. The Scottish Conservative representation in Scotland was halved in 1987 and then completely eliminated in 1997 when Labour returned to power. John Major resigned and the new Conservative leader, William Hague, announced that the Conservatives would no longer oppose devolution if it was the will of the Scottish people.

October 1974: SNP consolidate their success in the February 1974 election by increasing their MPs from seven to eleven, gaining 30% of the votes. Labour government commits itself to devolved government for Scotland and Wales.

July 1978: *Scotland Act* secures Royal assent. Amendment to the Act requires a referendum to be held with a qualification that 40% of the Scottish electorate give their consent.

March 1979: Referendum is held and despite a majority of Scots voting for a Scottish Parliament, the Yes vote does not meet the required 40%. (See Table 7.2.) This ensures defeat for those in favour of devolution.

28 March 1979: The SNP withdraws its support for the minority Labour government. The Labour government is defeated on a vote of confidence and a general election is held.

May 1979: The Conservatives, under Margaret Thatcher, win a landslide victory. The SNP's support is significantly decreased and their MPs are reduced from eleven to two. The Conservatives are totally opposed to devolution.

May 1997: Labour, under Tony Blair, wins a landslide election. The Conservatives are wiped out in Scotland, with all eleven MPs losing their seats. Labour commits itself to create a Scottish Parliament and a Welsh Assembly.

amount of 'tinkering' (minor reforms) with the arrangements for the 'government of Scotland', usually in response to indications of Scottish dissatisfaction with existing arrangements expressed through voting behaviour and the party system. Nonetheless, the 'British' dimension in the government of Scotland prevailed over the 'Scottish' until the 1960s. Then the two important developments of Scotland swinging to Labour from the 1959 election onwards and the dramatic impact of the SNP in the 1970s set in motion political forces which could no longer be contained by 'tinkering'.

The establishment of a Scottish Parliament and Executive represents a decisive strengthening of the Scottish dimension and a profound reform of the British Constitution. The question which remains, and which will dominate discussions about Scottish politics for years to come, is whether the Scottish Parliament and government will permanently keep Scotland within the United Kingdom or if this is a final step which will lead to independence and the ending of the 'UK connection'.

DISTINCTIVE SCOTTISH INSTITUTIONS

The Scottish dimension was prominent from the outset of the British state. The social institutions which were retained at the time of the Treaty of Union 300 years ago are still significantly Scottish today.

Scotland's 'distinctiveness' was not insignificant. It led to Scotland being granted representation in the British Cabinet and a separate government department to look after its interests—the Scottish Office was established in 1885. Later Scotland would have legislative recognition through the establishment of a Scottish Grand Committee in the House of Commons. Scotland retained a national consciousness which refused to die in spite of the loss of independence and the growth of a strong, centralised British state with its centre in Westminster and Whitehall.

The distinctive Scottish identity was maintained by several cultural and social institutions which survived the transition from independence to Union. Foremost among these are:

▲ the educational system
▲ the Church of Scotland
▲ the legal system.

Education

Education remains one of the most significant functions of government in Scotland involving local authorities, the Scottish Government Education Department and the Scottish Qualifications Authority (formerly the Scottish Exam Board). Decisions about subject curricula, teachers' salaries, and reform of examinations have long been among the most significant to be taken within the 'Scottish political system', although autonomy has not been absolute when British governments have been adamant about comprehensive education and the publication of school league tables.

The Scottish legal system

The Scottish legal system and Scots Law constitute the third defining characteristic of Scottish distinctiveness inherited from the independent Scotland which existed before 1707. The legal system has perhaps been the most significant politically because it has required the passage of separate Scottish legislation through the British Par-

The Church of Scotland

The Church of Scotland is Presbyterian in character and is the product of a much stronger Reformation than occurred south of the border. It is Scotland's Established Church though by no means its only Church. The influence of the Church was particularly strong until the mid-nineteenth century in relation to education, poor relief and moral and social welfare. Today the Church functions politically as a pressure group, especially at the time of meetings of its General Assembly when the views of the Church are extensively reported by the Scottish media. Scotland has become much more heterogeneous in terms of religion. 16% of the Scottish population is Roman Catholic (30% in Glasgow). Significantly, the elevation of Archbishop Winning to Cardinal in 1994 was regarded as a matter of national pride and a recognition by the Vatican of Scotland's independence from England in terms of Church affairs.

liament and its implementation by devolved governmental institutions in Scotland itself.

Occasionally the distinctive features of Scots Law such as the majority verdict and the 'Not Proven' verdict hit the headlines. There have been efforts to abolish the 'Not Proven' verdict which may demand a greater burden of proof in order to convict on serious offences than would be the case if it did not exist. The separate Scottish legal system has meant that the education of lawyers and the practice of law have both remained rigorously Scottish. English lawyers are not qualified in or familiar with Scots Law (the reverse is also true) and therefore cannot practice in Scotland without acquiring the necessary training and qualifications.

National consciousness

What is significant about education, the law and the Church of Scotland is that decision making in those areas has been largely a matter for Scots living in Scotland and for Scottish institutions based in Scotland. The fact that this has happened generates the belief that this is how it should be. Also, it has maintained a degree of national consciousness which extends beyond the regionalism associated with Geordies in the North-east of England or Yorkshire Tykes. Such national consciousness has also been kept alive by Scottish culture which supports a Scottish element in the broadcasting and news media and by Scottish sport which enjoys separate national status in some sports such as soccer (the World and European Nations Cups), rugby (the Six Nations Championship), golf (the Dunhill Cup) and so on.

1997 Devolution Referendum

The 1997 devolution referendum provided a vastly different outcome from that held in 1979. Held at the beginning of a Labour government elected by a massive majority, the referendum resulted in comfortable majorities in favour of both the Scottish Parliament and the proposed tax-varying powers. Labour was united—there was no 'Labour Votes No' campaign this time. The SNP and the Liberal Democrats both supported the proposals, even though this was a short-term tactic on the part of the SNP whose objective remained Independence. Unlike 1979, there was no '40% rule' in 1997. Close

The Scottish Party System: Votes and Seats 1955–2005

Percentage Share of the Vote in British General Elections

	1955	1959	1964	1966	1970	[1]1974	[2]1974	1979	1983	1987	1992	1997	2001	2005
Labour	46.7	46.7	48.7	49.9	44.5	36.6	36.2	41.5	35.1	42.4	39.0	45.6	43.9	38.9
Conservative	50.1	47.2	40.6	37.7	38.0	32.9	24.7	31.4	28.4	24.0	25.7	17.5	15.6	15.8
Liberal	1.9	4.1	7.6	6.8	5.5	7.9	8.3	8.7	24.5	19.0	13.1	13.0	16.4	22.6
SNP	0.5	0.8	2.4	5.0	11.4	21.9	30.4	17.3	11.0	14.0	21.5	22.1	20.1	17.7

Number of Westminster Seats Won

	1955	1959	1964	1966	1970	1974[1]	1974[2]	1979	1983	1987	1992	1997	2001	2005
Labour	34	38	43	46	44	40	41	44	41	50	49	56	[3]56	[3]41
Conservative	36	32	24	20	23	21	16	22	21	10	11	0	1	1
Liberal	1	1	4	5	3	3	3	3	8	9	9	10	10	11
SNP	0	0	0	0	1	7	11	2	2	3	3	6	5	6

Table 7.1 Note: There were two elections in 1974 in February[1] and October[2]; [3] includes the Speaker

Four significant developments in Scottish electoral politics, which explain the radical changes in the arrangements for the government of Scotland proposed by Labour in 1997, are illustrated in Table 7.1.
- Scotland has developed a four-party system which has implications for the government of Scotland under the proportional electoral system of the Scottish Parliament.
- The Scottish Conservatives have suffered a long-term decline since the late 1950s. Scotland was a 'Tory-free zone' after the 1997 general election and had only one MP after the 2001 and 2005 general elections.
- The Liberal Democrats and the SNP have been beneficiaries of the move from two-party to four-party politics in Scotland.
- Labour has maintained a dominant position in spite of the existence of four parties because the first-past-the-post electoral system employed for the Westminster Parliament works in its favour. In 2001 Labour won 78% of Scotland's seventy two seats with 43.9% of the vote. In 2005 Labour won 73% of Scotland's fifty nine seats.

National consciousness in Scotland was traditionally expressed on football terracings.

to three-quarters of those voting in 1997, almost 45% of the registered electorate, supported devolution. However, slightly less than two-thirds, only 38.3% of the registered eletorate, voted for tax-varying powers. (See Table 7.2.) The 1997 vote emphasised the near to impossible constraint imposed in 1979 by the '40% rule'.

Support for the Parliament ranged from 84.7% in West Dunbartonshire and 83.6% in the City of Glasgow to 57.3% in Orkney and 60.7% in Dumfries and Galloway. Support for the tax-varying powers ranged from 75% in Glasgow to 47.4% in Orkney and 48.8% in Dumfries where the 'Noes' won, narrowly, their only 'victories'. Some local council areas on the 'periphery', the regions furthest away from the densely populated urban and industrial central belt, were least enthusiastic about the prospect of a devolved Scotland in which they might have different interests from the majority. Thus the Scottish Liberal Democrat leader, Jim Wallace, at that time MP for Orkney and Shetland and a strong devolutionist, represented an area suspicious of what devolution might bring.

ELECTION OF THE SCOTTISH PARLIAMENT

The first elections to the Scottish Parliament were held on 6 May 1999 using the two-ballot, mixed electoral system laid down in the *Scotland Act*. The 129 Members of the Scottish Parliament (MSPs) are selected by two distinct methods. Every voter has two ballots to cast. In the first ballot the traditional British 'first-past-the-post' system returns seventy three constituency MSPs. These single-member constituencies are identical to the seventy two Westminster constituencies in British general elections prior to 2005, except that Orkney and Shetland count as separate constituencies in the Scottish Parliament (hence seventy three rather than seventy two constituency MSPs). A radical redrawing of boundaries and a reduction of Scottish seats from seventy two to fifty nine was carried out before the 2005 British general election. Nevertheless, it is the pre-2005 Scottish Westminster constituencies which are used in the first ballot in Scottish Parliament elections.

In the second ballot another fifty six MSPs are elected from party lists in eight regional constituencies (seven MSPs per regional constituency) by the additional member system (AMS). In 1999 and 2003 the two ballots were printed on separate pieces of paper. In 2007 the two Scottish Parliament ballots were printed on one single piece of paper which led to claims that voters were confused, causing many to record their votes incorrectly. (See Chapter 1.)

The government's White Paper on Devolution justified this system on the grounds that its "greater proportionality" would "build stability into the overall settlement". However, the government stopped short of the high level of proportionality associated with STV in multi-member constituencies. (The operation of the AMS, which allocates list seats in the second ballot, is explained on page 123.). The major trends in voting behaviour and the degree of proportionality achieved in the first three elections to the Scottish Parliament are described in Tables 7.4–7.7

The Scottish political system has been extended and transformed by devolution. The Parliament has added an extra layer to party

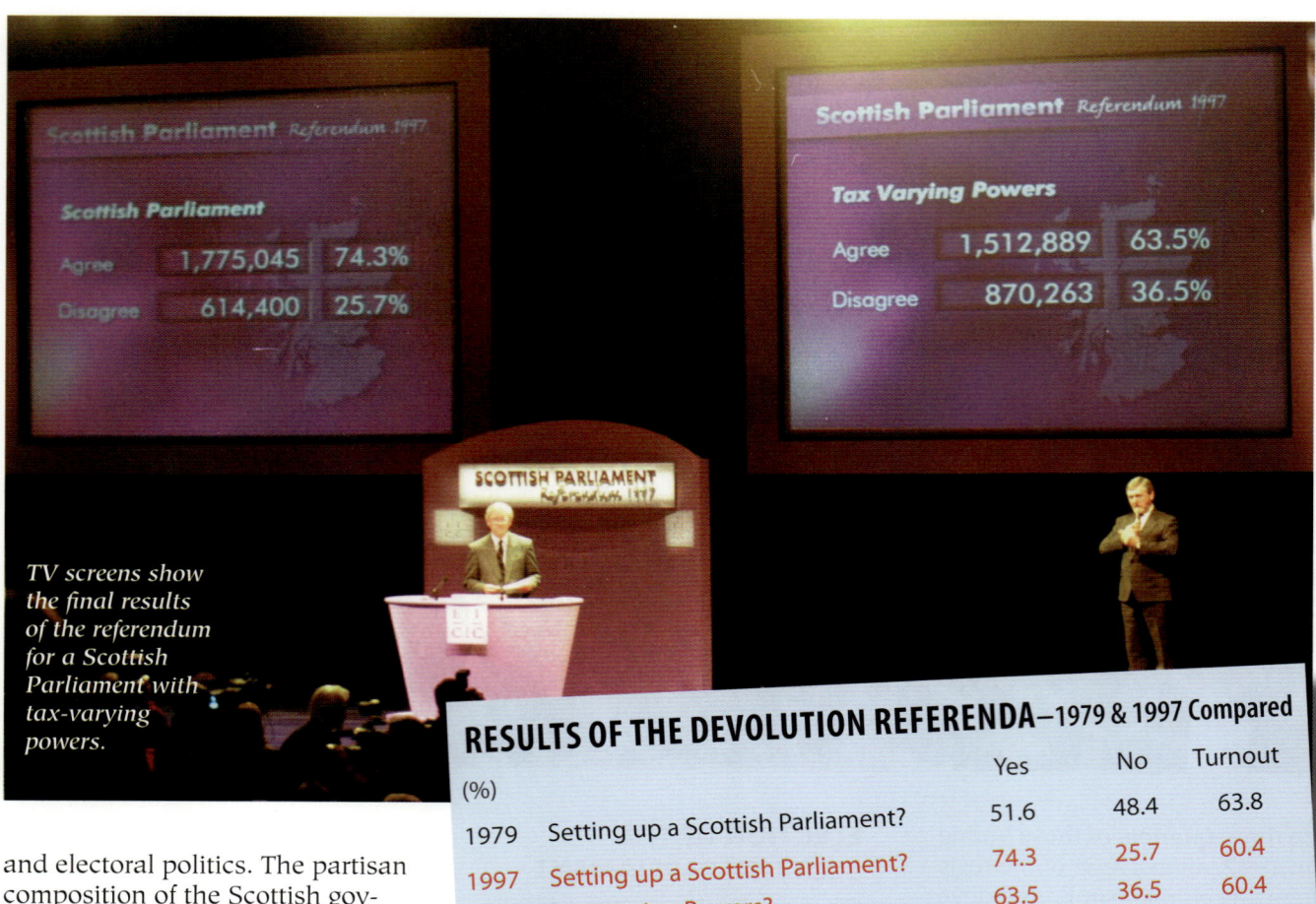

TV screens show the final results of the referendum for a Scottish Parliament with tax-varying powers.

RESULTS OF THE DEVOLUTION REFERENDA—1979 & 1997 Compared

(%)		Yes	No	Turnout
1979	Setting up a Scottish Parliament?	51.6	48.4	63.8
1997	Setting up a Scottish Parliament?	74.3	25.7	60.4
1997	Tax-Varying Powers?	63.5	36.5	60.4

Table 7.2

and electoral politics. The partisan composition of the Scottish government has been transformed because elections have so far led to government by coalition, 1999 to 2007, and government by a minority party, the SNP, since May 2007, rather than government by a single majority party which has been the British norm. The emergence of an SNP minority government led by Alex Salmond as First Minister was not generally foreseen three years earlier given the SNP's poor voting performance in both the 2004 European elections and the 2005 general election. One political commentator was moved to claim in 2004 after the European Parliament elections that "Scottish nationalism seems to be in the grip of an inexorable decline…" (A Macleod *The Times* 15 June 2004). The SNP subsequently changed its leader with Salmond, then a Westminster MP representing Banff and Buchan, replacing John Swinney.

The constituency and regional structure of membership of the Scottish Parliament is illustrated in Table 7.3. The seventy three single-member constituencies are usually listed under the eight second ballot regions when election results are reported. Of the eight regions, Glasgow and Central Scotland each have ten constituencies; the Highlands and Islands has eight; and the remaining five regions have nine constituencies each. The eight regions each elect seven list MSPs in the second ballot.

The three Islands seats have the smallest electorates; in 2007 Orkney and Shetland both had fewer than 20,000 voters and the Western Isles had 22,051. The five Highlands seats include Inverness East, Nairn and Lochaber with over 70,000 voters, one of the highest electorates. Glasgow with ten seats had the third lowest electorate and an average of 47,759 voters, well below the national average of over 53,000 voters per constituency.

The Main Contest: Labour against SNP

Labour has been the strongest Scottish party in Westminster elections since 1959, including in 2005. That status was maintained in 1999 when the Scottish Parliament was first elected. Labour was again the strongest party in 2003, but by a narrower margin. However, the most significant trend shown in Table 7.4 is the decline since 1999 in Labour's share of both votes and seats which in 2007 pushed the previously dominant party into second place behind the SNP and out of control of the government.

Table 7.4 illustrates clearly the divergent effects of the two electoral systems employed in the election of the Scottish Parliament. The first constituency ballot uses the familiar first-past-the-post system (FPTP). The second regional list ballot employs the

The Scottish Parliament: Constituencies and Regions

Region	Electorate 2007 (average size)	No of Seats	Constituencies
Highlands and Islands	337,794 (42,224)	8	Orkney; Shetland; Western Isles; Caithness, Sutherland and Easter Ross; Ross, Skye and Inverness West; Inverness East, Nairn and Lochaber; Moray; Argyll & Bute
North East	506,600 (56,296)	9	Aberdeen Central; Aberdeen North; Aberdeen South; Angus; Banff and Buchan; Dundee East; Dundee West; Gordon; West Aberdeenshire and Kincardine
Mid-Scotland & Fife	513,443 (57,049)	9	Dunfermline East; Dunfermline West; Fife Central; Fife North East; Kirkaldy; Ochil; Perth; Stirling; North Tayside
Lothians	519,115 (55,679)	9	Edinburgh Central; Edinburgh East and Musselburgh; Edinburgh North and Leith; Edinburgh Pentlands; Edinburgh South; Edinburgh West; Linlithgow; Livingston; Midlothian
Central	559,452 (55,945)	10	Airdrie and Shotts; Coatbridge and Chryston; Cumbernauld and Kilsyth; East Kilbride; Falkirk East; Falkirk West; Hamilton North and Bellshill; Hamilton South; Kilmarnock and Loudon; Motherwell and Wishaw
Glasgow	477,586 (47,759)	10	Anniesland; Baillieston; Cathcart; Govan; Kelvin; Maryhill; Pollok; Rutherglen; Shettleston; Springburn
West of Scotland	475,073 (52,786)	9	Clydebank and Milngavie; Cunninghame North; Dumbarton; Eastwood; Greenock and Inverclyde; Paisley North; Paisley South; West Renfrewshire; Strathkelvin and Bearsden
South of Scotland	514,105 (57,123)	9	Ayr; Carrick, Cumnock and Doon Valley; Clydesdale; Cunninghame South; Dumfries; East Lothian; Galloway and Upper Nithsdale; Roxburgh and Berwickshire; Tweeddale, Ettrick and Lauderdale

Table 7.3

additional member counting system (AMS) described in Chapter 1 and illustrated on page 123. In 2007 Labour won the narrowest of majorities among constituency MSPs, thirty seven of the seventy three available, in spite of winning 15,831 fewer votes than the SNP who won twenty one seats. Labour fell behind the SNP in the popular vote overall because Labour's victory margins over the SNP in its best regions, Glasgow, Central Scotland and West of Scotland, were narrower than the SNP's victory margins over Labour in the North East, the Highlands and Islands and the South of Scotland.

Table 7.1 illustrates the roller coaster character of SNP support in British general elections since the early 1970s. The SNP has also experienced fluctuating fortunes in Scottish Parliament elections. In 1999 the SNP was clearly Scotland's second party, behind Labour but significantly ahead of both the Liberal Democrats and the Conservatives. In 2003 the SNP lost ground, as did Labour, when the Scottish Socialist Party (SSP) and the Greens competed more strongly, increasing their votes and winning seats in the second ballot. Nevertheless, the SNP remained a clear second to Labour, well ahead of the Conservatives and Liberal Democrats.

The SNP made a major breakthrough in 2007, beating Labour in the percentage of the popular vote gained in both ballots and emerging as the largest party at Holyrood. The most immediate effect of the 2007 result was to give the SNP control of the Scottish government although this was as a minority administration. The SNP could not find a coalition partner with enough seats to achieve a majority in the Parliament. The SNP's commitment to Independence and an eventual referendum on this issue meant that possible partners, especially the Liberal Democrats, would not cooperate with the SNP.

Potentially the most significant feature of the 2007 results was the SNP's capture of nine seats from Labour in the first ballot. For years the SNP had been struggling to win seats in Labour's urban and industrial heartlands, but with very little success. However, the SNP's 2007 gains from Labour included seats of this kind in several regions. These SNP gains may represent a significant and permanent breaching of Labour's stronghold, an interpretation encouraged by the decline in the Labour vote in both 2003 and 2007. On the other hand, the gains may be attributable to short-term political forces at work in 2007. Which interpretation is valid may be decided by how public opinion assesses the performance of the SNP minority administration.

Conservatives and Liberal Democrats

Table 7.4 illustrates an interesting contrast in how the other two 'major' Scottish parties win seats in the Scottish Parliament under the AMS electoral system. Support for the Conservatives and the Liberal Democrats has been remark-

Scottish Parliament Election Results: 1999, 2003 & 2007

| | FIRST BALLOT (Constituencies) | | | | | | SECOND BALLOT (Regional List) | | | | | |
| | Share of Vote(%) | | | Number of Seats | | | Share of Vote(%) | | | Number of Seats | | |
	1999	2003	2007	1999	2003	2007	1999	2003	2007	1999	2003	2007
Labour	38.8	34.6	32.2	53	46	37	33.6	29.3	29.2	3	4	9
SNP	28.7	23.8	32.9	7	9	21	27.3	20.9	31	28	18	26
Liberal Democrat	14.2	15.4	16.2	12	13	11	12.4	11.8	11.3	5	4	5
Conservative	15.6	16.6	16.6	0	3	4	15.4	15.5	13.9	18	15	13
Greens	0	0	0.15	0	0	0	3.6	6.9	4	1	7	2
SSP/Solidarity	0	6.2	0.03	0	0	0	2.0	6.7	2.2	1	6	0
Others	2.7	3.4	1.8	1	2	0	5.7	9.0	8.4	0	2	1

Table 7.4 Source: Electoral Trends in Scottish Parliament Elections 1999–2007

ably consistent, with both winning around 15–16% of the vote in the first ballot and sixteen to eighteen seats overall. The third and fourth parties thus end up with almost identical representation at Holyrood, although they get there by different routes. The Liberal Democrats win most of their seats in the first ballot; in 2007 they won eleven first-past-the-post seats whereas the Conservatives managed only four. The Liberal Democrats won four of the eight Highlands and Islands constituencies, two each in Lothians, Mid Scotland and Fife, and the North East and one in the South of Scotland. They lost a seat to the Conservatives, Roxburgh and Berwickshire, in the Scottish Borders, an area traditionally loyal to the Liberals. The Liberal Democrats also lost two seats to the SNP, Argyll and Bute and Gordon, which they had won in 1999 and 2003. The Conservatives could win first ballot seats only in the South of Scotland (Ayr, Galloway and Upper Nithsdale, and Roxburgh and Berwickshire) and in Lothians (Edinburgh Pentlands). Conservative weakness in the first ballot in Scottish Parliament elections is consistent with their poor success rate in Scotland in British elections since 1997. (See Table 7.1.)

The two parties experienced different fortunes in the second ballot when the AMS counting system came to the rescue of the Conservatives who won one or two list seats in every region. In sharp contrast the Liberal Democrats have been winning only a small handful of list seats since 1999. (See Table 7.4.) They won no list seats in two regions where they were successful in the first ballot, Lothians and Mid Scotland and Fife.

The operation of AMS may be illustrated by comparing Liberal Democrat and Conservative fortunes in Lothians in 2007. The Liberal Democrats and the Conservatives won 12.7% and 13.1% of the vote respectively in the second ballot. The Liberal Democrats won two first ballot seats, Edinburgh South and Edinburgh West; the Conservatives won Edinburgh Pentlands. In the first second ballot count the Liberal Democrat share of the vote was divided by three, while the Conservative's share was divided by two. The 4.25% now accruing to the Liberal Democrats was lower than the vote share of the Greens, at 7%, who won the second list seat, and lower than Margo MacDonald's 6.7% which won the third list seat. It was also lower than the SNP's totals in the first, fourth and sixth counts and lower than Labour's total in the seventh count. So the Liberal Democrats won no list seats in Lothians. The Conservatives' 6.55%, 13.1% divided by two, was high enough to win them the fifth list seat.

Winning first ballot seats may lead to a party not winning list seats if it does not win enough votes in the region in the second ballot. How this works may be illustrated by comparing SNP and Liberal Democrat fortunes in the Highlands and Islands in 2007. Both won four of the eight seats available in the first ballot. The SNP then picked up two list seats and the Liberal Democrats none because the SNP won almost 35% of the popular vote in the second ballot compared to the Liberal Democrats' 19.9%. The SNP share was high enough, even after being divided by five, to win the fourth and sixth list seats. The seventh list seat was won by Labour whose vote was 5.69% after winning the first and third list seats, higher than the Liberal Democrats' 3.98% after its popular vote share was divided by five. (Work it out!).

These contrasting Conservative and Liberal Democrat fortunes focus attention on the degree of proportionality achieved by AMS compared to FPTP. Just how proportional these results are may be measured by a comparison with the results of the 2005 British general election in Scotland under FPTP. (See Tables 7.5 and 7.6.)

Proportionality in Scottish Parliament Election, 2007

	% Vote 1st Ballot	% Vote 2nd Ballot	% Seats in Scottish Parliament
SNP	32.9	31	36.4
Labour	32.2	29.2	35.7
Conservative	16.6	13.9	13.2
Liberal Democrat	16.2	11.3	12.4
Greens	0.15	4	1.6

Table 7.5

Proportionality in British Election in Scotland, 2005

	% Vote	Share of Scottish Seats in House of Commons
Labour	39.5	67.8
Liberal Democrat	22.6	18.6
SNP	17.7	10.2
Conservatives	15.8	1.7

Table 7.6

Labour has been the big winner in Scotland under FPTP, the Conservatives the big losers. AMS clearly produces much more proportional results.

Smaller Parties and Independents

The new electoral system provides opportunities for minor parties which have traditionally not done well under the FPTP system. Table 7.4 shows that parties such as the Greens and the SSP have not prospered in the first ballot but have experienced some degree of success in the second ballot, especially in 2003. Both parties, which follow different electoral strategies, were represented at Holyrood from 1999 until 2007 although their fortunes have fluctuated. The Greens contested almost no first ballot constituencies (only Glasgow Kelvin in 2007) whereas the SSP contested most of them in the first two elections. Both managed to win one list seat in 1999, the SSP in Glasgow and the Greens in Lothians. Both parties achieved a major breakthrough in 2003. Again neither won at the single-member constituency level but the Greens won seven list seats and the SSP won six.

Both parties were 'squeezed' in 2007 by the intensification of the mainstream struggle between Labour and the SNP for control of the Executive. The Greens dropped from almost 7% to 4% of the vote nationally. They also dropped below the threshold needed to retain the list seats won in 2003 except in Lothians where Robin Harper was re-elected with 7% of the vote and Glasgow where Patrick Harvie was re-elected. The SSP fell away because of a bitter internal dispute between their former leader, Tommy Sheridan, and others. Sheridan's new party, Solidarity, won more votes in 2007 than the SSP but no seats in the Scottish Parliament. The SSP's only electoral success in 2007 was in the local government elections where Ruth Black was elected un-

The AMS system encourages single issue candidates. At the 2007 election candidates organised around the issue of NHS reform.

der STV in the four-member Glasgow Craigton constituency.

John Swinburne, representing the Scottish Senior Citizens Unity Party, won 6.5% of the vote in Central Scotland in 2003, enough to win a list seat. Winning 2.5% in 2007 was not enough for him to retain the seat.

There have been a few individual Independent successes. Dennis Canavan and Dr Jean Turner have, in the past, been elected in the first ballot and Margo MacDonald in the second. These people represent different individual or independent routes to Holyrood. Canavan and MacDonald were both highly recognised experienced party politicians who fell out with their party hierarchies. Canavan first entered the Westminster Parliament in October 1974. He was re-elected in the subsequent elections up to and including the 1997 Labour landslide when he represented Falkirk West. Canavan, who always had a strong interest in Scottish affairs, wished to stand for the Scottish Parliament in 1999 while still in the House of Commons. Labour did not select him to run for the Scottish Parliament, so he stood in the first ballot (FPTP) and won as an Independent in 1999 and 2003. He stood down in

Party Representation in the Scottish Parliament 1999–2007

	1999	2003	2007
Labour	56	50	46
SNP	35	27	47
Conservative	18	18	17
Liberal Democrat	17	17	16
Green	1	7	2
SSP/Solidarity	1	6	0
Others	1	4	1

Table 7.7

2007 when Labour regained what had been regarded as a 'safe seat'. Canavan's success was based on retaining the loyalty of Labour supporters in his local constituency in spite of the Scottish party's refusal to select him.

Dr Jean Turner, elected in the first ballot in 2003 for Strathkelvin and Bearsden, illustrates the occasional power of single issue politics in elections. Dr Turner, a retired GP, represented the views of protesters against the proposed closure of Stobhill Hospital in the north of Glasgow. She won by only thirty eight votes in a traditional Labour constituency but lost in 2007 when Labour regained the seat.

Another major party dissident to enter the Scottish Parliament is Margo MacDonald, a long-standing SNP member who, like Canavan, fell out with her party over selection procedures. MacDonald achieved nationwide recognition by winning Govan for the SNP in a November 1973 by-election. She then became a media personality and was elected in Lothians from the SNP regional list in 1999. She fell out with her party over her position on the regional list as the 2003 election approached. MacDonald decided to stand as an Independent list candidate in Lothians. She secured election with 10.2% of the vote and repeated that success with 6.7% in 2007.

The Partisan Composition of the Scottish Parliament

Scotland's devolved system of government is, like its British counterpart, a parliamentary system. However, there is one significant difference. The AMS electoral system is clearly less likely than FPTP to produce a majority party in the legislature and a Scottish government based solely on that majority party.

The distribution of the 129 MSPs among the competing parties since 1999 is to be found in Table 7.7. No party has yet won an absolute majority. Labour won 43.4% of Holyrood seats in 1999 and 38.8% in 2003; the SNP won 36.4% in 2007. The SNP had the second highest number of seats in the first two elections, but it was the Liberal Democrats who joined with Labour to form the Scottish Executive whose overall majority was eight in 1999 but only three in 2003. In 2007 the coalition parties of the previous eight years fell three short of an overall majority. The SNP, the only party to gain seats compared to 2003, did not have a majority. The SNP made clear that it would not drop its commitment to holding a referendum on the Independence issue. This stance ruled out the three other major Scottish parties as coalition partners. The two Greens agreed to support the SNP in Parliament in return for the convenership of a Holyrood committeee and SNP support on environmental issues.

IMPACT OF THE NEW VOTING SYSTEM: CONCLUSIONS

The additional member electoral system, incorporating a strong element of PR, was introduced to reduce the alleged deficiencies of the first-past-the-post system. What have been the principal consequences for Scottish politics of its operation since 1999?

A fairer result

There is no doubt that AMS increases proportionality by reducing the gaps between shares of votes and shares of seats. In 1999, for the first time since 1955, Labour did not win a majority of seats in a Scottish-wide election, an outcome which was repeated in 2003 and 2007. In sharp contrast, in 2005 the first-past-the-post system awarded Labour almost 70% of Scottish seats in the House of Commons with only 39.5% of the Scottish vote.

Coalition government or Minority Party government

The second consequence of AMS was apparent immediately in 1999 with the formation of a Labour–Liberal Democrat coalition led by Donald Dewar (Labour) as First Minister and Jim Wallace (Liberal Democrat) as Deputy First Minister. To enjoy the barest majority in the Scottish Parliament on its own (sixty five MSPs), a party would have to win almost half of the overall composition of the Parliament (129 in total) in the first ballot. In 1999 Labour won fifty three seats in the first ballot which left it twelve seats short of an overall majority. The second ballot gave Labour only three of the fifty six list seats available, leaving the party nine seats short of a majority at Holyrood. Coalition government rather than Labour attempting to govern on its own as a minority Executive was the outcome of inter-party negotiations in the immediate aftermath of the election.

The 1999 result was repeated in 2003, although the coalition had a smaller majority, and coalition government for Scotland began to be regarded as a permanent feature of the AMS system. The 2007 election took the government of Scotland in a different direction when the SNP overtook Labour as the strongest party in the Parliament, but only by a single seat. Labour and the Liberal Democrats did not have a majority. The SNP could not find a coalition partner with enough seats to provide a parliamentary majority because of its stance on Independence and its stated intention to hold a refer-

Proliferation of Parties: Glasgow Region Second Ballot 2007

Winning 10% of the vote	Winning 5-10% of the vote	Winning 4-5% of the vote	Winning 1-2% of the vote	Winning Less than 1% of the vote
Labour	Liberal Democrats	Solidarity	British National Party	Scottish Unionist Party
SNP	Conservatives		Scottish Senior Citizens Unity Party	Publican Party
	Greens		Scottish Christians Party	United Kingdom Independence Party
			Socialist Labour Party	Scottish Voice
			Christian People's Alliance	SACL
			Scottish Socialist Party	Communist Britain
				9% Growth

More parties stood in other regions including:
Free Scotland, Scottish Jacobite, Raving Looney, Equal Parenting Alliance
Peace Party, Had Enough, Scottish Enterprise, Save NHS

Table 7.8

endum on this issue. The only two parties with enough seats to form a majority coalition were Labour and the SNP and they were always unlikely to be coalition partners because of the bitter rivalry between them. There was a widespread feeling that since the SNP had 'won' the election it should be allowed to form the new Scottish Executive even if it could not find a partner to establish a majority coalition. Thus Scotland moved from the novelty of coalition government to the novelty of minority party government.

Small parties encouraged and sometimes rewarded

The third tendency of AMS in practice has been the occasional capture of a few seats by small or minor parties with relatively small shares of the popular vote. In 2003 the Greens and the SSP won thirteen out of fifty six seats in the second ballot. The presence of Green and SSP MSPs in the Scottish Parliament would not have been achieved under first-past-the-post. This feature has been erratic in so far as the significant gains of both the Greens and the SSP in 2003 were almost eliminated in 2007 when they lost votes and seats as the SNP surged into first place. Thanks to AMS the Greens hung on with two list seats, one each in Glasgow and Lothians.

The electoral fortunes of Tommy Sheridan, the former leader of the Scottish Socialist Party, illustrate the differential impact of the various electoral systems employed in Scotland in recent years. Sheridan represented the Pollok ward of Glasgow City Council from 1995 to 2003. Although these elections were decided by the first-past-the-post system, Sheridan defeated the major party candidates because he built up strong support in a small, relatively deprived area where he was well known. In 1999, on the same day as the Scottish Parliament elections, Sheridan won his local government seat (2,972 voted) with 42.5% of the vote, beating the Labour candidate into second place. In the first ballot of the Scottish Parliament elections (first-past-the-post), Sheridan stood in the Pollok parliamentary constituency (26,080 voted) winning 21.5% of the vote and coming third behind the Labour/Co-op and SNP candidates. The AMS counting system in the second ballot in the Glasgow regional constituency, with an electorate exceeding half a million, returned Sheridan and the Liberal Democrat Robert Brown to the Scottish Parliament with 7.25% and 7.21% of the vote respectively. Sheridan's electoral success came to an end in 2007 due to a spectacular court case and the breakup of the SSP into warring factions. Sheridan established a new party which he named Solidarity.

Solidarity did best in Glasgow winning 4% of the vote in the second ballot, down from the SSP's 16% in 2003 and not enough to get Sheridan elected.

Greater voter choice

There has been a large increase in the number of parties and individual candidates competing for seats in the second ballot. No fewer than twenty three parties and Independents contested the second ballot in both Glasgow and the Lothians in 2007 compared to fourteen and seventeen respectively in 2003. (See Table 7.8.)

The second ballot and the proliferation of parties have given voters the opportunity to vary their allegiance by voting for more than one party. The four major parties have all experienced a drop in support between the two ballots as some voters move to support other parties in the knowledge that their votes might not be 'wasted'. In addition to the parties which won second ballot seats, the Scottish electorate gave 8% of its votes to parties like those listed in Table 7.8 in 2003 and 2007.

The Greens and the SSP have been the principal beneficiaries of the second ballot counting system, along with the Independent Margo MacDonald and in 2003 the Scottish Senior Citizens Unity Party. However, the 2007 results emphasise that smaller parties are not guaranteed representation if the major party battle intensifies and their second ballot regional vote shares fall below 5–6%.

Parties rewarded for votes achieved

AMS has maintained the four-party character of Scottish politics by coming to the rescue of the Conservatives. In 1999 the Conservatives won eighteen list seats compared to none in the first ballot. Unlike Westminster, the Scottish Parliament has not been in danger of becoming a 'Tory Free Zone'. The SNP has also performed strongly in the second ballot. In 1999 the SNP won exactly half of the fifty six second ballot list seats compared to only seven individual constituencies. In 2007 the SNP was the most successful party in terms of making the most of the two sections of the Scottish Parliament electoral system.

Gender Representation in the Scottish Parliament

One of the most striking features of the first election to the Scottish Parliament in 1999 was that forty eight of the 129 MSPs were women, 37% of the total membership. This was double the proportion of women in the House of Commons and close to the 40% achieved in Sweden.

The number of women MSPs had fallen slightly by 2007, down from forty eight in 1999 to forty three, one-third of the membership. Slightly more women, proportionately, were elected in the first ballot. Labour had the highest proportion of women MSPs, exactly 50% of Labour representation at Holyrood. More than half the Labour MSPs elected in the first ballot were women. Labour and the SNP were more successful than other parties at getting women elected in the first ballot.

Women MSPs were evenly distributed among the eight regions, between five and seven per region, other than the Highlands and Islands where only two women MSPs were elected (Mary Scanlon, Conservative, and Rhoda Grant, Labour).

Women Candidates and MSPs by Party: 2007

	Constituency Seats (73)		AMS List Seats (56)	Totals	
	Nº of Women Candidates	Nº Elected	Number of Women Elected	Nº	%
Labour	33	20/37	3/9	23/46	50
SNP	24	5/21	7/26	12/47	26
Conservative	15	0/4	5/13	5/17	29
Liberal Democrat	22	1/11	1/5	2/16	12.5
Others	NA	0	1/3*	1/3*	
Totals		26/73	17/56	43/129	33

Table 7.9
* 'Others' are the two Greens, both male, and the Independent Margo MacDonald

Illustration of the Additional Member Counting System

The counting method for the additional member system is described in the White Paper on the Scottish Parliament.

1. "Each elector will be entitled to cast two votes: one for a constituency MSP and one for the party of his/her choice."

2. "Votes for constituency MSPs will be counted on a 'first-past-the-post' basis."

3. "The fifty six additional members will be elected in eight 7-member constituencies (the existing European constituencies) as follows:"
   - "The number of votes cast for each party … will be counted."
   - "The number of votes cast for each party will then be divided by the number of constituency MSPs gained in Parliamentary constituencies … plus one".
   - "The party with the highest total after the (above) calculation is done gains the first additional member."
   - "The second to seventh additional members are allocated in the same way but additional members gained are included in the calculations."

The operation and impact of the AMS counting system is illustrated below by working out the counting of votes from the second ballot and the subsequent allocation of the seven additional list seats for the Glasgow regional constituency in 1999.

1999 Glasgow Voting Results in Scottish Parliament Elections

	No. of MSPs from 1st ballot	Votes from 2nd ballot
Labour	10	112,588
SNP	0	65,360
Conservative	0	20,239
Liberal Democrat	0	18,473
SSP	0	18,581
Greens	0	10,159

Table 7.10

Allocation of MSPs from the Second Ballot using the formula: $\dfrac{\text{Number of Second Ballot Votes}}{\text{Number of MSPs} + 1}$

	1st Count	2nd Count	3rd Count	4th Count	5th Count	6th Count	7th Count
Labour	$\dfrac{112{,}588}{10+1} = 10{,}235$	$\dfrac{112{,}588}{10+1} = 10{,}235$	$\dfrac{112{,}588}{10+1} = 10{,}235$	$\dfrac{112{,}588}{10+1} = 10{,}235$	$\dfrac{112{,}588}{10+1} = 10{,}235$	$\dfrac{112{,}588}{10+1} = 10{,}235$	$\dfrac{112{,}588}{10+1} = 10{,}235$
SNP	$\dfrac{65{,}360}{0+1} = \mathbf{65{,}360}$	$\dfrac{65{,}360}{1+1} = \mathbf{32{,}680}$	$\dfrac{65{,}360}{2+1} = \mathbf{21{,}786}$	$\dfrac{65{,}360}{3+1} = 16{,}340$	$\dfrac{65{,}360}{3+1} = 16{,}340$	$\dfrac{65{,}360}{3+1} = 16{,}340$	$\dfrac{65{,}360}{3+1} = \mathbf{16{,}340}$
Conservative	$\dfrac{20{,}239}{0+1} = 20{,}239$	$\dfrac{20{,}239}{0+1} = 20{,}239$	$\dfrac{20{,}239}{0+1} = 20{,}239$	$\dfrac{20{,}239}{0+1} = \mathbf{20{,}239}$	$\dfrac{20{,}239}{1+1} = 10{,}119$	$\dfrac{20{,}239}{1+1} = 10{,}119$	$\dfrac{20{,}239}{1+1} = 10{,}119$
Liberal Democrat	$\dfrac{18{,}473}{0+1} = 18{,}473$	$\dfrac{18{,}473}{0+1} = 18{,}473$	$\dfrac{18{,}473}{0+1} = 18{,}473$	$\dfrac{18{,}473}{0+1} = 18{,}473$	$\dfrac{18{,}473}{0+1} = 18{,}473$	$\dfrac{18{,}473}{0+1} = \mathbf{18{,}473}$	$\dfrac{18{,}473}{1+1} = 9{,}236$
SSP	$\dfrac{18{,}581}{0+1} = 18{,}581$	$\dfrac{18{,}581}{0+1} = 18{,}581$	$\dfrac{18{,}581}{0+1} = 18{,}581$	$\dfrac{18{,}581}{0+1} = 18{,}581$	$\dfrac{18{,}581}{0+1} = \mathbf{18{,}581}$	$\dfrac{18{,}581}{1+1} = 9{,}290$	$\dfrac{18{,}581}{1+1} = 9{,}290$
Greens	$\dfrac{10{,}159}{0+1} = 10{,}159$	$\dfrac{10{,}159}{0+1} = 10{,}159$	$\dfrac{10{,}159}{0+1} = 10{,}159$	$\dfrac{10{,}159}{0+1} = 10{,}159$	$\dfrac{10{,}159}{0+1} = 10{,}159$	$\dfrac{10{,}159}{0+1} = 10{,}159$	$\dfrac{10{,}159}{0+1} = 10{,}159$
MSP awarded to	**SNP**	**SNP**	**SNP**	**Conservative**	**SSP**	**Lib Dem**	**SNP**

Table 7.11

Labour won all ten of Glasgow's constituency MSPs in the first ballot, so Labour's second ballot vote is divided by eleven in the first count; the vote totals for all other parties are divided by one because none of them won a seat in the first ballot.

Thus Labour with over 40% of the popular vote in the second ballot won no list seats because its monopoly of seats in the first ballot meant that its second ballot vote total was divided by eleven. The votes of four other parties exceeded Labour's 10,235 votes in the first count. The SNP won four Glasgow list seats because it came a strong second in the second ballot with 25.5% of the popular vote. This enabled the SNP to win the first three list seats. The Conservatives, the Liberal Democrats and the SSP each won about 7% of the vote, enough to win one list seat. The Greens would have won the ninth seat if there had been two more list seats available.

Chapter 8
The Scottish Government

What you will learn.
1. The Scottish Parliament as an arena for cooperation and decision making.
2. The distribution of powers between the Scottish and UK Parliaments.
3. Cooperation and conflict between the Scottish and UK Parliaments.

The structure and functions of Scotland's devolved government are to be found in the White Paper 'Scotland's Parliament' which was published in July 1997 and in the *Scotland Act* passed by the British Parliament in 1998. It is made clear in the White Paper that Scotland's devolved institutions are to follow British constitutional and political practice and traditions: "The Scottish Executive will operate in a way similar to the UK government and will be held accountable to the Scottish Parliament."

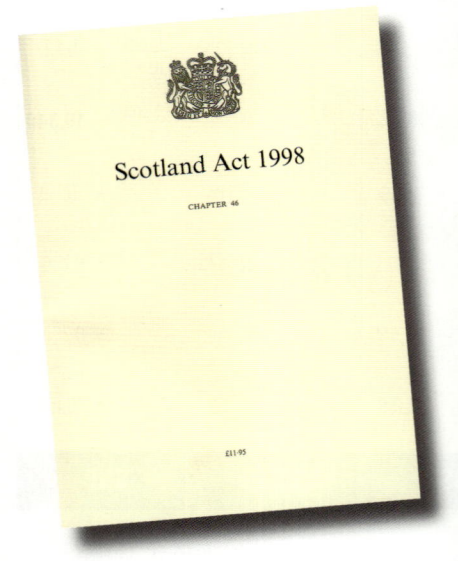

There are clear differences between the British and Scottish Parliaments. Scotland has a unicameral parliament and the relationship between the political parties is less oppositional. Unlike Westminster, the debating chamber is arranged in a semicircle, which reflects the desire to encourage consensus amongst MSPs. The Scottish Parliament reflects a new kind of politics, most obviously in terms of proportionality and gender balance.

FOUNDING PRINCIPLES OF THE SCOTTISH PARLIAMENT

The Scottish Parliament has four founding principles agreed by the consultative steering group established by the Secretary of State for Scotland in 1997. The group sought to create founding principles which would result in an effective and accountable Parliament answering the needs of the Scottish people. The founding principles are:

Sharing Power
Power should be shared between the Parliament, the Scottish Executive and the people of Scotland. The Presiding Officer sets aside all party loyalties and acts as a neutral chairperson in debates in the Scottish Parliament. The Presiding Officer also chairs the Parliamentary bureau which is made up of representatives from the political parties and which controls the programme of business for the Parliament. The committee system (see pages 125–126) promotes power sharing since MSPs from all parties are represented both on the Committees and as Conveners and Deputy Conveners. Furthermore, the public have direct access to influence parliamentary legislation.

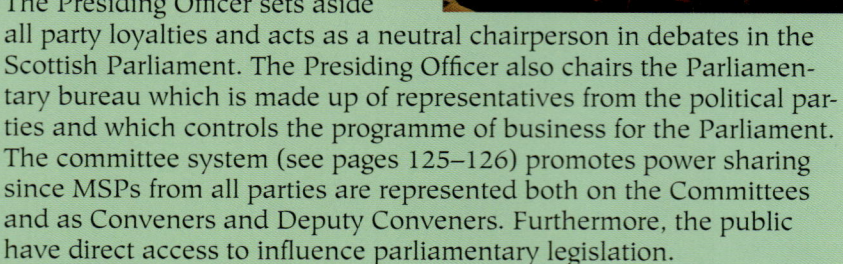

Accountability
Clear guidelines and structures through a rigorous code of conduct for Members of the Scottish Parliament and the strong role of Committees create accountability.

Accessibility, openness and participation
The Parliament's Research and Information Group (RIG) is influenced by the above principle. The RIG provides research services, information services and participation services. Parliament sittings take place during normal business hours and chamber debates and Committee meetings are open to the public and are often held in places other than Edinburgh.

Equal Opportunities
Through the Parliament's Equal Opportunities Committees, equal opportunities for all are promoted. The working hours are family friendly and parliamentary sessions take place on a regular, programmed basis. This has encouraged more women to enter politics.

UK Politics Today

SCOTTISH PARLIAMENT COMMITTEES

One of the success stories of the Scottish Parliament has been the workings of the Scottish Parliament Committees. (See Committees in Action, page 126.) Much of the work of the Scottish Parliament is done in Committees and this reflects their greater importance and influence compared to Westminster Committees. This system compensates for the fact that there is no revising chamber.

The key functions of Committees are:

- to consider proposals for legislation;
- to conduct inquiries and publish reports; and
- to hold the Scottish government/executive to account.

Committees have between six and eleven MSPs and are selected with regard to the balance between the parties in the Parliament. Convenerships are also shared between the political parties. The Transport, Infrastructure and Climate Change Committee is chaired by Patrick Harvie of the Green Party. This was part of the deal struck with the SNP in return for the support of the Green Party. The SNP should have had convenership of this Committee. Committee meetings usually take place in the Parliament's committee rooms on Tuesdays and Wednesdays when Parliament is sitting. Committees can also meet at other locations throughout Scotland.

There are two types of Committees. Mandatory Committees must be set up under the Scottish Parliament's standing orders, while Subject Committees are established at the beginning of each parliamentary session. Private Bill Committees can also be set up to scrutinise Private Bills submitted to the Scottish Parliament by an outsider, either an individual or an organisation. For example, in 2003 a Private Bill Committee dealt with the complex legislation for the underground ex-

The Committees of the Scottish Parliament: Convenerships October 2007

Party	Convener	Deputy Convener
SNP	5	5
Labour	5	6
Lib Dems	2	2
Conservatives	2	2
Green	1	–

Table 8.1

MANDATORY COMMITTEES
- Finance
- European and External Relations
- Public Petitions
- Standards and Public Appointments
- Subordinate Legislation
- Audit
- Equal Opportunities
- Procedures

SUBJECT COMMITTEES
- Justice
- Transport, Infrastructure and Climate Change
- Economy, Energy and Tourism
- Education, Lifelong Learning and Culture
- Health and Sport
- Local Government and Communities
- Rural Affairs and Environment

Report by the Scottish Parliament Health Committee on Free Personal Care for the Elderly: June 2006

The Committee praised the free care policy for improving services for the elderly, helping to reduce the problem of bed blocking in hospitals and allowing many people to be supported in their own homes.

In 2005 local authorities were given £153 million to pay for free personal care for the elderly. This figure will rise to £169 million for 2007–08.

Committee's recommendations
- a detailed executive review of the finances of free personal care for the elderly
- an end to the legal loopholes which allow councils to 'ration' free personal care
- new guidelines to ensure that services such as food preparation are provided free
- Ministers should prevent councils from delaying assessments

tension to the National Gallery of Scotland.

Committees can conduct inquiries and can publish reports. Committees can call Ministers, civil servants, members of organisations and members of the public to give evidence. In 2005, for example, the Health Committee initiated an inquiry into the Scottish Executive's policy of 'free personal care for the elderly.' (See page 125.)

In December 2007 the Education Committee voted to reject government plans to scrap the student graduate endowment. The Committee was evenly split on whether to back it, but it's convener, Labour MSP Karen Whitfield, used her casting vote against the Bill. The government stated that the final decision on the proposals would be made by the Scottish Parliament.

Public Petitions Committee

The Public Petitions Committee considers petitions which have been submitted to the Scottish Parliament and may decide to refer them to other Committees for further consideration.

Petitions are submitted by individuals and groups who want to raise an issue. The public petition system is a key part of the Scottish Parliament's commitment to openness and accessibility.

All Committees have a responsibility to consider and report on any petitions referred to them by the Public Petitions Committee.

Petitions can have positive outcomes. For example they can:
- lead to changes in the law
- be considered as part of a wider inquiry
- initiate parliamentary debates
- prompt action from the Scottish government or another public body
- provide essential information to help the scrutiny of legislation
- result in changes to regulation and guidance

Viewpoints on Committees in Action

Donald Gorrie, Liberal Democrat
"They (Committees) have done some really good work and stuck to their guns against the Executive, unlike in the House of Commons. The Local Government Committee got good concessions from the Executive on the Ethical Standards Bill, on rights of appeal for councillors and extending the provisions to many quangos."

Brian Taylor BBC
"The Executive and civil servants are chilled at developments in the committee, especially when dealing with Bills. At the House of Commons Ministers are part of the committees considering legislation but at Holyrood they are just interested onlookers. They can seek to influence but ultimately they can't control them, nor can civil servants. They must win their case, and that's the importance of the new politics."

Margaret Smith Liberal Democrat
"The Committees have done an incredible job in terms of scrutiny, compared to Westminster. But we're seriously under-resourced; my Committee has half a researcher to assist us in scrutinising a budget of more than £3 billion."

Justice Committee
Convener – Bill Aitken (Conservative)   Deputy Convener – Bill Butler (Labour)

The Justice Committee considers matters which fall within the responsibility of Justice Secretary Kenny MacAskill. It can examine criminal and civil matters and community safety. It also looks at the functions of Scotland's senior law officer, Lord Advocate Elish Angiolini, other than her responsibility to investigate deaths and as head of the criminal prosecution service.

Finance Committee
Convener – Andrew Welsh (SNP)   Deputy Convener – Elaine Murray (Labour)

Regarded as one of the most powerful Holyrood Committees, a point proved by its SNP convenership, finance considers government proposals and other issues concerning budgets, public spending and tax-varying resolutions.

Health and Sport
Convener – Christine Grahame (SNP)   Deputy Convener – Ross Finnie (Lib Dem)

This Committee covers matters which fall within Health Secretary Nicola Sturgeon's remit, including the NHS in Scotland. It also deals with the relevant responsibilities of Stewart Maxwell, the Minister for Communities and Sport. Its Deputy Convener was the Environment Minister under the previous government.

In September 2007 the Health and Sport Committee supported the raising of the legal age for buying cigarettes from 16 to 18 and this was passed by the Scottish Parliament. The Committee also considered two petitions calling for changes to the ban on smoking in enclosed public places as part of their post-legislature scrutiny of the measure. The petitioners want smoking to be permitted in designated areas within pubs and clubs.

LEGISLATIVE PROCEDURES IN THE SCOTTISH PARLIAMENT

All new laws start life in the Parliament as Bills. These can be initiated by the Scottish government, a Scottish Parliament Committee, any MSP through a Members' Bill and any person or organisation through a Private Bill. To become law, any Bill must successfully negotiate three stages in the Scottish Parliament.

The vast majority of Bills passed by the Parliament are presented by the Scottish government. MSPs can put forward a Member's Bill. For example, Tommy Sheridan attempted to have a Members' Bill passed which would have introduced free school meals to all pupils in Scotland. More recently, Members' Bills were put forward to abolish prescription charges (both bills failed).

The government may consult with the relevant Committee, other interested parties and the general public.

Stage 1: General Principles

The general principles of the Bill are sent for consideration to the relevant subject Committee, known as the Head Committee. The Finance Committee is usually involved at this stage to provide detailed financial information. A debate follows in Parliament and if the general principles are acceptable the Bill goes on to stage 2.

Stage 2: Detailed Examination

The Bill is given a more detailed line-by-line consideration by one or more Committees, one of which will be the relevant subject Committee. Any MSP can put forward an amendment but proposed amendments must articulate with the general principles of the Bill. The Committee will then vote on which amendments to accept.

Stage 3: Final Consideration of the Bill

If the Bill proceeds to stage 3, Parliament will consider the Bill as amended at stage 2 and may make further amendments. If Parliament passes the Bill it is then submitted by the Presiding Officer to the Sovereign for royal assent.

Receiving Royal Assent

At this stage the Bill becomes an Act of the Scottish Parliament.

PARLIAMENT AT WORK, SESSION 2006 – 2007

Debates

Sixteen half days are allocated to non-Executive political parties. Debates on the following issues took place:

- Trident (SNP)
- Council Tax (Conservative)
- Scottish Water (Green Party)

Legislation

- Parliament examined fourteen new (draft) Bills. Of these six were Members' Bills which enable backbench MSPs to raise issues of concern
- Twenty seven Bills received Royal Assent and became Acts of the Scottish Parliament. Of these Acts twenty were Scottish Executive Bills, four were Private Bills, two were Members' Bills and there was one Committee Bill.

Committees

- Committees met on 324 occasions
- They worked on twenty nine inquiries and scrutinised twenty eight Bills and 297 pieces of subordinate legislation
- 1,460 witnesses gave evidence to Committees

SEWEL MOTIONS

Sewel motions were introduced while the *Scotland Act* was being passed in the House of Lords. Lord Sewel argued that "there will be instances where it would be convenient for legislation on devolved matters to be passed by the UK Parliament."

Today there are conflicting views over the use of these motions. One view is that they diminish the importance of the Scottish Parliament and the democratic process; others argue that Sewel motions operate to the benefit of the people of Scotland.

What is certain is that Sewel motions play a very important part in the legislative process. In the Parliament of 1999–2003, two-thirds of the Bills were dealt with under Sewel motions and were not discussed in the Scottish Parliament.

Critics of Sewel motions claim that the Scottish government is using Westminster to legislate on controversial issues. In 2004 the Scottish Executive used the Sewel motion to legislate on gay marriages, thus avoiding debate in the Scottish Parliament and in the Scottish media. Lord Elder, who helped draw up the *Scotland Act*, supports this criticism as he feels that contentious issues are being by-passed for debate through the use of Sewel legislation.

The then coalition Executive of Labour and Liberal Democrats defended Sewel. It argued that Scotland had the best of both worlds—it could adopt UK legislation it liked while concentrating on more important measures, such as the banning of smoking in public places in March 2006. An Executive spokesperson stated in 2004: "There is no question of power drifting to Westminster. The boundaries between reserved and devolved matters remain those set out in the *Scotland Act*."

The election of a minority SNP government in 2007 raises interesting issues about the future of Sewel motions. The SNP want in the short term to increase the powers of the Scottish Parliament and in the long term to establish an independent Scotland.

KEY EVENTS IN THE SCOTTISH PARLIAMENT 1997-2007

May 1999 
Donald Dewar became First Minister and Labour and the Liberal Democrats formed a coalition government. Jim Wallace, leader of the Liberal Democrats, became Deputy First Minister.

July 1999   Tuition Fees
The Cubie Committee, set up by the Scottish Parliament, rejected the UK Parliament's decision to introduce higher education tuition fees. It recommended that graduates pay into a Graduate Endownment Fund once they had graduated and reached a certain level of income. The Scottish Executive accepted the Cubie Recommendation.

May 2000   Repeal of Section 28
Section 28, Clause 2A of the *Local Government (Scotland) Act* 1986 prohibited the "promotion of homosexuality in schools". The new 1997 Labour government had pledged to repeal this legislation. In Scotland the religious establishments and the Conservatives were against repeal. The millionaire Brian Souter financed a 'Keep the Clause' campaign which was supported by the *Daily Record*. The Bill divided Scotland. Critics of the Bill argued that it was destroying the moral and religious fibre of Scottish society; supporters argued that it would create a more tolerant and equal Scotland.

July 2000   John Swinney, new SNP leader
Alex Salmond resigned as leader of the SNP. In the fight for the leadership, John Swinney defeated Alex Neil.

October 2000   Death of Donald Dewar
On 11 October Donald Dewar, the 63-year-old First Minister, died suddenly. In the leadership contest for the Labour Party, Henry McLeish defeated Jack McConnell and became the new First Minister.

November 2001   Resignation of Henry McLeish
McLeish resigned over the 'officegate scandal'. He had failed to disclose that he had sub-let his constituency office and had used the income to fund Labour's electoral campaigns. Jack McConnell became the new Labour leader and new First Minister.

2002 Free personal care for the elderly introduced

May 2003   Scottish Parliament Elections
Once again Labour was the largest party and continued its coalition government with the Liberal Democrats.

July 2004   Resignation of John Swinney
In a surprise development Alex Salmond once again became the leader of the SNP.

October 2004   Opening of the new Parliament
The Queen formally opened the new Scottish Parliament building. It opened three years late at a cost of £431 million (the original estimate had been £40 million).

May 2005   New Liberal Democrat Leader
Jim Wallace resigned as leader of the Liberal Democrats. Nicol Stephen became the party's new leader and the new Deputy First Minister.

October 2005   Resignation of Conservative leader
David McLetchie, leader of the Scottish Conservatives, resigned, stating that the recent press coverage surrounding his expenses claims had been damaging and a major distraction from efforts to rebuild support for the Conservative Party. Annabel Goldie was elected the new leader.

March 2006   Ban on Smoking in public places

April 2006   Introduction of free eye tests

May 2007   Scottish Parliament Elections
A historic victory for the SNP as it became the largest party and formed a minority administration with Alex Salmond as First Minister.
Scotland's first Asian MSP, Bashir Ahmad, was elected to the Scottish Parliament as an SNP regional list MSP.

September 2007
Wendy Alexander replaced Jack McConnell as leader of Scottish Labour.

October 2007
Age for buying cigarettes raised to 18.

UK Politics Today

TENSION BETWEEN CONSTITUENCY AND LIST MSPs

One consequence of the electoral system is that the traditional link between constituents and their representatives is now more complex. The constituency MSP represents a specific area and, having defeated other party candidates in a straightforward FPTP contest, he/she can claim to be the legitimate person to represent the constituents in an area, for example West Renfrewshire. In the 2007 elections Trish Godman, Labour, was elected as the constituentcy MSP. However, voters in West Renfrewshire are also represented by seven list MSPs. These are the list MSPs for West of Scotland who are elected by the second, regional list, vote. Among these seven is Annabel Goldie, leader of the Scottish Conservatives and a resident of West Renfrewshire. As a leader of a political party, Annabel Goldie has a far higher profile than Trish Godman. Constituents in West Renfrewshire can contact either Labour's Trish Godman about issues in their own area or instead they may contact any of the additional 'list MSPs' who may belong to another party and who serve the wider 'regional' area.

Both constituency and list MSPs carry out the same duties and have the same responsibilities. However, party politics ensures ongoing tension. In 2001 Andrew Wilson, an SNP list MSP, appeared before the Parliament's Standards Committee. The constituency MSP, Labour's Cathie Craigie, had raised a complaint that Wilson had described himself as the 'local' MSP on party posters in the Cumbernauld and Kilsyth constituency. Mr Wilson apologised to the Standards Committee, and no further action was taken.

Both constituency and list MSPs complain about each other's actions. Constituency MSPs are convinced that list MSPs 'cherry pick' local issues and conduct electioneering with the purpose of winning the seat at a future election. In contrast, list MSPs argue that constituency MSPs regard them as 'second class politicians' and that they work just as hard as constituency MSPs.

In 2003 Brian Wilson, who at the time was a Labour Westminster MP and a former government Minister, created controversy when he stated that list MSPs "were under-employed wastes of space" and that he "would not weep any tears if the list system was done away with." Peter Peacock, list MSP for the Highlands and Islands and Scotland's then Education Minister said "I am neither under-employed nor a waste of space and I'm on my way to give evidence to a parliamentary Committee so I have to go."

WHAT IS THE SCOTTISH EXECUTIVE?

Under paragraph 44 of the *Scotland Act* 1998, there "shall be a Scottish Executive".

The Scottish Executive is the government in Scotland for devolved matters and is responsible for formulating and implementing policy in these areas.

However, after the Scottish Parliament elections of 2007 the new SNP administration announced that the Scottish Executive was to be renamed and rebranded as the 'Scottish government'. While this is now the case, the name 'Scottish Executive' is still the legal name since any change must come about with an amendment to the *Scotland Act* and not by the wishes of the First Minister, the Scottish Executive or the Scottish Parliament.

Nevertheless, the original symbol of the Scottish Executive, which had the Royal Arms for Scotland and the words 'The Scottish Executive' in both English and Scottish Gaelic has been replaced with the flag of Scotland and the words 'The Scottish Government'.

The Scottish government building in Edinburgh showing the new logo.

The Scottish government therefore is the executive branch of government in Scotland and in practice is formed from the party or parties holding a majority of seats in the Scottish Parliament. It is led by the First Minister who is nominated by the Parliament and who in

Extract from the Scotland Act 1998
The Scottish Executive
(1) There shall be a Scottish Executive whose members shall be—
(a) the First Minister,
(b) such Ministers as the First Minister may appoint, and
(c) the Lord Advocate and the Solicitor General for Scotland.
(2) The members of the Scottish Executive are referred to collectively as the Scottish Ministers.

Lord Advocate excluded from new Cabinet

SCOTLAND'S top law officer will no longer sit in the Scottish Executive Cabinet, it emerged last night.

The Lord Advocate has sat in on Cabinet meetings for the past eight years but Alex Salmond has decided he wants to de-politicise the post.

Elish Angiolini, the current Lord Advocate, will have to stay out of the Cabinet.

Mr Salmond said he wanted law officers who were "independent of politics".

However, under UK law, the Lord Advocate remains both a member of the Scottish government and its legal adviser.

Adapted from *The Scotsman* 23 May 2007

Choosing the First Minister and the Executive

After a Scottish Parliament election, a First Minister is formally nominated by the Parliament before being officially appointed by the Monarch on the advice of the Presiding Officer. The Scottish Parliament has twenty eight days in which to nominate one of its members for appointment as First Minister who in turn appoints the Scottish Ministers to make up his/her Cabinet with the agreement of Parliament and the approval of Her Majesty the Queen.

The current First Minister of Scotland is Alex Salmond of the Scottish National Party (SNP). He made political history after becoming the first Nationalist to be elected First Minister of Scotland. The SNP leader was voted into office by Parliament after seeing off a final challenge from Scottish Labour leader Jack McConnell by forty nine votes to forty six, after he was supported by the Greens while the Liberal Democrats and the Conservatives abstained. Consequently, Parliament nominated him to be First Minster on 16 May 2007 following the Parliamentary elections held on 3 May 2007 and he was officially appointed by the Queen on 17 May 2007.

turn appoints Scottish Ministers to make up a Cabinet, but only with the agreement of Parliament and the approval of the Monarch.

As First Minister, Alex Salmond is the head of the devolved Scottish government. He leads the Scottish Cabinet and is responsible for development, implementation and presentation of government policy, for constitutional affairs, and for promoting and representing Scotland. He is also directly accountable to the Scottish Parliament for his actions and the actions of the Scottish government.

There is no fixed term of office for the First Minister, unlike the four year maximum term for Members of the Scottish Parliament. Instead, after appointment the First Minister can remain in position until s/he resigns, is dismissed or dies. There have only been four First Ministers in the short history of Scotland's Parliament: the first, Donald Dewar, died in office and the second, Henry McLeish, resigned. In both these circumstances, it was the responsibility of the Presiding Officer to appoint someone to serve as First Minister in the interim, until the Scottish Parliament decided on a new nominee to be presented to the Monarch for formal appointment. The third, Jack McConnell left office after the 2007 election which saw the SNP become the biggest party in the Parliament. Alex Salmond is the fourth and current First Minister.

The term 'Scottish Ministers' collectively refers to the First Minister, the Ministers, the Lord Advocate and the Solicitor General who together make up the Scottish government. Each Minister or Deputy Minister is responsible for a particular department and will indicate to the Parliament what actions it intends to take and what legislation (laws) it wants the Parliament

Scotland's First Ministers 1999–2008

First Minister	Term of Office	Reason for end of office
Donald Dewar	7 May 1999–11 October 2000	Died
Henry McLeish	27 October 2000–8 November 2001	Resigned
Jack McConnell	22 November 2001–17 May 2007	Lost Election
Alex Salmond	17 May 2007–?	

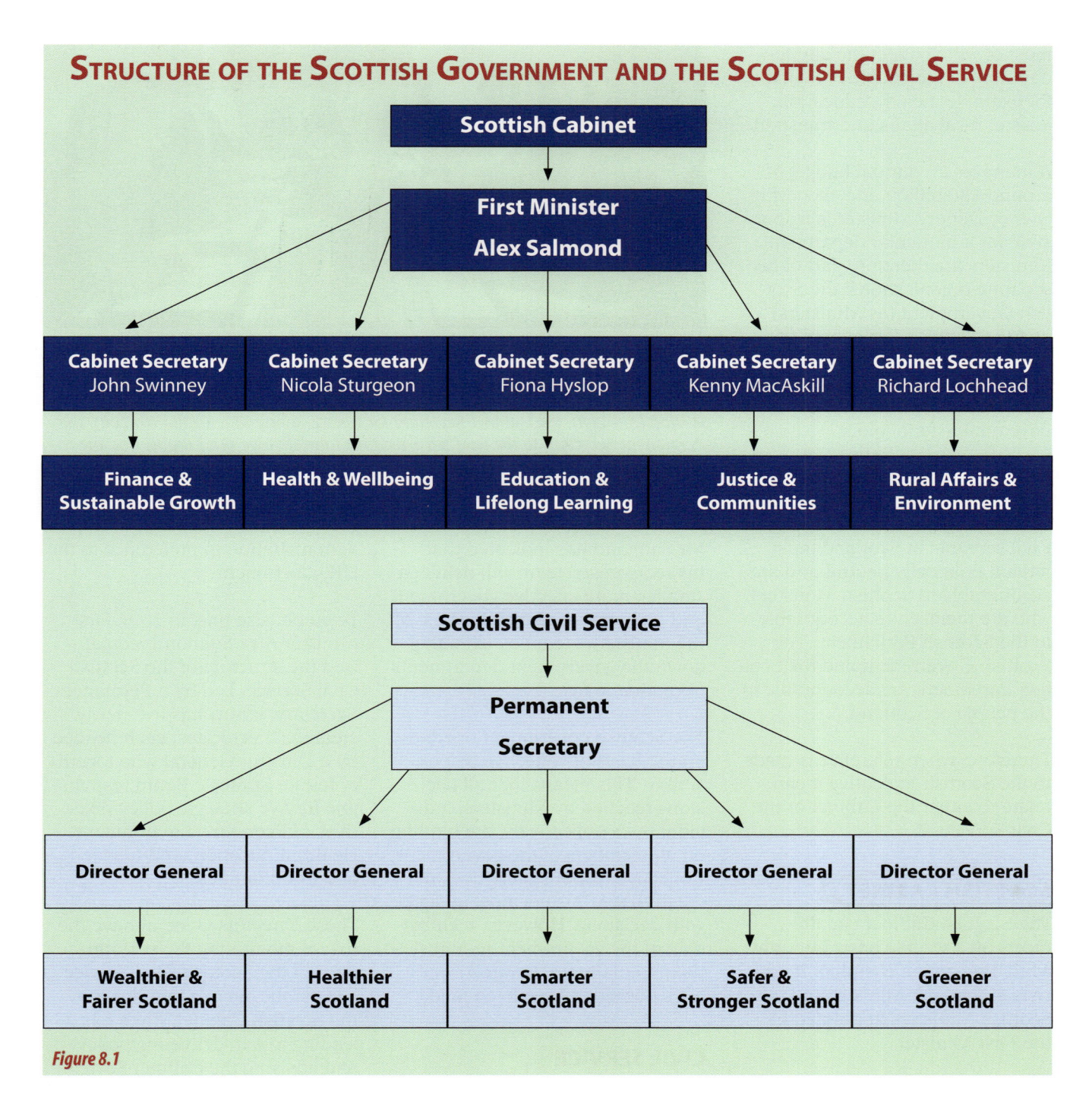

STRUCTURE OF THE SCOTTISH GOVERNMENT AND THE SCOTTISH CIVIL SERVICE

```
Scottish Cabinet
      ↓
First Minister
Alex Salmond
```

Cabinet Secretary John Swinney	Cabinet Secretary Nicola Sturgeon	Cabinet Secretary Fiona Hyslop	Cabinet Secretary Kenny MacAskill	Cabinet Secretary Richard Lochhead
Finance & Sustainable Growth	Health & Wellbeing	Education & Lifelong Learning	Justice & Communities	Rural Affairs & Environment

```
Scottish Civil Service
         ↓
  Permanent Secretary
```

Director General	Director General	Director General	Director General	Director General
Wealthier & Fairer Scotland	Healthier Scotland	Smarter Scotland	Safer & Stronger Scotland	Greener Scotland

Figure 8.1

to agree to. The government is accountable to the Parliament for its actions.

With Alex Salmond as First Minister, the Scottish National Party currently forms a single-party minority Scottish government. After the May 2007 elections the SNP emerged as the largest single party in the Scottish Parliament with a majority of seats—forty seven of the 129 seats. However, if the other parties vote together they have a majority over the government and can prevent it passing legislation.

Mr Salmond heads the first minority administration since devolution and so begins a new form of consensus and inclusive politics in Scotland as he will have to seek Parliament's approval 'policy by policy' across the chamber. This may make it difficult for the SNP to achieve its goals, one of which is to hold a referendum on Scottish Independence.

The Lord Advocate (currently Elish Angiolini), is the chief legal officer of the Scottish government. The Solicitor General (currently Frank Mulholland) is the deputy of the Lord Advocate. Their role is to advise the Scottish government on Scots law.

Both are members of the Scottish Executive, as set out in the *Scotland Act 1998*. However, after becoming First Minister, Alex Salmond decided that the Lord Advocate should no longer attend the Scottish Cabinet, stating that he wished to "de-politicise the post". (See *Scotsman* article on page 130.)

Overall, the Scottish government is responsible for devolved matters most of which affect the day-to-day lives of the people of Scotland, for example, health, education, justice, rural affairs and transport.

It manages an annual budget of around £30 billion and each Minister or Deputy Minister is responsible for a particular department. Ministers are therefore part of two separate organisations: the Scottish Government (as Ministers) and the Scottish Parliament (as MSPs). In addition to a constituency or regional office dealing with local matters, a Minister may also have a ministerial office.

The term 'Scottish Executive' is also used as the name for the civil service administration in Scotland. Civil servants in Scotland must remain politically neutral and are accountable to Scottish Ministers, who are themselves accountable to the Scottish Parliament. The Scottish Government and the Scottish Parliament are accountable to the people of Scotland.

Therefore, when reference is made to the Scottish Executive it can relate to either the Cabinet or the Civil Service.

SCOTTISH CABINET

The Scottish Cabinet usually meets on a weekly basis but only while Parliament is sitting. It consists of the First Minister and other Scottish Ministers appointed by the First Minister.

When it came to voting in Alex Salmond's new Cabinet in Parliament, approval was only given after opposition party MSPs (Labour, Conservatives and Liberal Democrats) abstained.

The new Scottish government comprises sixteen ministerial posts in all. This will see First Minister Alex Salmond being joined in Cabinet by five Cabinet Secretaries, each presiding over their own departments and ministers. Along with two Law Officers this makes a total of eighteen compared to a total of twenty for the previous administration. (See Figure 8.1.)

The Cabinet Secretary for Rural Affairs and the Environment Richard Lochhead (Left), the Cabinet Secretary for Finance and Sustainable Growth John Swinney (2nd Left), the Cabinet Secretary for Education and Lifelong Learning Fiona Hyslop (3rd Left), the Cabinet Secretary for Justice Kenny MacAskill (4th Left), the Permanent Secretary to the Scottish Executive John Elvidge (2nd Right) and the SNP deputy leader Nicola Sturgeon (Right) attend the first formal meeting of the new Nationalist Cabinet at Bute House in Edinburgh.

Mr Salmond has indicated that his reorganised team will deliver a smaller, more effective government and he hopes to reduce the cost of the ministerial team by slimming down the government departments from nine to five.

The Scottish government operates on the basis of collective responsibility. This means that all decisions reached by Ministers, individually or collectively, are binding on all members of the government. Collective responsibility does not mean that Ministers must all agree with decisions. However, membership of the government requires them to maintain a united front once decisions have been made.

CIVIL SERVICE

The civil service is a matter reserved to the UK Parliament rather than being a matter devolved to the Scottish Parliament. Therefore, the civil service in Scotland is part of the wider UK Home Civil Service. While the Permanent Secretary of the Scottish Civil Service, Sir John Elvidge, is the most senior civil servant in Scotland who heads the Strategic Board of the Scottish Executive, he remains answerable to the most senior civil servant in the UK, the Cabinet Secretary. However, some people argue that those civil servants who work for the Scottish government primarily serve the devolved administration in preference to the UK government.

To emphasise this, in 2007 First Minister Alex Salmond reorganised the structure of the Scottish Civil Service. Led by a Permanent Secretary, it now has five newly created Directorates, each headed by a Director General who together form a Strategic Board responsible for five strategic policy objectives of Economy, Environment, Health, Education, and Justice and Communities.

These Directors General have the role of monitoring the performance of the Scottish Civil Service against the agenda laid down by the Scottish Cabinet. Each has a leading role in delivering policy and advising the Cabinet Secretaries of the Scottish government.

Arena for future Conflict

Overall, it is the duty of civil servants to remain politically neutral, to serve objectively, and to obey the government of the day. This is a duty to the office and not to the individual who holds that office. However, the effectiveness of the government can be affected by the personal relationships between the office holder and the civil servant.

Furthermore, while the Civil Service Code (Scottish Executive version) lays down that civil servants in Scotland are "accountable to Scottish Ministers who in turn are accountable to the Scottish Parliament", it also advises that they are at the same time "an integral and key part of the government of the United Kingdom".

> "The Civil Service is an integral and key part of the government of the United Kingdom. It supports the UK Government and Devolved Administration of the day in developing and implementing their policies, and in delivering public services and is accountable to Scottish Ministers, who in turn are accountable to the Scottish Parliament."
>
> Adapted from the Civil Service Code (Scottish Executive Version)

The civil service in Scotland therefore remains part of the Home Civil Service, although some people argue that civil servants working for the Scottish government owe their loyalty to the devolved administration rather than to the UK government.

Under the situation in 2008, civil servants in Scotland were working directly for an SNP administration while their colleagues in London were working directly for a Labour administration. Consequently, civil servants no longer exchanged information informally, as they did previously when Labour was in control of both the UK and Scottish Parliaments.

According to Scotland's most senior civil servant, Sir John Elvidge, the election of the SNP brought an end to the informal contacts which used to be commonplace between the Scottish Executive and the UK government. This could lead to future conflict if London and Edinburgh begin to operate as separate administrations, breaking the powerful civil service links that used to bind Scotland into the rest of the United Kingdom.

In fact, the Permanent Secretary at the Executive has disclosed that he has plans to create a separate Scottish Civil Service, severing the link with Whitehall that has existed for more than a century. However, Whitehall still has power over Scottish civil servants who are currently part of the UK Home Civil Service and any changes to this situation must be agreed by Westminster.

For government to work effectively there must be open communication and trust between the two administrations. However, the core problem is the reality that the civil service is, in effect, serving two governments of different political ideologies at the same time.

A situation of conflict could develop, then, when a civil servant serving a Labour Minister in Westminster has to talk to or brief a civil servant in Edinburgh who serves an SNP Minister. If the matter is a confidential one the exchange of details may be restrained and limited because they both know that the information will be shared with the opposing Minister.

The civil service in Scotland produced the detailed legislative analysis required for the White Paper on Scotland's constitutional future for the SNP administration. However, this work on a document that is helping to prepare the ground for the break-up of the United Kingdom was carried out by civil servants who are also members of a common United Kingdom civil service.

DEMANDS FOR FURTHER DEVOLUTION

While the SNP minority government in Scotland would like independence, it knows that it cannot push for this without holding a referendum. To do this it needs the approval of the Scottish Parliament. Despite being the largest party in the Scottish Parliament the SNP still has a minority government. Together Labour, the Liberal Democrats and the Conservatives have the majority in Parliament and, therefore, can block any plans for a referendum on independence. Their united front is based on an outright rejection of full independence and

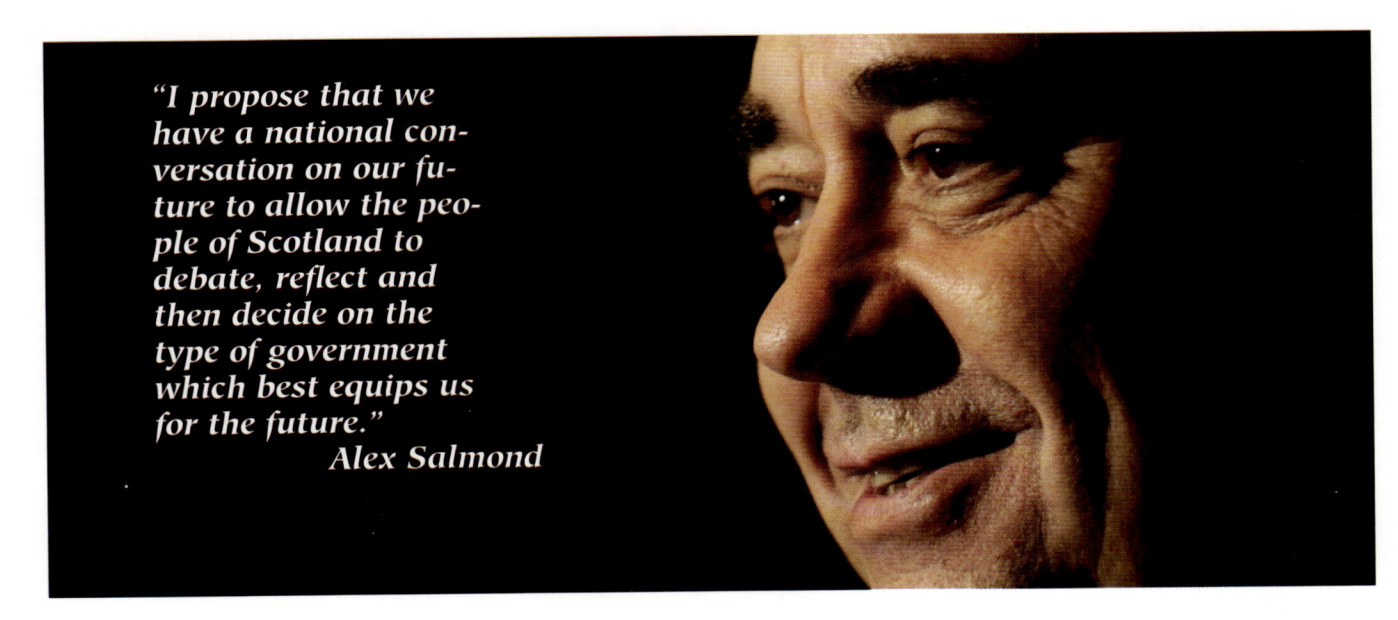

> "I propose that we have a national conversation on our future to allow the people of Scotland to debate, reflect and then decide on the type of government which best equips us for the future."
> *Alex Salmond*

Secretary of State for Scotland

In 1999, the Scottish Parliament took on the legislative powers for devolved matters. Ministerial functions for such matters were transferred to Scottish Ministers who are accountable to the Scottish Parliament. Today the Scottish government is responsible for all devolved matters and most of the responsibilities previously held by the Scottish Office have become part of the remit of the Scottish government. At the same time, the Secretary of State for Scotland remains a member of the UK government and is accountable to the UK Parliament. The Secretary of State for Scotland holds this post jointly with another post in the UK Cabinet. (In 2008 Des Browne, pictured opposite, held the posts of Secretary of State for Defence and Secretary of State for Scotland.) In addition to his other ministerial duties, he represents the interests of Scotland in the UK Cabinet as Secretary of State for Scotland, particularly in those matters reserved to the UK government. He is also responsible for the smooth running of Scotland's devolution settlement and acts as guardian of the *Scotland Act*.

a willingness to work towards a stronger Parliament, not separation from the rest of the UK.

This 'unionist coalition' of the opposition parties has changed the nature of Scottish politics from being Right against Left to Nationalists against Unionists because the only way to defeat the SNP's independence drive is through cooperation.

In response, SNP leader Alex Salmond launched a 'national conversation' on Scotland's future. The formal White Paper, or draft legislation, lays out what the SNP sees are the three choices for the country's future.

1. Maintain the current devolved arrangement.
2. Extend devolution by increasing the powers of the Scottish Parliament.
3. Full independence.

While none of the parties are happy with the current devolved arrangement, all the opposition parties reject full independence, but would like more powers for the Scottish Parliament. The Liberal Democrats want increased powers for the Scottish Parliament and more control over tax. Both Scottish Labour and the Scottish Conservatives also want increased powers but Labour wants a limited form of fiscal federalism while the Scottish Conservatives are wary of transferring too much power.

In effect, the three main opposition parties are attempting to gain the upper hand and isolate the SNP by showing that they are willing to consider reforms, short of an independence referendum. In the end though, any changes to Scotland's powers or even full independence would involve changes to the *Scotland Act* which can only be done by Westminster.

SCOTLAND IN THE BRITISH CONSTITUTION

In constitutional terms the British dimension remains dominant in the post-devolution era. In spite of the significant constitutional reform of a Scottish Parliament and Welsh Assembly, Britain remains a unitary state. The constitutional relationship between the Scottish Parliament and the British Parliament is defined clearly in Section 28 of the *Scotland Act 1998* which states that the Scottish Parliament's power to legislate "does not affect the power of the Parliament of the United Kingdom to make laws for Scotland".

In other words, in post-devolution Britain the UK Parliament's power to legislate with regard to Scotland remains and Westminster retains absolute parliamentary sovereignty. This means that it could legitimately, as a last resort, overrule or veto the enactments of the elected Scottish (and Welsh) legislatures. When devolution was chosen as the preferred type of constitutional reform, federalism was deliberately rejected. In a federal state like the United States the sub-national territorial units, the American states, are constitutionally assigned legislative powers which in theory cannot be overruled by the national government. Disputes between the two levels of government often have to be resolved by the Supreme Court.

The provisions of the *Scotland Act* in effect point to a critical distinction between the 'constitutional' and the 'political'. What is permissible and legitimate constitutionally may not be viable politically especially now that the relationships between the British and Scottish institutions of government are no longer in their infancy.

While there was a Labour government in London and a Labour–Liberal Democrat coalition in Scotland, the relationship was fairly amicable and it was never necessary to use the right to veto Scottish legislation. However, under the current situation, the relationship between a Labour government in London and an SNP government in Scotland is more likely to stimulate its use. This may lead to variations in popular support for Scottish independence which in turn would exacerbate the impact of any conflicts of economic and other interests between Scotland and Britain.

Scotland's Representation at Westminister

The 2005 general election returned fifty nine Scottish MPs to the UK Parliament. The party with the largest number was Labour with forty one, followed by eleven Liberal Democrats, six SNP and one Conservative. Scottish MPs represent the interests of their constituents on reserved matters in the House of Commons. Scottish MPs also sit on the Scottish Affairs Committee which examines the expenditure and administration of the Scotland Office.

West Lothian Question

The Conservative Party at Westminster is questioning the rationale of Scottish MPs voting on issues that affect only England and Wales when English MPs cannot vote on issues devolved to the Scottish Parliament. This is known as the West Lothian Question, so named as it was originally raised by the West Lothian MP Tam Dalyell. The fact that the Prime Minister is a Scot from a Scottish constituency has raised the temperature over this controversy. The Labour Party under Tony

SCOTTISH RESPONSIBILITIES

Devolution established a Scottish Parliament and gave it responsibility for 'devolved' matters while the UK Parliament remains responsible for 'reserved matters' in Scotland. The Scottish Parliament can pass both primary and secondary legislation across a wide range of devolved matters.

The 1998 *Scotland Act* does not set out devolved matters but instead lists 'reserved matters' for which the UK Parliament retains responsibility. By definition, devolved matters on which the Parliament can legislate are all those which are not specifically reserved.

Devolved matters include:
- Health
- Education and training
- Local government
- Social work
- Housing
- Planning
- Tourism, economic development and financial assistance to industry
- Some aspects of transport, including the Scottish road network, bus policy and ports and harbours
- Law and home affairs
- The police and fire services
- The environment
- Natural and built heritage
- Agriculture, forestry and fishing
- Sport and the arts
- Statistics, public registers and records

UK RESPONSIBILITIES

The UK Parliament continues to legislate for Scotland on reserved matters. It may also legislate on devolved matters in Scotland.

Reserved matters include:
- Constitutional matters
- UK foreign policy
- UK defence and national security
- Fiscal, economic and monetary system
- Immigration and nationality
- Energy: electricity, coal, gas and nuclear energy
- Common markets
- Trade and industry, including competition and customer protection
- Some aspects of transport, including railways, transport safety and regulation
- Employment legislation
- Social security
- Gambling and the National Lottery
- Data protection
- Equal opportunities

Blair used Scottish MPs to push through legislation such as Foundation Hospitals and university top-up fees for students at English universities—legislation which does not exist in Scotland.

Implications for Scotland of Government policies in reserved areas

The Scottish Parliament legislates for Scotland on devolved matters while the UK Parliament at Westminster continues to legislate for Scotland on reserved matters. However, in certain circumstances the Scottish Parliament may give its consent for Westminster to legislate for Scotland on devolved matters. This procedure is known as a Sewel Motion, named after the former Scottish Office Minister Lord Sewel.

Nevertheless, a principle has been adopted whereby the UK Parliament will not normally legislate in relation to devolved matters in Scotland without the agreement of the Scottish Parliament. This may happen where, for example, it is considered sensible and appropriate to put in place a single UK-wide directive or where the Scottish Parliament supports proposed legislation but no Parliamentary time is available because of separate Scottish priorities.

Some government policies on reserved matters can have significant implications for Scotland through their potential impact on the policies of the Scottish government since it will have to implement them in Scotland (for example, European Union regulations). They can also impact on the exercise of ministerial functions which are devolved and may need to take account of the separate Scottish legal system.

FINANCING THE GOVERNMENT OF SCOTLAND

How should the policies and expenditure of the Scottish government departments be financed? This is one of the most difficult questions facing politicians on both sides of the border. Differences of opinion over it can threaten good relations between Scotland and the rest of the United Kingdom. It is not a new question in so far as it has long been claimed that Scotland received more than its fair share of British public expenditure in the pre-devolution era. Treasury figures released in 2006 suggest that public expenditure per capita (the most common test of 'fairness') was higher in Scotland than in any other British 'region' except Northern Ireland.

Such 'discrepancies' are partly based on different levels of deprivation across British regions. In respect of Scotland's apparently favoured and privileged position, part of the explanation lies in its relatively large territorial size and low population density outside the central belt which means that expenditure per person for the same level of services such as education and health care is higher

Issues over British public expenditure continually stimulated political debate along regional and party political lines while there was a Labour administration in Westminster and a Labour–Liberal Democrat coalition in Holyrood (1999–2007). For electoral and political reasons Labour was sympathetic to Scottish claims that differences in expenditure were justifiable. Now, with an SNP administration at Holyrood there is an intensification of the controversy along national lines. The English regions have renewed their complaint that they are unfairly treated with the Scots replying that the differentials are justifiable on the grounds of needs coupled with Scotland's contribution to the British Treasury from North Sea Oil revenues. The ultimate Catch 22 for any English politician looking for a reduction in Scottish public expenditure is that reducing Treasury-sourced Scottish expenditure might strengthen the SNP's case for independence.

Public spending per head
Treasury Figures 2005–06

England	£6762
Northern Ireland	£8925
Scotland	£8265
Wales	£7702

Table 8.2

The Barnett Formula

The main source of finance for the Scottish Parliament is a block grant, or assigned budget, from the Treasury calculated according to the Barnett formula (named after the Treasury Minister who devised the formula in 1979). This gives Westminster the power to decide on the level of the Scottish Parliament's budget. Under the Barnett formula, Scotland currently gets around £1,500 more to spend on public services for each member of the population than England. The Barnett formula dictates that Scotland, which has around 8% of the UK population, gets a fixed quota of 10% of the money available for public services. Official figures in 2006 put public spending per head in England at £6,762, but in Scotland it was £8,265 per head, a difference of £1,503.

The Barnett formula takes no account of the amount raised by taxation in each of the home nations, nor issues such as sparsity of population, unemployment and health factors. English politicians and newspapers have criticised Barnett as being unfair to England. On BBC's Question Time in October 2007 and again on BBC Five Live Radio, a *Daily Mail* columnist, Kelvin McKenzie, declared that Scots were ripping off the English. He stated: "Basically the Scots exist solely on the handouts of the clever English generating wealth in London and the South-east."

However, this viewpoint has been challenged in Scotland. The SNP highlights "the Barnett squeeze". It argues that rather than protecting the favourable spending position of Scotland, Barnett is a formula which steadily erodes that advantage. In the period 2003 to 2006

English public spending per head increased by 13.8%; in Scotland by 12.5%.

The Herald newspaper also challenged the view that Scots are the UK's 'subsidy junkies'. In an article in November 2007 it examined Scotland's financial contribution to the UK economy. Based on figures from Oxford Economics, it argued that Scotland does not receive a disproportionate amount. Using 2005–06 Treasury figures, Oxford Economics estimated that the tax revenue from Scotland was £49 billion compared with total spending of £49.2 billion. These figures include revenue from North Sea Oil. In terms of spending, it argues that after Northern Ireland, London has the second highest level of spending. Crossrail, the scheme to improve commuter services to and across London, will cost an estimated £15 billion.

One crucial feature of the Scottish block grant is that it allows Ministers to decide how the annual budget is spent. Expenditure is allocated en bloc, not per service (health, transport, etc.) thereby giving Ministers the opportunity to reallocate funds between services in line with their priorities.

However, all the opposition parties are calling for some restraint on these powers over the budget which allow only Ministers to make changes to how it is spent. They are arguing that having a minority government alongside a new politics based on consensus and compromise also needs a new rule over budget control that takes account of the new party balance in the Scottish Parliament. With a minority government, any refusal by the SNP to allow parliamentary proposals for budget changes would be in danger of appearing undemocratic.

Scottish Taxation Powers

The Scottish Parliament has the power granted by the *Scotland Act* to vary income tax rates. Tax rates, which are normally determined by the Chancellor of the Exchequer, can be varied in Scotland by up to three pence in the pound up or down. This power has so far never been used but the Scottish government and Parliament could decide to increase the rate of income tax levied in Scotland by 3p in the pound. (If currently deployed, Scots would pay 25% rather than 22% at 2007 rates.)

If it was decided to increase income tax in Scotland, the extra income would be additional to the Scottish block grant from the Treasury. If it was decided to decrease the rate of tax paid by individuals living in Scotland, which would mean that Scots would contribute less to the British Treasury from which the block grant comes, then the loss in revenue would be subtracted from the amount given to the Scottish block grant. The Scottish Parliament also has the power to vary the business rate.

Conflict with Westminster

In October 2007 a row broke out between the Chancellor, the Scotland Office and Labour MSPs in the one corner and SNP Ministers in the other, over Scotland's share of UK funding. The Scottish government felt that the funding allocation was the worst under the Barnett Formula since devolution began and means that Scotland is effectively being both squeezed and short-changed by the Treasury. This is happening at a time when Scottish oil revenues over the next five years are due to reach £55,000 million in comparison with £38,000 million over the last six years. On the other side, the Chancellor stressed that Scotland received exactly what it was entitled to under the Formula.

However, the row has not gone away and goes deeper than that. Some SNP MSPs believe that Scotland is being punished for voting SNP by a Labour government in Westminster which decides on the level of Scotland's budget. Others though, see it as a need by the SNP to blame Westminster for the difficulties it is having in keeping its manifesto promises. Some big schemes that were planned have had to be deferred e.g. the reduction of class sizes in early years. This may ultimately push the SNP into demanding greater control over how the Scottish government raises its income (fiscal autonomy) for Scotland.

One key SNP manifesto pledge is to replace the council tax with a local income tax, a reform which has been backed by the majority of the Scottish Parliament. This has already led to conflict between the SNP and Westminster as Mr Salmond becomes increasingly keen to push through both this and other promised SNP reforms. Despite the backing of the Scottish Parliament for the reforms, the UK government has threatened to withhold more than £400 million if they go ahead. The Prime Minister made it clear that Holyrood would not be getting any more money from central government beyond the current block grant including holding back the council tax rebate, worth about £400 million, if Scotland does change the system of local taxation.

Wesminster's argument is that the council tax rebate is a benefit paid in relation to the council tax. If there is no council tax in Scotland then there cannot be any council tax benefit. If the system of local taxation is changed, the £400 million currently reserved for council tax benefit would not be diverted from direct spending to the Scottish block grant, where it could be used to help meet any shortfall in tax revenue. This means that if the Scottish government changed the system of local taxation, it would have to fund any shortfall itself from its current budget of around £30 billion. This would mean less for Scotland's schools, hospitals and roads.

However, the SNP insists that the £400 million is part of assigned Scottish funding and should therefore remain in the block grant. Also, the council tax rebate is designed to reduce the amount of local taxation that local people pay,

Demonstrators called for an immediate suspension of 'dawn raids' on asylum seekers in Glasgow in October 2005. The rally followed the deportation of a Kosovan family who were removed from their home in the city after five years. The Scottish government was powerless to do anything to change the raids.

regardless of the type of local taxation.

Another example of the First Minister's funding plans causing conflict with Westminster is over his scheme to raise finance through a bond issue scheme. A scheme of this nature involves borrowing and Westminster has insisted that the Scottish government has no powers to borrow money and that there are no plans to change this.

These issues show the control that Westminster has over Scottish finances and the lack of fiscal autonomy that the Scottish Parliament has. Any perceived reduction in the block grant could push the Scottish government into raising income tax to make up the shortfall. However, every party is very wary of doing this as it would be very unpopular with the public and would almost certainly lead to electoral defeat at the polls.

These issues around funding and fiscal autonomy could create greater divisions between Scotland and the rest of the UK. Regardless of who is in power north and south of the border, both governments need to work constructively together because if either government uses the financial issue for partisan reasons, Scotland will be the loser.

Overall, the whole conflict could be viewed as backtracking by the SNP who, some say, promised things in their election manifesto that they knew they could never deliver, and now they are desperately blaming everyone but themselves for the lack of funding and the inability to deliver.

Nevertheless, this may give more weight to the calls for the Barnett formula to be scrapped and the Scottish Parliament to be given fiscal autonomy with greater powers to raise its own revenue. However, in an attempt to stave off any further confrontation with the SNP administration at Holyrood, the Prime Minister has boosted the status of the Scotland Office with a Minister of State to help ensure that Whitehall departments work with Ministers from Holyrood.

SOME CONTENTIOUS ISSUES

Debate on the war in Iraq

The Scottish Parliament can, and does, debate reserved matters, even though it cannot legislate on them. While MPs at Westminster were waiting to be allowed to debate the crucial issue of whether there should be a fresh mandate from the United Nations before war was declared on Iraq, the Scottish Parliament was debating it—even though it had no direct responsibility for defence or foreign affairs.

Asylum seekers

Asylum is one of the few issues with local effects that is run entirely from London rather than being a devolved matter.

Campaigners against Dungavel (a detention unit in Scotland for asylum seekers) said the Scottish Executive should have the power to close it or at least to speak out against it. However, the Executive can only refer people to the Home Office because it had no powers over this area of policy since immigration is a reserved matter.

MSPs, human rights groups and church leaders mounted a Scotland-wide campaign against the detention centre which led to the Bishop of Paisley travelling to London to present the Home Secretary with a petition calling for its closure.

In addition, Westminster has refused Scotland the power to have a separate protocol on the forced removal of failed asylum seekers despite objections to the continued use of dawn raids and the detention of asylum seekers in Dungavel. Immigration is reserved to the UK government and the Scottish government has no power to act in the matter even to the point of having to accept specialist teams being sent to Scotland to deal with asylum applications.

Fresh Talent Initiative

The Scottish government has had to negotiate a special deal with the Home Office, so that overseas students in Scottish colleges and universities can remain in Scotland for two years after they graduate (in other areas of the UK it is just six months). This is because immigration is a reserved matter and the Scottish Parliament has no control over it. Some argue that with Scotland's declining population the Parliament needs a much bigger say in how immigration is controlled in Scotland. This could be done either by making special exceptions for people who want to settle in Scotland or by devolving power over immigration to the Scottish Parliament.

Trident

In October 2007, The First Minister arranged a summit on the future of the Trident nuclear weapons programme, which is based in Scotland.

Plans for the summit were announced as the Scottish Parliament voted against renewing Trident (SNP, Liberal Democrats and Greens are all against). However, the issue of renewing Britain's nuclear deterrent is reserved to Westminster and in March 2007 the UK Parliament voted in favour of plans to renew the country's nuclear submarine system. In retaliation, Alex Salmond has caused conflict by suggesting that since the matter is reserved and therefore the Scottish government cannot prevent the renewal programme, the UK government should be charged for transporting the warheads through Scotland. He has done this because while defence is reserved, transport is a devolved matter.

In October 2007 Alex Salmond called for Scotland to have observer status at the 2008 Nuclear Non-Proliferation Treaty talks. This outraged the Scotland Office with David Cairns, a Scotland Office Minister, criticising Salmond "for cavorting across the world stage with his discredited looney left policies".

Health

The Scottish government suffered a defeat in Parliament over its policy on legally binding NHS waiting time guarantees and therefore cannot continue with its planned reform.

Government Ministers argued that a legal guarantee was the only way of ensuring that promises to patients were actually kept. On the other hand, the Liberal Democrats claimed that the move would only lead to a 'litigation culture' in the health service and voted against it. So too did the other opposition parties except the Greens. Consequently the government lost the vote by forty eight votes to seventy seven.

Housing Transfer

A debate on Glasgow's housing stock transfer that ended in deadlock was only resolved when the Presiding Officer used his casting vote twice.

An opposition call for the government to intervene to push forward the second stage of the transfer to local housing groups was tied at sixty votes to sixty when the Presiding Officer voted against the motion.

A government motion criticising the original Glasgow housing stock transfer was also defeated in the same manner. This is because convention dictates that the Presiding Officer can use his vote when there is a dead heat—and he must cast it in favour of the status quo.

Trams

A plan for trams in Edinburgh was put back on the agenda after opposition parties joined forces to demand that the scheme go ahead.

The SNP administration had cancelled the plan over concerns that the project did not represent value for money. Regardless, Labour, the Tories and the Liberal Democrats voted in unison to support the scheme. More importantly, government Ministers indicated they may not be bound by parliamentary votes amid fears that they would face certain defeat in any debate on the issue.

HAS DEVOLUTION MADE A DIFFERENCE?

Pre-May 2007

Up until 2007, devolved policy in Holyrood mainly mirrored policy in Westminster, with the 'Sewell motion' acting as an instrument for fast-tracking UK legislation into Scottish law and a means by which UK-wide uniformity on certain matters was ensured. It also enabled EU or international obligations to be ratified and helped to ease the legislative burden in Scotland allowing more urgent matters to be prioritised. There were two reasons for this. Firstly, Labour was the main party of government at Westminster and at Holyrood and potential problem issues were more often than not solved through party channels. For example, the Secretary of State for Scotland acted as a link between the Labour majorities in Westminster and Holyrood. Secondly, there has been significant civil service continuity, with civil servants working for the Scottish Government being part of a common UK Home Civil Service with Whitehall.

Policy Divergence

However, devolution has made a significant difference in policy terms between Scotland and the rest of the UK. The main policy differences compared to Westminster are:
- Raising the legal age to buy cigarettes
- Ban on smoking in public places introduced over a year earlier
- Free long-term personal care for the elderly
- Abolition of up-front tuition fees for students in higher education
- Three-year settlement for teachers pay and conditions
- Less restrictive *Freedom of information Act*
- Abolition of fox hunting
- 'One stop shop' for Public Sector Ombudsman
- Abolition of the ban on 'promoting homosexuality' in schools by repeal of Section 28 / Clause 2A of the *Local Government Scotland Act* 1986

The Scottish Parliament has led the way with these policy differences and has created a gulf between Holyrood and Westminster. The successful use of devolution by the Scottish Parliament to legislate caused UK-wide resonance and helped to set the terms for future policy debate throughout the UK. For example, Holyrood delivered on tuition fees, Section 28 and fox hunting which had eluded Westminster for a long time.

A good example of Westminster catching up with Holyrood is over the issue of the ban on smoking in public places. In Scotland the ban came into force on 26 March 2006; in England it took almost another year and a half (July 2007). The contrast could not be more stark.

The UK Cabinet struggled to agree a deal on banning smoking in workplaces. The Department of Health said Ministers had tried to strike a balance between freedom of choice and protecting non-smokers. This was also tied to anxieties over criticisms of the 'nanny state' from the press which did not happen in Scotland.

Also, a public health expert said England lacked a champion to push the case for a ban, while in Scotland, the First Minister gave it his full support. Furthermore, in Scotland it was about health and economics whereas in England the rights of smokers were taken into consideration.

Post-May 2007

Following the May 2007 elections things have been less smooth. The election of an SNP administration has introduced the potential for party political conflict into inter-governmental relations. The different party majorities in Westminster and Holyrood are already putting a strain on the ethos of shared responsibility found in the UK Home Civil Service. There is a call for a separate Scottish Civil Service, which suggests that there is a decline in the unifying force of the common UK Home Civil Service.

The SNP government has also been critical of the Sewel Motion because it felt it does not allow the Scottish Parliament to have a say in a Bill in Westminster that may have an impact on Scots Law. If the SNP pushes for changes to this procedure it may lead to Scotland having to formulate all of its own policies from scratch which will increase pressure on the parliamentary timetable.

The SNP has also been active in its opposition to what it perceived to be a programme of privatisation by the former Labour/Liberal Democrat Executive—for example, the issues surrounding the privatisation of the Scottish prison service and programmes funded by the Private Finance Initiatives (PFI). The alternative SNP policy is for a 'Scottish Futures Trust', which would be financed through a bond scheme, counteracting any need to pay high levels of interest payments and allowing these funds to be put back into public services rather than being used for private profit.

Mr Salmond is also calling for the Scottish Parliament to be given extra powers over broadcasting in Scotland, a matter which is reserved to the UK government. This has the backing of MSPs who support broadcasting being devolved and a commission is being set up to look into Scottish broadcasting.

He also wants control over elections to be handed to Holyrood, following the problems in May 2007.

Policy Convergence and Differences

Despite some differences in policy between Holyrood and Westminster there are also examples of policy convergence. For instance, arrangements for incorporating Scottish issues into UK issues have transferred smoothly from the pre to the post-devolution situation. However, in EU matters, despite the Scottish government making a significant contribution to the debate on European regions at the European Convention on behalf of the UK, the Scottish Parliament remains unable to deal directly with the EU on issues such as health and the environment even though these are devolved matters. As a result, the SNP is now beginning to seek a distinctive Scottish profile in Europe.

Airgun Ban

The Scottish government and Westminster have clashed over the issue of airguns. The Scottish government has called for more powers from Westminster to deal with the rising number of airguns in Scotland.

Although new rules governing the ownership of airguns came into effect in October 2007 throughout the whole of the UK, the Scottish government believes that Scotland has a distinctive problem with the weapons. It is therefore putting the case that Holyrood needs more powers to tackle the issue head-on.

In response, the Secretary of State for Scotland said that Westminster's priority was to work with Holyrood to ensure that all communities were protected from gun crime. The issue of firearms is one of the areas which remains reserved to Westminster and Scottish Ministers are not allowed to legislate on it without the clear consent of the UK government. Nevertheless, the Scottish government believes it could obtain powers over airguns in one of two ways. Either Westminster could devolve firearms legislation permanently to Edinburgh, or a one-off procedure could occur whereby Westminster would agree to Holyrood legislating in this area. This would be a reverse of the Sewel convention.

Chapter 9
Local Government

What you will learn.

1. The role, functions, finance and reform of local government in Scotland.
2. Powers and responsibilities of Scottish local authorities.
3. The extent of co-operation and conflict between local authorities and the Scottish government.
4. The effects of the electoral system on local authority decision making and on the composition of Scottish councils.

THE STRUCTURE OF LOCAL GOVERNMENT IN SCOTLAND

Local councils impact on the daily lives of all Scottish citizens. They provide schools for our children and care for the elderly and they maintain our roads. The range of services provided by our councils is extensive (see page 144) and the money to pay for them comes mostly from general taxation and our council tax. We elect councillors to represent our interests and to manage budgets of millions of pounds.

The last thirty years have witnessed dramatic changes in the role, structure and influence of local councils. Under the Conservatives (1979–1997), local authorities suffered a reduction in their income and range of services which led to financial crises and continual conflict with central government. The election of a Labour government in 1997 saw a new partnership with local authorities, and the creation of a Scottish Parliament in 1999 under the control of a Labour and Liberal Democrat coalition (1999–2007) which provided both opportunity and challenge for local councils to redefine their role and to restore their credibility with the Scottish people. In 2007, the election of a new Scottish National Party-controlled Scottish government, coupled with a change to the political control of Scotland's local authorities signalled an exciting time ahead.

The structure of local government has also witnessed significant changes in recent years. Between 1975 and 1996, local government in Scotland was a two-tier system. It consisted of nine large regional councils along with fifty three district councils on the Scottish mainland, while Orkney, Western Isles and Shetland had 'all-purpose' islands councils responsible for all local government functions.

The *Local Government (Scotland) Act 1994* led to a reorganisation of local government in 1996, resulting in the structure that exists today. The three island councils remain unchanged, but the regional and district councils have been replaced with twenty nine single tier (or unitary) bodies. Overall, there are thirty two unitary councils with councillors who are elected every four years by registered voters in each council area or Ward. The councils have full responsibility for the provision of all local government services with the ex-

Split of Public Sector employment in Scotland 2006

- NDPBs & Public Corporations 8%
- Armed Forces 3%
- Civil Service 10%
- NHS 26%
- Local Government 53%

Figure 9.1

Employment in Local Government

The largest single group of people employed in local government is teachers who make up 20%, with other education staff including classroom assistants, music instructors, laboratory assistants, library and clerical staff making up a further 16%. Social work staff account for 17%, and police and fire-related services 10% of those employed by local authorities. Figure 9.2 illustrates the breakdown of employment in local government in Scotland for 2006.

The remaining local government staff are classed as 'other'. These include corporate services; central support; planning and economic development; housing; roads and transport; arts, sports and leisure; libraries, museums and galleries; trading standards; staff of district court; environmental services; and Direct Labour Organisations (DLO)/Direct Service Organisations (DSO).

Breakdown of employment in local government in Scotland, 2006

- Education –Teachers– 20%
- Education –Other– 16%
- Social Work 17%
- Police & Fire Related Services 10%
- Others 37%

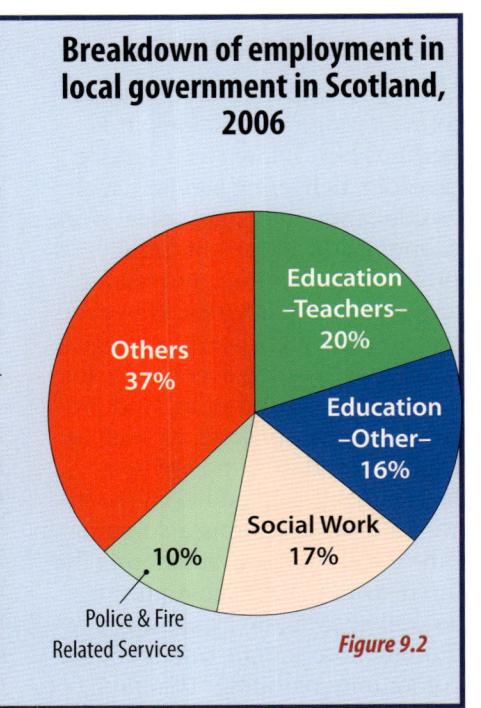

Figure 9.2

ception of water and sewerage and the Reporters to Children's Panels (the Scottish Children's Reporters Administration has responsibility for this).

There are three levels of government in Scotland: the Westminster government, the Scottish Parliament and local government. Local government is the democratically elected part of government in Scotland at the local level. There are 1,222 councillors within Scotland's thirty two unitary authorities. In 2005–06 total expenditure by Scottish local government was £18.4 billion.

The number of people who work in local government is 262,000. These include teachers, police, fire services and social work services. This accounts for 53.1% of public sector jobs in Scotland. The next biggest public sector employer is the National Health Service (NHS) employing 126,000 people and accounting for just over a quarter of public sector jobs in Scotland. The civil service accounts for 10%, Non-Departmental Public Bodies and Public Corporations account for 8% and the Armed Forces account for 3% of public sector jobs in Scotland. Figure 9.1 illustrates how public sector employment was split in Scotland in 2006.

THE ROLE AND FUNCTION OF LOCAL GOVERNMENT

Local government in Scotland performs a range of functions. It is perhaps best known as a service provider, delivering services such as education, housing, social work, economic development, public protection, planning, and leisure and recreation facilities. However, local authorities also play a regulatory role, issuing licences to, for example, taxis and pubs, and providing regulatory services such as trading standards and environmental health. In addition, the local authority performs a community leadership role, promoting the interests of its local communities, as well as fulfilling its statutory requirement to initiate and facilitate community planning. This range of functions is illustrated in the workings of Renfrewshire Council on page 144.

Prior to devolution in Scotland in 1999 the Westminster Parliament controlled all legislation relating to local government in Scotland. The Scottish Office had an input in formulating this legislation but had no power of its own to do so. However, since 1999 Scotland has had its own Parliament which, with its devolved powers, can enact its own legislation relating to local government. As a result, local authorities in Scotland must operate within the powers given to them by the Scottish Parliament.

Local authorities carry out their role within the powers prescribed under various Acts of Parliament. (See above.) Their functions are comprehensive with some being mandatory. A mandatory service

(continued on page 145)

TIMELINE OF IMPORTANT **LEGISLATIVE FOUNDATIONS** OF LOCAL GOVERNMENT IN SCOTLAND

Local Government (Scotland) Act 1973
Legislation that implemented the two-tier structure of local government which was later abolished in 1996. Also established the Local Government Boundary Commission for Scotland and Accounts Commission for Scotland. This Act has been greatly amended but many elements remain in force (for example, provisions relating to local government finance and the role of community councils).

Civic Government (Scotland) 1982
Details the regulatory and licensing functions of local authorities in relation to a range of activities such as taxis, shops and public houses.

Local Government Act 1988
Introduced Compulsory Competitive Tendering (now replaced by Best Value) and a range of other miscellaneous provisions.

Local Government and Housing Act 1989
This Act has also been substantially amended although some elements remain in force such as provisions dealing with the procedures of local authorities in relation to party political organisation and the appointment of staff.

Local Government Finance Act 1992
Legislation to introduce the council tax.

Local Government etc. (Scotland) Act 1994
Legislation to introduce the current structure of thirty two unitary local authorities.

Local Government in Scotland Act 2003
The 2003 Act placed a duty on local authorities to achieve best value and provided them with a new power to improve the quality of life of local people. It also put community planning on a statutory basis.

Local Governance (Scotland) Act 2004
The Local Governance (Scotland) Act 2004 provided for the election of councillors via the Single Transferable Vote (STV) system of election to multi-member wards consisting of three or four members. It also established remuneration arrangements for councillors and provided for severance payments to be made to councillors who were not standing for re-election in 2007.

THE 1996 LOCAL GOVERNMENT STRUCTURE

Scotland's Local Authorities

	Population	Area (hectares)
Aberdeen City	212,494	18,216
Aberdeenshire	226,871	631,736
Angus	108,400	218,396
Argyll & Bute	91,306	702,300
Clackmannanshire	48,060	15,809
Dumfries & Galloway	147,800	644,567
City of Dundee	145,663	5,500
East Ayrshire	120,820	127,527
East Dunbartonshire	108,240	17,551
East Lothian	90,640	66,558
East Renfrewshire	82,780	16,802
City of Edinburgh	448,620	26,001
Falkirk	145,610	29,300
Fife	349,200	134,045
City of Glasgow	577,869	17,472
Highland	208,900	2,611,906
Inverclyde	84,990	16,724
Midlothian	80,910	34,966
Moray	86,940	223,694
North Ayrshire	135,020	88,755
North Lanarkshire	321,750	47,648
Orkney Islands	19,245	102,498
Perthshire & Kinross	134,470	539,479
Renfrewshire	172,970	26,250
Scottish Borders	104,300	472,749
Shetland Islands	21,930	147,097
South Ayrshire	112,960	123,021
South Lanarkshire	302,100	177,789
Stirling	86,230	224,320
West Dunbartonshire	93,790	17,573
West Lothian	158,730	42,664
Comhairle nan Eilean Siar	26,510	307,005

Table 9.1

A Inverclyde
B Renfrewshire
C East Renfrewshire
D City of Glasgow
E West Dunbartonshire
F East Dunbartonshire
G North Lanarkshire
H Clackmannanshire

Figure 9.3

The regions and districts were replaced by twenty nine all-purpose councils on the mainland, with three islands authorities. (See Figure 9.1 and Table 9.1.) The thirty two councils can be divided into different categories:

* the three distinctive islands councils of Orkney, Shetland and the Western Isles
* the unitary authorities based on former regions, such as Dumfries and Galloway, Fife, Highland and Scottish Borders
* the unitary authorities almost completely based on former district councils, such as Argyll and Bute, Dundee, Glasgow, Inverclyde, Moray and Stirling
* unitary authorities based on amalgamations of former councils, such as Aberdeenshire, East Ayrshire, North Lanarkshire and South Lanarkshire

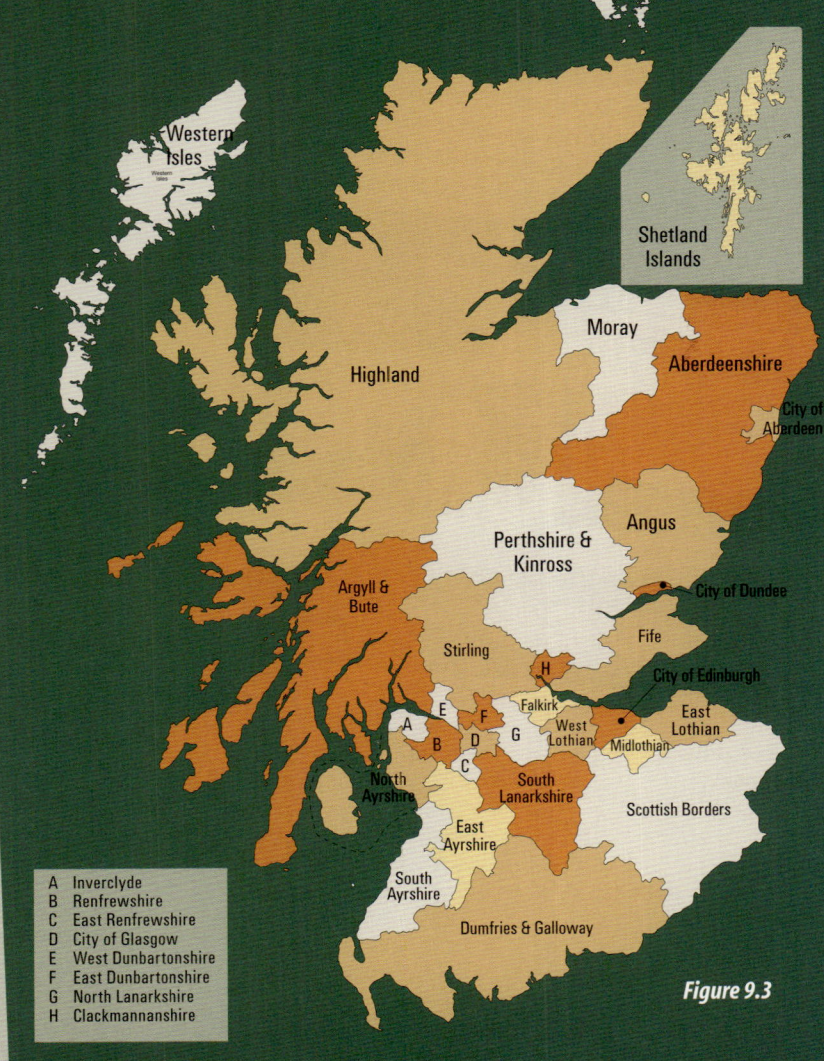

The Establishment of Joint Boards

The abolition of the regions and the transfer of their powers to the small councils led to the setting up of joint arrangements between authorities in public services which involved strategic functions or in cross-authority services such as police and fire services. Critics of joint boards argue that they weaken democratic accountability as a council's involvement in a joint board is seldom subject to public scrutiny. A further criticism is that joint arrangements enable larger councils to dominate the decision making process with their larger resources thus disadvantaging smaller and weaker authorities.

Renfrewshire Council

Renfrewshire Council has a population of 173,000 and covers an area of around 270 square kilometres. Its main towns are Paisley and Renfrew and it includes rural areas such as Lochwinnoch and Kilbarchan. The council has eight departments which provide the full range of local authority services to the people of Renfrewshire.

Chief Executive's Department
Key Responsibilities
- corporate strategy and planning
- community planning
- best value policy and coordination
- performance planning and management
- urban regeneration
- social policy
- Paisley partnership
- corporate communications and marketing
- press and publicity
- emergencies planning

Social Work
Key Responsibilities
- community care, including home care, day care, occupational therapy, residential and respite services for older people and those with disabilities
- children and family services, including child protection, fostering and adoption, children with special needs and family-based support
- criminal justice social work providing a range of diversionary services, probation, reports to court and support for victims of crime

Corporate Services
Key Responsibilities
- committee and member services, including servicing joint committees/boards and the children's panel advisory committee
- registration of births, deaths and marriages
- organising elections
- responding to the ombudsman on complaints of alleged maladministration
- community councils
- litigation, legal advice, contracts and conveyancing
- licensing and Renfrewshire District Court
- personnel services
- training and development
- skillseekers programme management
- health and safety

Planning and Transport
Key Responsibilities
- planning and building control
- roads and public transport
- economic development
- tourism
- European matters
- flood prevention
- conservation of the natural and built heritage of Renfrewshire
- management of the council's internal transport operations

Education and Leisure Services
Key Responsibilities
- primary schools
- secondary schools
- early education
- community education provision for youths and adults
- libraries
- museums and the arts
- provision for those with special educational needs
- swimming pools and sports centres
- childcare and out of school care
- support services like the psychological service or educational development
- halls and community facilities

Environmental Services
Key Responsibilities
- control of pollution, noise, pets and litter
- food safety, food standards, weights and measures, counterfeit goods
- refuse collection and disposal, street cleaning, public conveniences, civic amenity sites and recycling
- building cleaning, janitorial services, catering, and school crossing patrols
- research and development, information, advice and health promotion
- sustainable development and environmental issues
- maintenance of parks, cemeteries and other open spaces
- animal health and welfare

Finance and IT
Key Responsibilities
- preparation and monitoring of revenue and capital budgets
- preparation and publication of financial reports and annual accounts
- internal audit and treasury management
- administration of the billing and enforcement of council tax and non-domestic rates, debt recovery
- provision of information technology services

Housing & Property Services
Key Responsibilities
- housing allocations
- repairs and improvements
- rent collection and arrears recovery
- homelessness
- tenant participation
- capital investment
- private sector grants
- safer communities initiative
- management of building stock and estate
- improvement of energy consumption
- maintenance of commercial and industrial portfolios
- disposal of surplus property by way of sale or lease
- provision of project management, professional and technical services
- provision of a cost-effective construction service

is one that the local authority is required by law to provide, for example primary and secondary education. More recently, local authorities have been required by law to ensure that their service provision secures 'Best Value' and they must also facilitate community planning.

Other services are discretionary. A discretionary service is one which the local authority is allowed to provide if it wishes, for example providing an outing for the elderly.

Finally, others are permissive. A permissive service is one which the local authority is not required to provide by law but it is legally allowed to provide if it wishes, for example swimming pools and theatres.

Government at a local level has a variety of roles and functions which can be said to fall into four main categories.

Provision of Services

Local authorities are responsible for the planning, resourcing and direct provision of a wide range of services and are legally responsible for them. These services are illustrated in the workings of Renfrewshire Council (see page 144) and include education, housing, social work, economic development, public protection, planning, and leisure and recreation.

Local government has the additional responsibility to work in partnership with other public agencies and commissioning services from the voluntary and private sectors. This may include community planning partnerships and local economic forums. For example, the Glasgow Community Planning Partnership operates across the local authority area to bring together a range of organisations which are committed to working together to ensure an inclusive Glasgow. The role of its Forums is to agree a programme of action for the streamlining and improvement of the local delivery of services.

In order to fulfill its role of service provider local government is now working more and more in partnership with the private and voluntary sectors as well as with Scottish government agencies, such as Communities Scotland. (See below for how Communities Scotland and Glasgow City Council work in partnership.)

Strategic Planning

Local authorities publish a strategic plan in which they lay out the long-term objectives for their local

A Plan for Partnership

Below is an extract from Renfrewshire Council's Community Plan (A Pattern for Partnership 2000–2010).

"Lots of different organisations provide services to local people. Many of the issues which affect people's quality of life, such as employment, childcare, crime, drugs and health, cannot be dealt with by organisations working on their own. If services are to be provided in ways that people want and we are to address the issues people are concerned about, it is important that the public, private and voluntary sectors work closely together and combine their resources and expertise to achieve more for the people of Renfrewshire."

Glasgow Community Planning Partnership Members

Glasgow Community Planning Partnership brings together the public sector, partners and the community to agree priorities on the planning and provision of services. Below are members of Glasgow's Community Planning Partnership.

- Glasgow Community Volunteer Service
- Glasgow Housing Association
- Scottish Government
- Communities Scotland
- Strathclyde Passenger Transport Executive
- Glasgow Chamber of Commerce
- Glasgow City Council
- Glasgow Colleges Group
- Scottish Enterprise
- NHS Greater Glasgow
- Strathclyde Police
- Jobcentreplus
- Strathclyde Fire & Rescue

Communities Scotland and Glasgow City Council work in Partnership

Communities Scotland is a Scottish government agency whose aim is to work with others to ensure decent housing and strong communities across Scotland. Glasgow City Council is currently working in partnership with Communities Scotland to help homeowners who are having difficulty paying repair bills.
Tim Ellis of Communities Scotland said: "The scheme of assistance will change the way local authorities support owner-occupiers in dealing with repairs, improvements and adaptations."
Councillor George Ryan, who is involved with development and regeneration services at Glasgow City Council, added: "Communities Scotland and Glasgow City Council have worked together to introduce this scheme."

area and community. The purpose of these plans is to assess the priorities of local communities and to look at how their needs can best be met. Strategic or community planning is therefore a process whereby local authorities and other local agencies come together to develop and implement a shared vision for promoting the well-being of their area. These agencies include community, voluntary and private sector interests, for example businesses, charities and the NHS.

Renfrewshire Council published its Community Plan 2000–2010 which laid out its long-term plan covering a ten-year period prioritising its objectives to meet the needs of the local area and the people who live there. (See page 145.)

Regulation

Local authorities have a regulatory function. Their role in regulation is to issue licences such as those to taxi drivers, shops and public houses. They also have the role of providing regulatory services such as trading standards and environmental health.

Community Leadership

With the requirement on local councils to produce a strategic plan it could be argued that local government is moving away from its traditional role as a service provider and instead becoming a community leader. Ever since competitive tendering was introduced in the 1980s requiring local authorities to use the private sector to deliver services, they have developed a more 'enabling' role, making it possible for others to meet the needs of local people. Strategic planning combined with partnerships as a platform for the design and more importantly the delivery of services means that the council's role in providing services is diminishing as its role of coordinator of multi-agency provision increases.

POLITICAL CONTROL OF LOCAL AUTHORITIES

In May 2007 the Single Transferable Vote (STV) system of election was used for local government elections in Scotland to elect councillors to multi-member wards consisting of three or four members. These multi-member wards are larger geographical areas and therefore councillors now represent wider groups of people. However, the total number of councillors remains unchanged at 1,222.

The *Local Governance (Scotland) Act 2004* provided for this change from the traditional first-past-the-post (FPTP) system to a form of proportional representation (PR). It resulted in substantial change in both the composition and political control of Scottish local authorities.

The first significant change happened even before the election took place. This was because there was a high number of councillors who did not stand for re-election at the 2007 election. Consequently, there was a significant change to the personnel elected with almost half (48%) being elected for the first time. The *Local Governance (Scotland) Act 2004* established remuneration arrangements for councillors and provided for severance payments to be made to those councillors who were not standing for re-election in 2007.

Number of councillors taking severance payments and number of new councillors elected in the 2007 Scottish Local Elections

2007 Scottish local elections

Councillors who took Severance Payment	Councillors who were elected for the first time
434 (35.5%)	586 (48%)

Table 9.2

However, the most significant factor in the change from using FPTP to using STV was the results of the elections. These showed that Labour either lost control of councils or had to run them with a minority, where before the old system of FPTP had given them comfortable majorities, for example East Lothian, Midlothian, Stirling, and Clackmannanshire. Moreover, in the former Labour stronghold of South Lanarkshire, Labour formed a coalition with the Conservatives. Overall, there was a dramatic reduction in Labour council representation and an increase in the number of SNP councillors in almost every council. Only Glasgow and North Lanarkshire remained under Labour majority administration control while Orkney, Shetland and the Western Isles (Comhairle nan Eilean Siar) continued to be controlled by Independent councillors.

Number of councillors and council control by party after the 2007 Scottish Local Elections

	Councillors Elected	Councils Controlled
SNP	363	0
Labour	348	2
Liberal Democrat	166	0
Conservative	143	0
Green	8	0
Scottish Socialist Party	1	0
Solidarity (Glasgow)	1	0
Others	192	3
No Overall Control		27

Table 9.3

THE IMPACT OF *PR* ON SCOTTISH LOCAL AUTHORITY CONTROL

- Out of thirty two councils, twenty seven were left with no single party being in overall control, while only Glasgow and North Lanarkshire remained in Labour hands after the use of STV.
- Labour's influence declined and it was no longer the majority party in many local authority areas including East Lothian, Midlothian, Clackmannanshire, and Stirling Councils.
- The increase in the number of councillors from small parties and the levelling out of results for parties other than Labour has been attributed to the use of PR.

Facts on selected areas

City of Glasgow
Labour kept control of Glasgow City Council with forty five councillors whilst the SNP won twenty two, the Liberal Democrats and Greens five each and Solidarity and the Conservatives had one councillor each.

City of Aberdeen and Aberdeenshire
In both Aberdeen and Aberdeenshire, the Liberal Democrats remained the biggest single party. There was no single majority party on either council, leaving both councils with no overall control. In Aberdeen the Liberal Democrats had fifteen councillors, the SNP twelve, Labour ten, the Conservatives five, with one Independent. In Aberdeenshire the Liberal Democrats had twenty four councillors, the SNP twenty two, the Conservatives fourteen, with eight Independents.

Midlothian
Midlothian is now being run under no overall control, with nine Labour, six SNP and three Liberal Democrat councillors. Prior to the use of STV, on the old council Labour controlled fourteen out of the eighteen wards.

Stirling
In Stirling, where control of the council has always been finely balanced—having twice been decided by cutting cards—the use of STV resulted in Labour gaining eight wards on the new council to the SNP's seven, the Conservatives' four, and the Liberal Democrats' three.

East Lothian
In East Lothian, Labour gained seven councillors as did the SNP, the Liberal Democrats had six, the Conservatives two, with one Independent. Prior to the use of STV, Labour controlled sixteen out of the twenty three wards.

Angus
In Angus, the SNP lost overall control after running the council since 1995, dropping from seventeen wards to thirteen on a council of twenty nine.

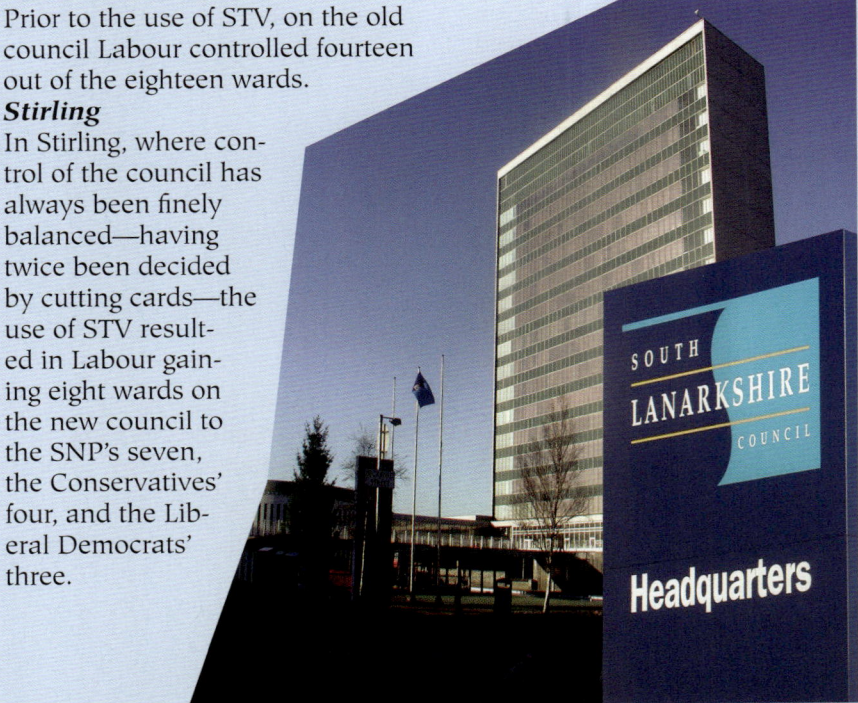

The decline of independent councillors

One of the major losers from STV is Independent councillors. It seems that the change in the voting system and a perceived resurgence in the influence of party politics have added to the decline of Independent councillors.

Despite the two Northern Isles councils, Shetland and Orkney, remaining strongly independent, this is not the case in other parts of the country. In Aberdeenshire, Moray, and Dumfries and Galloway the number of Independent council-

Comparison of the Number of Councillors Elected in 2003 under FPTP and in 2007 under STV *by party*

	2003	2007	Difference
Labour	509	348	-161
SNP	176	363	+187
Liberal Democrat	174	166	-8
Conservative	122	143	+21
Green	0	8	+8
Others	241	194	-47
Total	1,222	1,222	0

Table 9.4 Source: Electoral Commission 2003; BBC 2007.

lors was dramatically cut. For example, in Dumfries and Galloway only two Independent councillors won seats, a decline from twelve before the 2007 election.

This decline is most notable in the Scottish Borders where the Independent members of Scottish Borders Council showed a dramatic reduction. Before the 2007 election there were thirteen Independent councillors; after the election this number fell dramatically to five. Of the eight seats lost the SNP won four, the Liberal Democrats two and a new party, the Scottish Borders Party, won two—one in Galashiels and the other in Leaderdale and Melrose. The Conservative Party stayed unchanged with eleven councillors.

Losers

Tables 9.3 and 9.4 clearly show the decline of Labour's dominance at local elections. Labour had the largest fall in representation at local authority level with 161 fewer councillors (13.2% of all councillors) being elected in 2007 than in 2003.

'Others' which mainly consists of Independent councillors, also lost out with forty seven fewer councillors.

Winners

On the other hand, the main winners, or those who increased their number of councillors, were the SNP who gained 187 councillors (15.3% of all councillors), and the Conservatives who had twenty one more councillors than in 2003. The Greens also gained eight councillors where before they had none. (See Table 9.4.)

Control of Councils

In 2003 there were twenty local authorities with single-party 'majority' administrations. Labour controlled thirteen local authorities, the SNP one and the Independents six, with eleven having no overall control resulting in a coalition.

Local Authorities with single-party majority administrations after 2007 local elections

Local Authority	Party
Comhairle nan Eilean Siar	Independent
Orkney Islands	Independent
Shetland Islands	Independent
Glasgow City	Labour
North Lanarkshire	Labour

Table 9.5

Local Authorities with single-party minority administrations after 2007 local elections

Local Authority	Party
Clackmannanshire	Labour
Inverclyde	Labour
Midlothian	Labour
North Ayrshire	Labour
East Ayrshire	SNP
South Ayrshire	Conservative

Table 9.6

Involvement of parties in multi-party coalitions forming governing administrations after 2007 local elections

Party	Number
SNP	11
Liberal Democrats	12
Conservatives	8
Labour	7

Table 9.7

In 2007 things were entirely different. There were only five local authorities with single-party 'majority' administrations (three of these were formed by groupings of 'Independent' candidates) and six with single-party 'minority' administrations. The remaining twenty one local authorities had multi-party coalitions forming a governing administration. (See Tables 9.5–9.7).

REFORM OF LOCAL GOVERNMENT

From 1997 onwards, various suggestions for the reform of local government were made. Considerable problems were highlighted in the way that local government in Scotland was perceived by the public and the electoral system used to elect councillors was criticised. There were further problems of low turnout among the electorate and young people have felt increasingly alienated from local government politics. In 1999 the McIntosh Commission examined the "crisis in local government" and proposed that:

- PR be introduced for local government elections
- councillors should be paid
- community councils should be given a bigger role

In 2002 the Kerley Committee examined ways of making citizens more interested in participating in local government whether by standing for election as councillors or by voting in elections. It recommended that:

- STV be used in local government elections
- the age at which people can stand for election be lowered
- councillors should be paid

The *Local Government in Scotland Act* 2003 placed a duty on local authorities to achieve 'best value' and provided them with a new power to improve the quality of life of local people. It also put community planning on a statutory basis.

The *Local Governance (Scotland) Act* 2004 provided for the election of councillors via the Single Transferable Vote (STV) system of election to multi-member wards consisting of three or four members. It also established remuneration arrangements for councillors and provided for severance payments to be made to councillors who were not standing for election in 2007.

Following the Scottish Parliament elections in 2007, which saw the SNP in charge at Holyrood, Scottish local government could be subject to more change. According to its Manifesto, the SNP wanted to give local communities more control. The aim is to give individuals, families and communities more control of their own destiny by transferring power to the local level and finding ways to devolve power from local authorities to community level.

The SNP also aims to enhance the role of all of Scotland's 1,200 community councils with a view to giving them increased power over current local authority budgets. It would like them to have genuine decision making abilities affecting service provision and delivery and a greater role in the process of applying for anti-social behaviour orders (ASBOs).

RELATIONS BETWEEN LOCAL AND NATIONAL GOVERNMENT

In June 1997 the UK government signed the Council of Europe's Charter of Local Self-Government, thereby affirming its commitment to maintaining a strong system of local government. It also must ensure the political, administrative and financial independence of local authorities and must allow them to have the responsibility for managing local affairs. In theory therefore, local authorities should be independent bodies who are left alone to manage the daily business affairs of the authority without interference from the Scottish Parliament and government.

In reality however, the Scottish Parliament sets the agenda for most of the functions carried out by local authorities through Acts of Parliament. The Scottish Government sets the framework of government policy for local government to put into practice and also sets targets for local government to achieve.

EXTRACT FROM SNP MANIFESTO 2007

Communities in control
The SNP's aim is to give individuals, families and communities more control of their own destiny. We will opt for de-centralist policy solutions that devolve power to local level wherever that is possible and seek ways to devolve power from local authorities to community level.

New powers for communities
We will review the role of community councils to make them more responsive, dynamic and representative. Devolving greater responsibilities to community councils will be a central consideration of this review.
We will consult on proposals to make new local government ward boundaries the structural basis for new community councils, with increased powers. These powers could include directing a portion of current local spending in their area. As a starting point the consultation will seek views on a figure of £30,000 for every 1,000 Scots or £300,000 for a community of 10,000 people—approximately the size of Fort William.
We particularly want to empower Scots living in areas of deprivation. We will pilot a community empowerment scheme giving deprived communities the ability to opt for empowered status, allowing local people to co-manage a proportion of public spending and services. We believe that this will deliver better outcomes and build community capacity and self-reliance, enabling people in disadvantaged communities to have more control of their own futures.

More community level management and ownership
We will consult on measures to enable new models of community management of facilities within local authority control, such as parks or libraries, to ensure that local people get the best use out of them. We will also consider ways to transfer under-used public assets into community ownership without the need for ministerial approval, where community benefit can be clearly demonstrated.

For this relationship to work effectively there must be cooperation between all levels of government. Scottish government Ministers meet regularly with individual local authorities, or with their representative body the Convention of Scottish Local Authorities (COSLA), on specific and general matters of current interest or concern. Advice and help is also provided to local authorities by the Scottish government Departments whose Minister in charge has certain powers through being a member of the Scottish government.

A good and strong relationship between local government and the Scottish government is pivotal to the working of local government. Local government is a democratically elected body of councillors who represent Scotland's local communities in policy areas such as education and transport. Likewise, the Scottish government is selected from a democratically elected Scottish Parliament to set national policies in these very same areas.

This provides the potential for conflict between two democratically elected authorities. On the one hand we had the democratic bodies which comprise Scotland's thirty two local authorities, and on

PAYMENT OF COUNCILLORS

In May 2007 the Scottish Executive introduced the payment of salaries for elected council members. Prior to this, councillors were given allowances but did not receive a salary. The 'Basic Allowance' paid to all councillors depended upon the size of the council, and was payable up to a maximum of £7,321. On top of this, individual councils had the power to set 'Special Responsibility Allowances' for councillors with significant additional responsibilities. These were usually reserved for the leader or deputy leader of a political group within the authority.

Councillors' Salaries

A Scottish Executive Committee which was set up to look into Scottish Local Authority Remuneration reported that the Allowances System was in need of a complete overhaul. It stressed that change was essential for the following reasons:

- The Basic Allowance was too low and did not recognise the modern role of a councillor
- The Special Responsibility Allowance, which was set by councils themselves, was being overused
- There was ambiguity regarding the allowance set for different council posts
- There was a lack of uniformity because councillors with similar roles had different salaries

The committee felt that since significant changes were already being introduced to local government in May 2007, this was the right time to address the whole issue of remuneration and put in place a system that is straightforward, open, transparent, and fit for purpose.

Details of the new system:

- Basic councillors receive a salary of £15,452. (Basic councillors are those who have no additional responsibilities for policy development or decision making on the council. The majority of Scotland's councillors, about 62%, are basic councillors).
- Council leaders have four salary levels which are set nationally. These are £30,905, £36,055, £41,206 and £51,508.
- Senior councillors have their salaries set by councils within a clear national framework and limits. (Examples of senior councillors are Committee Conveners and opposition leaders).

the other is the equally democratic Scottish Parliament and Scottish government.

The Scottish Executive is essentially the government of Scotland and it needs local councils to implement government policy. Likewise, local authorities need the Scottish Government to give advice and assistance on their functions because of the legal constraints within which they must operate. More importantly, local government relies on the Scottish government for income through the Revenue Support Grant.

Similarly, good relations between local government and the Scottish Parliament are vital since it is Holyrood that legislates for Scotland. For this reason relationships between local authorities and MSPs, especially constituency MSPs, have been important in the past and will continue to be important in the future. This also involves COSLA as the main means by which all councils seek to influence both MSPs and the Scottish government.

Before May 2007 the Scottish Executive was Labour–Liberal Democrat controlled as were many councils either in whole or in part. In the same way COSLA was mainly made up of Labour and Liberal Democrat councillors with a Labour councillor as President. This helped to make relationships less confrontational, especially on ideological matters, and kept communication fairly good considering that the two bodies have competing interests.

PAT WATTERS COSLA PRESIDENT FOR RECORD THIRD TERM

COSLA President Pat Watters said he was honoured to have been voted President of the voice of Scottish local government for a record three times.

"I am absolutely delighted and deeply honoured to be given the opportunity to be leading COSLA at such an exciting time in Scottish politics.

"During the past four years, the organisation has changed a lot. We are a strong political organisation but we are not a party political organisation. We have tried to balance the range of opinions within COSLA to create solutions and policy positions which all of Scottish local government can sign up to.

"That was important then and it is arguably even more important now."

Councillor Watters highlighted his commitment to work with the new Scottish government.

He said: "There is an opportunity to work even closer with the new Scottish government and we must embrace that. We have already taken up the opportunity to meet with the new Cabinet and have already seen the benefits of these discussions.

"We must be committed to looking beyond our own political horizons and at the bigger picture of progressing Scottish local government as a key player in the governance of Scotland and the development of the public sector.

"Reform of the public sector has been a key platform for local government and we welcome statements made in recent weeks by the Cabinet Secretary and the Scottish government to embrace this agenda.

"I will be leading COSLA's work in this vital area and look forward to collaborative work with our colleagues in the Scottish government to ensure that Scottish citizens will enjoy and benefit from first class public services which Scotland can be truly proud of."

Adapted from News Room report of COSLA

The Convention of Scottish Local Authorities (COSLA) has existed since 1975 with the function of promoting and protecting the interests of Scottish local government. All of Scotland's thirty two local authorities are members of COSLA. Each elects councillors to represent them within COSLA which meets on a regular basis throughout each year. COSLA's main headquarters are in Edinburgh and are staffed by professionals experienced in local government.

COSLA has two key roles, a representative role and an employers' role.

Representative Role

COSLA represents local government interests to the Scottish Parliament and the Scottish government. It does this by providing a platform for discussion and communication between its thirty two member councils and the government and Parliament.

Employers' Role

COSLA acts as an employers' organisation for Scottish local authorities negotiating on salaries and conditions of service between trade unions and employees of local authorities.

Following the elections to both local government and the Scottish Parliament in May 2007, Scotland's political landscape at both a local and a national level changed dramatically. This had an impact on the role of and relationships within COSLA and between COSLA and the Parliament and Scottish government. Before the elections many councils were controlled by the Labour Party and there was a Labour–Liberal Democrat-controlled Scottish Parliament and Executive. This meant that local authority representatives on COSLA were predominantly Labour councillors, thus helping to make COSLA's role of intermediary straightforward.

Now however, the Scottish National Party (SNP) has the most councillors in local government with Labour only controlling two councils. Furthermore, with the SNP now the largest party in the Scottish Parliament there is a different Parliament and Government and an SNP First Minister. This new political landscape will require much more cooperation between parties as can be seen by the number of coalition administrations there are in local authorities. It has also had a knock-on effect on the political make-up of COSLA as a cross-party organisation and will present many challenges to the future role and justification of COSLA in representing the views of its membership to the Scottish Parliament and government.

Concordat between the Scottish Government and COSLA, December 2007

The SNP minority government intends to work in cooperation with rather than in conflict with COSLA, and a historic agreement was reached in December 2007 which "sets out a new relationship between the Scottish government and local government based on mutual respect and partnership".

The main terms of the Concordat agreement are as follows:

- A commitment that the Scottish government will not undertake structural reform of local government during the term of this Parliament.

- The publication of funding to be made available during the period 2008–2011(See page 156.)

- A move to a Single Outcome Agreement (SOA) for every council, based on the agreed set of national outcomes (underpinned by agreed national indicators); for example one of the national outcomes is that "we (local councils) have tackled the significant inequalities in Scottish society" and one of the national indicators to assess the performance of local government is "decrease the proportion of individuals living in poverty".

- Each year councils will be required to submit a single report setting out progress and achievements towards the national outcomes.

- Local authorities will be able to retain, for the first time, all of their efficiency savings.

- Local authorities will be given greater powers to decide where money received from the Scottish government should be allocated in order to achieve agreed national outcomes. The amount of funding 'ring fenced' for specific government initiatives will be significantly reduced.

The decision to give councils greater powers over their finances has raised fears that educational priorities might lose out. At present money is ring-fenced for national priorities and the money can only be used for specific purposes, for example spending in schools. Now councils can ignore guidelines and allocate according to local priorities.

The *Herald* newspaper declared that this concordat with the thirty two councils "could radically change the relationship between central and local government".

In December 2007 the Scottish government set out the local government finance settlement for 2008–2011 for each of the local authorities. The allocation of funds was decided according to the established formula which gives the biggest increases to those councils with population growth. Glasgow and Edinburgh will gain from a £119 million annual fund which will be allocated for affordable housing.

CONFLICT OVER FINANCE

The major area for possible conflict is finance. The Scottish government has the power to control finances by

- setting the Revenue Support Grant
- restricting capital expenditure
- deciding mandatory and permissive expenditure
- capping budgets
- ring-fencing grants

Conflict arises because some council leaders feel that these powers over finance deprive them of their independence to set expenditure priorities. They feel that in order to have the ability to manage local affairs under their responsibility, they must be free to do so and not be limited to merely putting into practice government policy and meeting government targets. Any power to be independent is worthless without the necessary financial resources. About 80% of council budgets come from the Revenue Support Grant, leaving councils in a rather dependent position. Any changes to the level of revenue funding made nationally by the Scottish government and Scottish Parliament can have a very serious impact on the priorities set by councils locally. It is estimated that a cut of 5% in total government grants to local authorities needs a 20% increase in council tax to compensate. This is known as the 'Gearing Effect' whereby cuts in central funding result in disproportionate increases in council tax to ensure the same level of income.

Since the Scottish government prescribes the mandatory services that local authorities must provide, council leaders feel it must also provide adequate finances to the local authorities so that they can provide these services effectively. For example, some council leaders felt that the Scottish Executive's decisions to implement the McCrone agreement on teachers' pay and conditions and to provide free personal care for the elderly were not fully funded, leading some councils having to find the finances by cutting other services.

Also, because local authority budgets can be capped, thus preventing councils from raising additional funding, they can be further forced to cut services in order to balance their budgets. This was the case in Edinburgh in August 2007 when council workers went on strike over threatened cuts and redundancies by Edinburgh City Coun-

LOCAL GOVERNMENT FINANCIAL STATISTICS (2005–06)

Local Authority revenue expenditure (£billion)
- Education: ~4.6
- Housing: ~2.8
- Social Work: ~3.0
- Protective Services: ~1.5
- Other Services: ~3.6

Figure 9.4

Breakdown of spending costs
- Operating Charges 48%
- Employees 36%
- Loan Charges 11%
- Miscellaneous 5%

Figure 9.5

Gross revenue income (£billion)
(including the income of housing & trading services)
- Government Grants: ~5.6
- Sales, Fees & Charges: ~2.0
- Non-domestic Rate: ~1.8
- Council Tax: ~1.6

Figure 9.6

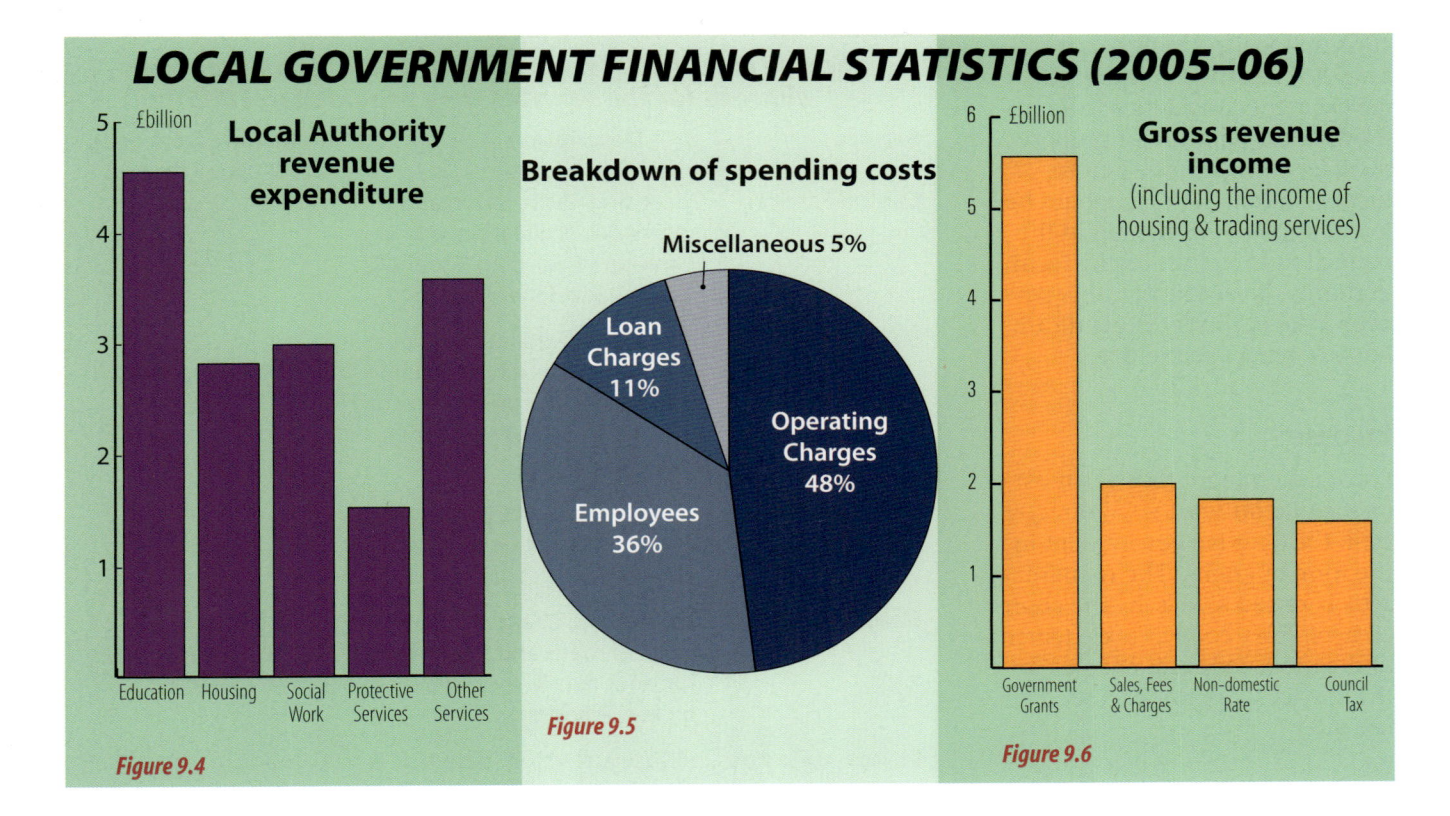

cil. The council's reasons were that it faced a serious financial situation and that it was essential to balance the books.

Expenditure

Local government expenditure can be split up into three general groups as follows:

Capital expenditure

This allows local authorities to purchase or invest in large assets which will benefit the community over many years, for example roads and schools. It is mainly financed from grants, loans and the proceeds from the sale of surplus assets.

Non-housing revenue expenditure

This is recurring expenditure which is financed through current income but not loans. It includes the day-to-day actual running costs of a local authority of which a major portion is employees' wages and salaries. The repayment of loans, including interest payments, is also part of revenue expenditure.

Local authority housing finance

All local authorities must maintain a 'ring fenced' housing account, known as the Housing Revenue Account (HRA). The HRA is the income, which mainly comes from rents, and the expenditure derived from the local authority's landlord function.

Holding local government in Scotland to account

Local government in Scotland spends around £29 billion of public money every year. It is not entirely free to spend this money without any controls or accountability. In reality, local authority expenditure is monitored and kept under control in various ways. Firstly, the Accounts Commission for Scotland has the role of checking that this public money is spent properly, efficiently and effectively. It does this by auditing all local authority accounts and monitoring their service provision for value for money while helping them to ensure efficient, effective and economic use of their financial resources.

Secondly, the *Local Government in Scotland Act* 2003 makes it a duty of local authorities to secure best value or a continuous improvement in performance. (See adjacent Best Value and Accountability.) It is now a legal responsibility of all local authorities to ensure that they get the best value for their money by maintaining a balance between the cost and the quality of service provision.

Finally, the Scottish government has reserve powers with which it

Best Value & Accountability

Duty to secure best value

1. It is the duty of a local authority to make arrangements which secure best value.
2. Best value is continuous improvement in the performance of the authority's functions.
3. In securing best value, the local authority shall maintain an appropriate balance between
   a quality
   b cost
4. In maintaining that balance, the local authority shall have regard to
   a efficiency
   b effectiveness
   c economy

Adapted from *Local Government in Scotland Act 2003*, Source: Scottish Executive can cap local authority expenditure. For instance, if the Scottish government considers a local authority's expenditure or proposed increase in expenditure to be higher than it thinks it should be, it can impose a reduction in the council tax level set by the local authority. Nevertheless, this power over local authority expenditure has not been used to date.

Income

Local government receives most of its income (around 80%) directly from the Scottish government in the form of grants. The remaining 20% is raised locally by the council itself from council tax payments and various fees and charges for the services it provides. (See Figure 9.6.)

Local authorities decide their own expenditure priorities from the income available to them and also set their own council tax levels. However, the local authorities have to bear in mind the powers of the Scottish government to control their expenditure.

In order to ensure a fair and equitable distribution between councils, some local authorities receive more money from the Scottish government than others. This is because not all local authorities are the same size and therefore do not have the same revenue raising potential. For example, the largest local authority is the City of Glasgow which has a population of just under 600,000 people, while the smallest local authority is Orkney with a population of fewer than 20,000 people. Also, Glasgow is home to seventeen of the twenty poorest areas in Scotland, with the top ten most deprived council wards in Scotland all being in the city. Just over half of Glasgow's population lives in these areas. (See Tables 9.9 and 9.10.)

In addition, Scotland's thirty two local authorities are diverse with differing expenditure needs, ranging from the four large and heavily populated City authorities to the small, sparsely populated rural

Income received by local authorities for their fees and charges for the services they provided in 2005

Service	Description	Income from Fees & Charges (£m)
Central Services	Licensing; birth, death and marriage certification; administration of Housing Benefit & Council Tax Benefit.	120.2
Social Work	Accommodation (e.g. residential care, nursing homes, children's homes); respite care; day care for people with disabilities.	191.4
Education	School meals; adult education; music lessons; hire of school premises.	94.9
Roads & Transport	Car parking charges; inspections of roads and streetworks; harbour fees & dues; cycle locker deposits.	94
Environmental Services	Refuse collection (domestic & trade); charges for public conveniences; pest control; burial grounds.	77
Cultural Services	Sports ground and leisure centre use; hire of public halls & buildings; libraries; fees and sales from museums & galleries.	74.3

Table 9.8 Source: Scottish Executive, Scottish Local Government Finance Statistics 2004-05, Table 2A (2006)

TEN most deprived council wards in Scotland (all in Glasgow)

1. Barlanark
2. Ruchill
3. Possilpark
4. Garthamlock
5. Keppochhill
6. Cranhill
7. Shettleston
8. Parkhead
9. Laurieston
10. Ruchazie

Table 9.9

TEN least deprived wards in Scotland

1. Giffnock, East Renfrewshire
2. Chapeltown, East Dunbartonshire
3. Midstocket, Aberdeen
4. Queens Cross, Aberdeen
5. South Morningside (1), Edinburgh
6. South Morningside (2), Edinburgh
7. Craigleith, Edinburgh
8. Westhill, Aberdeenshire
9. Netherlee, East Renfrewshire
10. Craiglockhart, Edinburgh

Table 9.10

FINANCING RENFREWSHIRE COUNCIL 2005–2006

Tables 9.11–9.13 show how much it cost Renfrewshire Council to provide its local services for the period between April 2005 and March 2006, and where the money came from to pay for these services.

Expenditure of Renfrewshire Council

Where the money is spent	£ millions
Education Services	147.5
Cultural Services	19.3
Environmental Services	16.3
Roads and Transport Services	26.3
Planning and Development Services	4.4
Social Work	69.5
Contribution to the police and fire boards	26.2
Other public services	17.1
Total amount spent on services	326.6

Table 9.11

Source of Income of Renfrewshire Council

Where the money came from	£ millions	%
Scottish Executive support grant	184.4	57
Business rates	64.1	21
Council Tax	69.3	21
Money from general reserves	1.6	1
Total	319.4	100

Table 9.12

Renfrewshire Council had a total income in 2005–2006 of £319 million. As Table 9.12 shows, most of it (57%) came from the Scottish Executive. About 21% of the income came from the rates charged for business premises, the levels of which are controlled by the Scottish government. Council tax is also about 21% of total income and is the only part that Renfrewshire Council controls. £1.6 million was also used from general reserves.

Housing Accounts 2005–2006

The housing accounts deal mainly with the cost of providing, improving and managing housing. By law, all the money spent on these houses must come from rent.

Income	£ millions
Council house rent	39.8
Other Income	2.7
Total	42.5

Table 9.13

and island authorities. (See Table 9.1 and Figure 9.1.) For example, the City of Edinburgh receives 75% of its income in grants from the Scottish government and raises the additional 25% itself from council tax and fees and charges while Comhairle nan Eilean Siar, formerly the Western Isles, receives 92% from the Scottish government and only raises 8% by itself from council tax and fees and charges.

The reason for this is that the Scottish government assesses how much each local authority needs in order to provide similar levels of services. In doing so it takes into account factors like the size of the population and its dispersal, the number of school aged pupils, and deprivation and crime rates in the authority.

Each local authority is then given a specific sum of money called the Aggregate External Finance (AEF) as a means of equalising the financial resources available to each authority for service provision, taking account of its local taxation base. This is mainly because local authorities with a lower taxation base or greater needs generally face higher costs in providing services while wanting to avoid putting a heavy burden on local taxpayers. So, without this equalisation of financial resources, many smaller authorities would have difficulty in providing even the basic services without having very high levels of council tax.

The levels of AEF are set by the Scottish government during a Spending Review that takes place every two years and leads to a settlement which covers a three-year period. This AEF is mainly made up of the Revenue Support Grant and income from non-domestic rates. (While non-domestic rates are collected by the local authority this is done on behalf of the Scottish Government which also sets their levels.) The three-year settlement allows local authorities to plan their expenditure priorities with some stability and certainty. Furthermore, the equalisation mechanism is 'needs based' and in proportion to the diverse characteristics of local council areas.

Fees and Charges

This includes payments to the local authority for the provision of services such as nursing and residential care homes, school meals, sports facilities, parking and trade waste collection.

Table 9.8 shows examples of the income received by local authorities for their fees and charges for the services they provided in 2005.

LOCAL GOVERNMENT PERSONNEL

Local councillors represent the interests of the people in their electoral ward and if members of the public have a problem over the local school, vandalism in the street or repairs to their council house, they can approach their councillor for support and advice. Councillors often attend meetings of local organisations such as community councils, School Boards and local Gala Day Committees.

Councillors also attend council meetings and are members of the different committees which may exist, for instance education or health. Unless they are Independents, councillors will belong to a political party and will attend meetings of their party's councillors where policies are discussed and decisions made. Even if they do not agree with a decision, such as closing a local school or cutting services, they are expected to follow the party line. The leader of the council tends to belong to the party with the largest number of seats as does the Provost who chairs council meetings and represents the council at official occasions like a visit from a member of the Royal Family or a delegation from abroad.

SNP delivers historic deal with Local Authorities

In its budget of November 2007, the SNP government persuaded local authorities to accept a freeze on council tax increases in return for greater flexibility in how they allocate their settlement from Holyrood. Finance Secretary, John Swinney, allocated £70million (2.7% of the overall council allocation) to compensate for a freeze on council tax. The council tax freeze is intended to lead to lead to its replacement with a local income tax.

Councils can expect to get £34.7 billion in the period 2007 to 2010. This would take the Scottish government's allocation to local government to £12 billion by 2010. However councils are expected to make efficiency savings of 2% for each of the three financial years.

Councillors in 2003

Following the 2003 local government elections, two Reports looked at the profile of both candidates and sitting councillors who stood at these elections. Below is a list of their key findings.

- Only 22% of Scotland's councillors were women. This figure is much lower than the 38% of women who are MSPs and not in proportion to the 52% of the Scottish population who are women.
- The average age of Scotland's councillors was 55, and only around 1% of councillors was younger than 30, while 25% of the population of Scotland is younger than 30.
- Councillors were more likely to hold a professional qualification or a degree than the general population.
- Only 2% of candidates in the 2003 elections came from ethnic minorities. This is approximately in proportion to the ethnic origin of Scotland's population.
- Councillors tended to come from more affluent backgrounds and had higher incomes than the general population.
- Nearly 64% of candidates in the 2003 elections were in employment and 70% worked in professional or managerial occupations.
- 23% of councillors were retired.

RADICAL CHANGE TO ABERDEEN CITY COUNCIL

Councillors are most often male and over 50, but Scotland has radically changed the demographic after the 2007 local government elections. Kevin Stewart, Aberdeen City Council's deputy leader, said of the 2007 local government election results and the emergence of three young councillors: "When I was first elected in 1999, I was the youngest on the council and I was 30 years old. I don't consider 30 that young. I think the council has to be representative of the community at large. I would not have asked them to do these jobs if I didn't think they were capable, and remember the electorate wanted them. I think that most people are excited by this situation and we still have a way to go in terms of women and people from ethnic minorities. I think that councils in some places required radical change."

Adapted from 'Fresh-faced challenge' *The Guardian* June, 2007

Councillors in 2007

Between the 2003 and 2007 Scottish local government elections, 78% of the 1,222 councillors were male with an average age of 55, and only 1% of them were under the age of 30.

In a move to encourage more women and young people to become councillors, the Scottish Executive lowered the age limit for council candidates from 21 to 18 and offered severance payments to older or longer serving councillors who wished to retire.

As a result, in Aberdeen City John West, at the age of 18, was elected to the City Council, becoming Scotland's youngest councillor. Moreover, his sister Kirsty who is 21, and another young person, Callum McCaig who is 22, were also elected in neighbouring wards.

Now John West has become Aberdeen City Council's Depute Provost, the council's substitute civic head, his sister is education spokesperson and McCaig is convener of the licensing committee.

The Committee Structure

Unlike Parliament, local councils are executive bodies as well as legislative ones. While the full council is the supreme decision making body in a local authority, much of the work and powers are delegated to the committees which are controlled by the ruling party. The chairs or conveners of committees are elected by the full council but are usually selected from the majority party group. They chair the committee meetings and work with the full-time council officials to ensure that council policy is implemented by the various departments. Most councils have a committee known as the Policy and Resources Committee. This committee decides the overall policy of the council and the allocation of resources to departments. The chairperson of this committee is usually the council leader who works closely with the Chief Ex-

DECISION MAKING IN LOCAL GOVERNMENT

In 1998 the Secretary of State for Scotland set up a commission to report on local government relations with the new Scottish Parliament. It was led by Professor Neil McIntosh, the Chief Executive of the former Strathclyde Regional Council. One recommendation of the McIntosh Commission was that councils should consider moving away from a committee structure and towards a cabinet style of local government. This was not a new suggestion and was first proposed in a consultation paper on the internal management of local authorities by John Major's Conservative government in the 1990s. Below is a summary of the McIntosh Commission's findings relating to the committee system.

Committee System
One view is that the committee system works well, especially if the influence of 'backbench' councillors is compared with that of backbench MPs. The committee system enables councillors to have an impact on decision making and to develop an expertise in specific affairs.

An alternative view is that it diminishes the role of the full council and turns it into a 'rubber stamp' body. If councillors spent less time on committees, they would have more time to devote to the needs of their constituents and to monitor the quality of local services.

Cabinet System
This is similar to the existing central government model. An executive of elected councillors (Ministers) selected from the whole council would run the council. The other councillors, whether from the ruling party or from the opposition parties, would scrutinise the work of the executive and concentrate on constituency matters. This was favoured by Tony Blair.

Directly Elected Executive
Under this model the executive (Cabinet) would be directly elected by the local electorate rather than by the leader of the majority party. This would necessitate separate elections, one for the council followed by one for the Cabinet. Such a model would be expensive and time-consuming and could confuse the public.

Directly Elected Mayor
Under this arrangement, similar to that found in many cities in the USA, the 'mayor' would be elected separately from the council. In 2000, London elected its first mayor in controversial circumstances with the victory of Ken Livingstone. (See page 42.) The McIntosh Commission, while not ruling out the election of mayors in the Scottish system, argued that there is no public demand for the creation of such a post in Scotland.

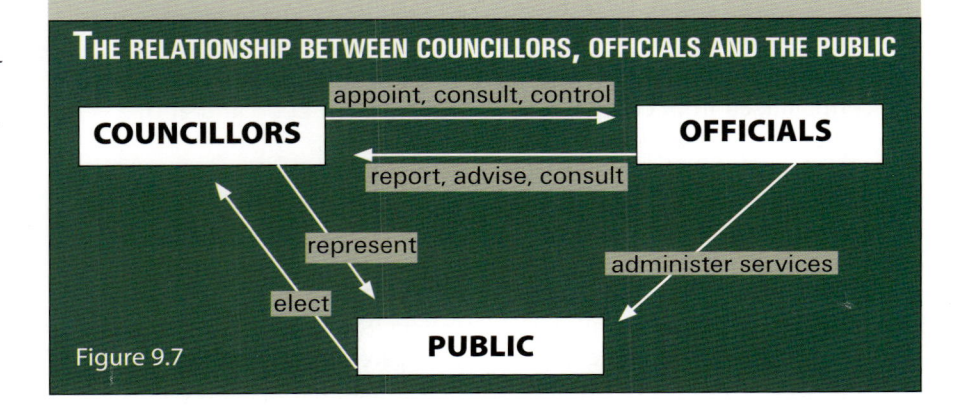

THE RELATIONSHIP BETWEEN COUNCILLORS, OFFICIALS AND THE PUBLIC

COUNCILLORS → appoint, consult, control → OFFICIALS
OFFICIALS → report, advise, consult → COUNCILLORS
COUNCILLORS → represent → PUBLIC
PUBLIC → elect → COUNCILLORS
OFFICIALS → administer services → PUBLIC

Figure 9.7

ecutive and the Director of Education.

Local Government Officials

All local authorities in Scotland appoint a Chief Executive who is head of the management team of directors of departments. In Renfrewshire Council the Chief Executive has his/her own department which covers the key corporate responsibilities of the council. (See page 144.)

The traditional view of the relationship between councillors and officials is that councillors make policy which officials implement in the same way that civil servants carry out the wishes of the Prime Minister and the Cabinet. In other words, power rests with the elected councillors.

An alternative view is that senior officials are involved in policy making. Directors of Education, Social Work, Finance, etc. have technical and professional expertise which councillors lack. Given the continuity of senior officials in office and the part-time nature of most councillors' role, it is not surprising that officials can influence policy making. It is important that senior officials have a good working relationship with senior councillors.

PAYING FOR LOCAL SERVICES–THE DEBATE

The way that local councils pay for the services they provide has always been the topic of much debate. Currently, local government receives around 80% of its income directly from the Scottish government in the form of grants. The remaining 20% is raised locally by the council itself from council tax payments and various fees and charges. It is the method of collecting this extra 20% that is the cause of disagreement. At the moment, each local authority has the power to set its own level of council tax, resulting in significant variations in the average council tax levels between Scotland's thirty two local authorities.

Average and increase in council tax for selected Scottish local authorities 1997-2007

Local Authority	Average Council Tax 1997	Average Council Tax 2007	Increase 1997–2007	increase (%) 1997-2007
Shetland Islands	376	817	441	118%
Aberdeenshire	596	1,114	518	87%
Highland	600	1,005	405	68%
North Ayrshire	556	898	342	61%
East Lothian	670	1,057	387	58%
Renfrewshire	650	990	340	52%
Inverclyde	614	906	292	48%
East Dunbartonshire	838	1,230	392	47%
North Lanarkshire	592	843	251	42%
Dundee City	658	894	236	36%
Scotland	651	980	329	51%

Table 9.14

For example, in 2007–08 East Renfrewshire had the highest average council tax bill in Scotland at £1,247. That was 70% higher than in Camhairle nan Eilean Siar (the Western Isles) which had the lowest average council tax bill in Scotland at £735. Furthermore, in 1997 the average council tax bill in Scotland was £651, while ten years later in 2007 it was £980, an increase of 51%. The biggest increases were on Shetland where bills had increased by 118% and Orkney where they had increased by 103%. This can be compared to West Dunbartonshire which had the smallest increase at only 21%. (See Table 9.14.)

Over the past ten years the cost to Scottish council tax payers of having their bins collected, maintaining their roads and providing their nursery education among other services has grown considerably more expensive and looks likely to continue to become even more so. Only one local authority, Inverclyde, reduced its council tax bill between 2006 and 2007.

Added to this is the cost of collecting council tax and also the rate of collection. Only 93.8% of total council tax due was collected in 2006–07 at a cost of £78 million. In fact, Scotland's local authorities have failed to collect £791 million in council tax since 1993–94, the equivalent of £400 for every household in Scotland. In 2006, £119 million went uncollected. Below are the key points from a Scottish Government Report on the figures for council tax collection by Scottish local authorities for the financial year 2006–07 and previous years.

- The total amount of council tax billed for all of Scotland's thirty two local authorities was £1.867 billion. Of this total, £1.751 billion was collected.
- This is a collection rate of 93.8%.
- This ranges from a low collection rate of 86% in Glasgow, to a high of 97.8% in Orkney.
- Since 1993–94, the overall total amount of council tax billed in Scotland was £18.487 billion, of which £17.661 billion, or 95.5% had been collected by 31 March 2007.

Source: http://www.scotland.gov.uk/News/Releases/2007/06/27093857

The Scottish Executive set up an independent Commission headed by Sir Peter Burt to look at ways of changing the local government tax system. The report, 'A Fairer Way' concluded that the council tax system should be replaced by a property-based tax by which each homeowner would pay an annual tax of 1% of their property's value. Given that the average Scottish property is currently worth approximately £140,000, this would mean the average Scottish local tax would be £1,400 per year. However, this system was rejected by the then First Minister Jack McConnell and the other main parties.

The Scottish Parliament has responsibility for local taxation in Scotland and so all the major political parties in the Scottish Parliament have proposed their own changes to the way of collecting local taxes to pay for council services while maintaining the levels of income currently raised from council tax. Below are the details of each party's way forward in the council tax debate.

At the moment the SNP has the most MSPs (but not a majority) in the Scottish Parliament and is in control of the Scottish government. The SNP is therefore the party most likely to attempt to change the method of local taxation.

SNP

The SNP wants to scrap the council tax which it says is unfair, and replace it with a local income tax (LIT) of 3 pence. This would mean it would be compulsory for all local authorities to levy an extra charge of 3p in the pound on income, with no local variation. The arguement is that the poor collection rate of the council tax is why an LIT would be more sensible. In 2007 the collection rate for income tax was 96.17% compared to 93.8% for council tax.

Critics say that since a local income tax is a tax levied on earned income and not on property it amounts to a tax on jobs and would be a disincentive to work. As such they say it would be a burden on hard-working families, the owners of small businesses and pensioners.

Liberal Democrats

Like the SNP, the Liberal Democrats favour an LIT but with an allowance for local variations. They estimate an average LIT of 3.625% among Scotland's local authorities.

Scottish Labour

Scottish Labour wants to keep the council tax, believing it to be the fairest means of local taxation, but wants to update the bandings which have not been changed since 1990. It also wants to introduce two new bands, one at the lower end and one at the top end, and to cut water and sewerage charges for the elderly.

Scottish Conservatives

Like Labour, the Conservatives in Scotland want to keep the council tax. Their proposed changes would include a discount of 65% for those over the age of 65.

Green Party

The Greens propose to scrap the council tax and replace it with a Land Value Tax. This is a tax set against the value of a person's land rather than the value of the property on the land.

Prospects for Change – Any Time Soon?

Any changes to the present system of council tax must be introduced to the Scottish Parliament as a Bill. If the SNP introduces a Bill to replace the council tax with an LIT it is highly unlikely that it will succeed in the current climate. Despite being in charge of the Scottish government, the SNP does not have overall power in the Scottish Parliament and therefore does not have sufficient MSPs or votes to get such a Bill through Parliament.

Despite the Liberal Democrats being in favour of an LIT, they do not back the SNP's proposal. This is because they see it as being undemocratic since it will introduce a fixed levy of 3 pence on income tax for all councils with no local variations or the ability for individual councils to set their own level. As a consequence they are unlikely to vote for it.

The Labour and Conservative Parties both support keeping the council tax and so will also vote against an SNP Bill.

The Green Party looks upon an LIT as an unfair tax on income and not a solution to the coun-

Party	Plans for Private Finance Initiatives (PFI)
SNP	Set up Scottish Futures Trust, a 'not for profit' trust, as an option. Authorities may choose to use PPP/PFI over the Scottish Futures Trust model if they wish.
Labour	Retain PPP but review it to ensure a level playing field between PPP and conventional borrowing.
Conservatives	Retain PFI
Green Party	Block use of PFI for new infrastructure schemes and develop municipal bonds to pay for schools, hospitals and public infrastructure.

Table 9.15

cil tax which they see as an unfair tax on property. They too will vote against it.

Under these circumstances any Bill should fail. Even if the Liberal Democrats are convinced by the government to support it, the other parties combined can still outvote them. In consequence, any changes to the way that local councils raise income to pay for the local services they provide is not likely to happen any time soon and the debate will rumble on for some time to come.

PRIVATE FINANCE INITIATIVES

Over the last thirty years there has been a decline in the influence and prestige of local authorities. One important reason has been the privatisation policies of both Conservative and Labour governments. The privatisation of local authority services has taken a number of different forms.

PFI was a Conservative policy which was enthusiastically embraced by New Labour. Under this initiative, private firms design, build and operate developments which require to be paid back over an agreed period of time. Labour changed the name to PPP (Public-Private Partnership) Programmes and argued that what mattered was the creation of state-of-the-art schools where pupils could be taught in well-resourced, modern buildings, and hospitals in which nurses could attend to patients in modern wards.

Now, with an SNP-controlled Scottish Parliament things look likely to change. The SNP's manifesto promised to introduce "a new system of infrastructure funding as an alternative to the costly and flawed PFI/PPP" in the form of the Scottish Futures Trust and soon after being elected stated that not just planned but current Private Finance Initiative (PFI) prison projects would be reviewed as a matter of urgent priority. It then announced that it was overturning plans for a privately run prison at Bishopbriggs in Glasgow.

However, the SNP's plans do not make the introduction of the Scottish Futures Trust mandatory. Instead, the manifesto says that procuring authorities may choose to use PPP/PFI over the Scottish Futures Trust model if they wish.

Nevertheless, the first 'not-for-profit' model has been used in Argyll and Bute Council's Education PPP. This model is set up in contractually the same way as a PFI project, but any surpluses generated are put back into education in the area rather than being paid out as profit to the equity holders. Also, in Comhairle nan Eilean Siar (the Western Isles) the whole education PPP project is owned by the council. Table 9.15 shows what each party represented in the Scottish Parliament has planned for PFI/PPP.

Scrapping council tax has £400m price tag– Browne

The UK government could withhold £400 million in benefits if the SNP-controlled Scottish Government scraps council tax, according to Scottish Secretary Des Browne.

The SNP administration wants to scrap council tax and replace it with a local income tax, but Mr Browne warned that the Scottish Government was likely to lose about £400 million in council tax benefits if it went ahead with these plans.

If the Treasury withholds the money, it would leave the Executive needing to find nearly £1 billion in new money to finance its plans.

Adapted from a report in the *Edinburgh Evening News* August 2007